Mary MacCracken

MILLION COPY BESTSELLING AUTHOR

A Safe Place for Joey

HARPER
element

This book recounts the essence of my experience and in that sense is a true story. However, it is not intended as a literal account, and it is not to be taken as a portrayal of any living person. All names (except for my family's and mine) of individuals, places, and institutions are fictitious.

HarperElement
An imprint of HarperCollins*Publishers*
1 London Bridge Street
London SE1 9GF

www.harpercollins.co.uk

First published in the United States as *Turnabout Children* by Signet, 1987
This updated edition published by HarperElement 2015

13 5 7 9 10 8 6 4 2

A catalogue record of this book is
available from the British Library

ISBN 978-0-00-755518-5

Printed and bound in Great Britain by
Clays Ltd, St Ives plc

MIX
Paper from
responsible sources
FSC™ C007454

FSC™ is a non-profit international organisation established to promote
the responsible management of the world's forests. Products carrying the
FSC label are independently certified to assure consumers that they come
from forests that are managed to meet the social, economic and
ecological needs of present or future generations,
and other controlled sources.

Find out more about HarperCollins and the environment at
www.harpercollins.co.uk/green

This book is dedicated to my own three children –
Susan, Nan, and Steve – and their families,
in small return for the joy they've given me.

And also to my four stepchildren –
Michael, Joan, Karen, and Mark –
and their families, who have enriched my life.

Contents

Acknowledgments

I particularly want to thank:

All the children I've worked with and their parents. This book might well have been titled "Lessons from Children."

My husband, Cal, for standing by, putting up with, and continuing to encourage me.

My daughter Susan, for reading every word of every draft and for offering insights, comments, and unfaltering faith.

My daughter Nan, for joining me in private practice, and sharing her talent for growing children.

Gene Young, my friend and first editor, for buying my first book, *The Lost Children*, and for thoughtfully editing both *Lovey* and *City Kid* and much of *A Safe Place for Joey*.

Fredrica S. Friedman, my current editor, for her hard work, enthusiasm, and careful guidance of this book in its final stages.

Carl Brandt, my agent, for watching over my books, both here and in other countries.

Ruth Watson, for reading, typing, and uncomplainingly retyping the many drafts of this book.

Meeting Myself

Maggie. Ten-year-old, bespectacled, beloved Maggie. She still couldn't tell time or remember her multiplication facts. She passed a spelling test if she studied the words long and hard, but a week later she was unable to spell most of the words on the test. But Maggie was desperately eager to learn and I was desperately lonely for children, which was why I was tutoring Maggie and a few others until I could get my "working papers" and return to teaching.

I was back in college now, not by choice, but by necessity. The private school where I had taught seriously emotionally disturbed children full time for over six years had become state approved, which meant that by law its teachers must be certified. I had left college 25 years before to be married at the end of my sophomore year, and, although I had been taking courses at night, these credits accumulate slowly and the school had its state approval before I did. I could not teach again until I had a bachelor's degree in education and teacher certification.

I decided to do it the quickest way I knew – by enrolling full time at the state college. Cal, my husband, supported and encouraged me. Our children were all grown, and some were in college themselves, the same age as my fellow students.

Continuing education for women was not yet popular, and I moved through my days in a sea of twenty-year-olds and dull undergraduate courses. That was okay. But as an education major I had expected to be surrounded by children. Not so. There were plenty of lectures, textbooks, quizzes, term papers, and tests – but no children. In the spring of our senior year, we would be sent into schools for six weeks as student teachers, but that was almost two years away and I knew that I couldn't wait that long to work with children again.

Before returning to college I had been teaching schizo-phrenic and autistic children in a small private school, and during those years I had come to love both the staff and the children. The children had been the beginning and end of my days, and without them there was an emptiness that nothing else could fill.

Consequently, when a psychologist I'd known at that little school asked if I'd be interested in tutoring, I jumped at the chance, sandwiching sessions with children between my college courses. And so, without plan or conscious intent, I began to work with a type of child I hadn't known before.

The first child to come was Bobby – seven years old, in second grade in public school, and seemingly bright, but totally unable to read. When I asked the psychologist who had sent Bobby to me how this could be, he shrugged and replied, "Suspected minimal brain damage."

Brain damage? The words hit hard. Bobby? I couldn't believe it. Bobby was bright, alert, bubbling with life, understanding subtleties without explanation – it didn't seem possible that his brain could be damaged. What I didn't know then was that in the late sixties and early seventies, learning disabilities was a new field and such medical terms as "brain damage" and "minimal brain dysfunction" were often still used. Now educators would use words like "dyslexic" or "learning disabled" to describe a child like Bobby.

In any event, I was sure that Bobby could learn to read. A friend helped me find an unused room in a nearby church, and Bobby and I met there twice a week. Almost immediately, he began to read. Not on grade level, of course, but within a few weeks he knew both the sounds and the names of the consonants, then the short sounds of *a* and *i* – and before one season changed to the next he could not only read, "A fat cat ran to a pit," he could write it as well.

It was a heady experience to be part of such phenomenal growth. Phenomenal to me, at least. I was used to months, sometimes years, of struggle before a child could acquire what Bobby learned in a few weeks' time.

It was not that I was doing anything so special. I was teaching the way I always had – moving slowly, sequentially – making sure each session ended with success. It was Bobby who was taking off, all by himself, and I was so caught up in the delight of his learning that I could hardly contain myself. Working with Bobby was my first experience with a child with learning disabilities, although I did not know it then.

Soon a friend asked if I would help Nancy, and someone else sent Henry, and Henry's mom referred Peter. And then a teacher who was also a friend sent me Maggie, and without knowing it she changed the course of my life. Maggie was small with a narrow little face and brown curly hair. She was a quiet, intense little girl, not especially pretty except when unexpectedly something she had been working on long and hard became clear to her – then her face lit up, and for a minute or two Maggie was beautiful.

A Safe Place for Joey

Maggie never complained, although sometimes her stomach ached before a test. She just kept on working diligently both in and out of school. She kept an alphabetical notebook of all her spelling words; she wrote multiplication facts in toothpaste on her bathroom mirror until she knew them by heart; she refused a gift of a digital clock, determined to learn to tell time the "usual" way. Maggie put in a lot more effort than most ten-year-olds, and still she struggled.

Why? What was wrong with Maggie? Her mother said she thought maybe Maggie had a learning disability and brought me an article from a magazine. Now, besides the escalating pleasure of being able to help these children, there was also a little tick of recognition.

Unable to spell correctly. Tick. Unable to tell time. Tick. Enormous difficulty putting a simple puzzle together. Tick. Tick. Tick. That was Maggie. That was also me.

In kindergarten the school nurse discovered I had almost no vision in my right eye. I was immediately taken to New York City to Dr. Sternhow, who had me look at his pencil, follow his flashlight, turn knobs to try to make things meet. I was given reading glasses, a black patch, a colouring book, and weekly remedial sessions. It did not seem serious. In fact, my mother and father seemed almost relieved. "No wonder she's never been able to catch a ball," they said to each other, smiling at me.

But despite the glasses and remedial sessions, I still couldn't skip or sing on key or remember a new phone number, or make my letters the right way.

As I got older, I was conscious of mixing up left and right, and was not able to set the table correctly unless I stood directly in front of each place and pointed my watch, which I knew I wore on my left hand, toward the spot where the fork should go. I was never sure in which direction to deal cards, and I had to work excruciatingly hard to learn the new steps at dancing school, practicing alone in my bedroom at night, saying everything out loud to myself in order to get it in the proper sequence. I was never a very good speller, and handwriting and artwork were a struggle.

As a young adult, I knew and tried to cover up the fact that I couldn't tell east from west or read a map. Even "before" and "after" were difficult, and I had tremendous trouble learning to tell time. Even now I say, "It's about ten to two," not sure whether it's actually twelve or eight minutes before the hour.

But I was lucky, I grew up in the safest of worlds – in a home full of love, warmth, good food, enough money, and tender care. I went to school in the same town year after year where there were small classes, good teachers, and loyal friends who picked me for teams despite my strikeout potential. So I was spared the loneliness and feeling of inadequacy that haunt the lives of so many learning disabled children. My language center was not affected – I could read, my grades were good – so I didn't have to deal with terms like "stupid" and "idiot." Hard as it was, I'm sure it would have been harder still for both my parents and myself if I had had to struggle in school. Then, as now, academic success and intelligence were considered synonymous. Instead I simply, though painfully, thought of myself as a klutz.

Still, I know what it's like, at least to a small degree – this feeling that the world is a little out of whack, slightly askew, and then one terrifying day you wake up and wonder if maybe it's not the world, but you.

A Safe Place for Joey

The day I met Maggie I met myself again, and I knew I had to find out why we were like that. Did we have learning disabilities? Why were we different from Bobby? Were we all brain damaged? Was there more than one kind of learning disability? What caused it? What could be done about it? And what was this word "dyslexia" that cropped up with increasing frequency?

I continued my dual major in special education and elementary education through my junior and senior years. The undergraduate courses remained dull and the professors uninspired. I still quaked silently through every quiz and exam, but in spite of it all I gradually found myself liking school – enjoying the books and journals, exploring the library stacks, discovering microfiche, talking with other students, becoming friends, Cal and I even partying with some, despite the gap in our ages.

But most of all, I liked tutoring the children – helping them learn, learning from them. I had always intended to return to the children I had first taught – to the strange, beautiful, haunting world of emotionally disturbed children. They were, after all, the reason I had returned to college in the first place. But now I found myself increasingly caught up in this new field of learning disabilities. I had to learn more, understand myself and Maggie, and the others. I was thoroughly and completely hooked.

I applied to a program offering a master's degree in learning disabilities and was accepted. I spent the next year and a half studying the historical development and theories of learning disabilities, the processes of the brain and the central nervous system, the techniques and tests involved in diagnosis, and the teaching strategies of individualized remediation. Unlike those of my undergraduate days, the courses fascinated and engrossed me and we had able professors to teach us.

We learned the electrical and chemical components of the brain, the functions of the right and left hemispheres, and the importance of such things as the development of the corpus callosum, the myelin-covered bundle of nerves that divides the two hemispheres. We learned that the delayed maturation of myelinization can slow down communication between the two hemispheres.

We learned that the cortex alone has over nine billion nerve cells and millions of interconnecting neural pathways. I marveled that there are millions of tiny neurons inside our brains, firing again and again during a single second – a colossal Fourth of July finale going off continuously inside our heads. I wondered that any of us got anything straight.

We learned that there is not just one single, simple learning disability, but many. The term "learning disabilities" covers disorders in written language (also known as dysgraphia), disorders in arithmetic (dyscalculia), and disorders in receptive and expressive language and reading (dyslexia), as well as difficulties in perception of spatial relations and organization. We learned that dyslexia is a specific condition with its own causes and symptoms and that special teaching techniques work. The problem is not a lack of intelligence, but an inability to process language.

We learned that there were many more boys than girls with learning disabilities, although no one was quite sure why or just how many more children in the United States were considered to be learning disabled.

Statistics now show there are five to ten million children, up to 20 percent of all our children, who have some type of learning difference, and probably even more who are not diagnosed. I know from practical experience that in almost every typical classroom there are one to two children who are destined to fall behind unless they are recognized, diagnosed, and given help. Recent studies give indications that there are more dyslexic boys than girls not only because of genetics but also because exposure to the male hormone testosterone affects boys during prenatal development of the brain.

I was continuing to see Bobby and Maggie and three or four other children at the church, and I was sure now that once I finished graduate school and had my learning disabilities certification, I wanted to set up a private practice.

Most of my fellow students were planning to work as learning disability specialists on state-mandated child study teams in public schools, and they urged me to do the same, citing the advantages of vacations, insurance, tenure, and pensions.

But I loved working in a one-to-one situation with a child. In the quiet I could almost hear what was going on inside the child without the need for words. I loved having it all together – doing both the diagnostic evaluation and the remediation, although of course at times I did just one or the other. I felt that there was a tremendous need to provide help for these bright, sensitive children who were so often misunderstood and thought stupid by some and lazy by others. Few understand the courage it takes for a child to return to a place where he failed yesterday and the day before and, in all probability, will fail again the next. I was moved time and again by the bravery of these children and joyous when they realized that they could learn and be successful. I loved them without reserve.

The difficulty of setting up a private practice in learning disabilities lay in the lack of models. I couldn't locate anyone who had actually done what I wanted to do, or even anyone interested in exploring the possibilities. I decided the thing to do was to be practical and just proceed one step at a time. I had some children – now I needed an office. If I was to be a professional, I had to have a place of my own.

I had been following newspaper ads and calling real estate salespeople without success when, unknowingly, one of my children, Fred, led me to my office.

With acuity and cruelty his fourth-grade classmates had dubbed Fred "the pig boy." He was not really a pig, of course – but when he was upset or angry he flared his nostrils and curled his lips until a kind of snout appeared while he snorted and grunted and crawled under his desk.

I worked with Fred on reading and writing, but he also saw Dr. Oldenburg, a clinical psychologist, for his deeper emotional problems. Rea Oldenburg was both respected and controversial. She was well known in the field for her work on the origins of children's fears, and almost as well known for her outspokenness. We conferred by phone several times a month about Fred's progress. During one of these conversations, shortly before my graduation, Rea Oldenburg mentioned that Fred's mother had told her that I was planning to open a practice in learning disabilities and was looking for office space.

I stalled, trying to choose my words, sure she would think me presumptuous. But instead she said, "If you're serious, there's office space opening up here in our building. It's only one room, but there's off-street parking. Dentists and eye doctors downstairs. Psychologists and psychiatrists upstairs. You'd be on the second floor with us. We all have patients like Fred, who have learning problems as well as emotional ones."

I was at the address Dr. Oldenburg had given me before nine o'clock the next morning. Any office building with Rea Oldenburg in it would have been attractive to me – but to have it on a quiet, tree-lined street in what was or had been a residential neighborhood seemed too good to be true. The building itself was wood shingled with a stone front and blue-shuttered windows. The dozen nameplates beside the wide front door announced its metamorphosis from home to business.

"It's small," Dr. Oldenburg's secretary repeated, opening a door to a room, off a small waiting room on the front side of the building. "And there's no bath – but Dr. Oldenburg would probably let you use ours."

"It's perfect," I said.

I scrounged up the security deposit and first month's rent. I furnished the office with a windfall of slightly inappropriate office furniture from a friend who was closing his BMW dealership. Not the small, welcoming round table and chairs and white wicker I'd visualized – instead a six-foot-long, black-walnut-topped desk with black swivel chairs behind and green leather chairs in front. I bought a secondhand file cabinet and had a phone installed, and I had a place of my own.

The children loved my office almost as much as I did – especially Michael. Eight years old, not yet reading, painfully shy – until he reached the desk. Once there he leaned back in the huge swivel chair, propped his feet on the desk, lit an imaginary cigarette, blew smoke rings, and proclaimed himself ready to begin. I sat beside him in a smaller chair – and Michael was right. He was ready and he began to learn to read. Michael was the first of a number of children referred to me by the psychologists and psychiatrists on the second floor. Maggie, Bobby, Fred, and two or three others whom I had been seeing at the church moved with me to my new office. Gradually, my practice grew.

I had been seeing twenty-year-old Tony at the church, and he too preferred my new office space and furniture. His father had bought Tony's way through private high school by paying tutors to write Tony's reports and by making donations to the school building fund in amounts large enough to bring him passing grades. Tony had been referred to me by a psychiatrist with the comment, "He wants to learn to read; he will also benefit from healthy mother figures in his life." Tony himself told me he was coming to me because he wanted to be able to read the "f ——— menus" when he went out on dates.

Then there was eight-year-old Adam – sandy-haired, freckle-faced, with the nicest parents in the world. "He's just like I was," his father said. "I had a terrible time learning to read. I still can't spell. Just help him as much as you can, make it as easy as possible for him. I know he's going to be all right. It just takes a while."

Next came Robin, six years old, referred to me by Dr. Oldenburg. "I don't think there's that much wrong," Rea said, "but she got a poor report at school – doesn't follow directions, reverses her letters. A lot of it is developmental, but she's an only child of older, well-to-do parents and she's under a lot of pressure. Be a buffer for her between school and parents. Give her some academic help. I think it will pay off." Robin looked just like my old Shirley Temple doll – the same blond curly hair, round brown eyes, and rosy cheeks. It was hard to believe I should be paid to work with Robin. But Dr. Oldenburg was right, and within six months she was in the middle reading group and blooming like an amaryllis.

I was beginning. Sometimes I feel as though I still am. I grew under the tutelage of Rea Oldenburg and the other profession-als on the second floor, but it is really the children who have taught me. Sometimes with joy, sometimes with sorrow, I learn a little more about how to help children from each child who enters my life.

There are many ways to write about children with learning disabilities. I have chosen to tell the stories of five children because this is the truest way I know to show what these children are really like. They are not all cut from one bolt of cloth – they have different disabilities and different degrees of disabilities. It is an injustice to lump them all under one broad term and assume they are all alike. Instead, it is necessary to know each child in detail, adding one tiny specific after another. Nothing ignored – everything important – until all of a sudden the child becomes clear to me and I can see what needs to be done. The label is the least important part, and I have finally stopped fussing over which term is best. It is the child who matters.

We all have our own protective devices, but these children have more than most. Because they are convinced that they are stupid and therefore unlovable, they cover themselves as much as they can. Of course, if they weren't intelligent, they wouldn't worry about it because they wouldn't be so painfully aware. But as it is they play the fool, act the clown, disrupt the class, figuring it's better to get in trouble than to look dumb. They slop their handwriting across the page – sometimes they can't help it, but often they do it so no one can prove they can't spell. They say they hate stupid games like Trivia because they can't remember non-meaningful facts. They have temper tantrums to show that they don't deserve to be loved. But all the time there is a silent cry for help from these children who, given the opportunity, will startle you with their insights, sensitivity, intelligence, humor, and ingenuity.

Mary MacCracken

Out of the hundreds of children I have known, the five I write about here are the ones who cried out the loudest – demanding to be heard, to have their stories told. They are unique, as every child is, but they are also universal in that I see dozens of Joeys, Bens, Alices, and Charlies every week of my life – and, every so often, another Eric. Their hair may be a different colour, and they may be taller or shorter, thinner or fatter, younger or older, from varying economic backgrounds and with different degrees of impairment – but I recognize them immediately and am continuously excited and challenged by how much they can learn.

Children with learning disabilities are just as bright as other children, but they will probably have to work harder than most to be successful in school. They need support and encouragement. I have seen that with love, remedial help, and a safe place somewhere in their lives, they will learn and grow.

Joey

"Zap! Wham! Zappo!" A water pistol pointed at me through the branches of a rhododendron bush. "That did it. I gotcha now." A thatch of red hair and a small freckled face emerged momentarily between the leaves.

"Joey," a voice called. "Stop that! Come out. Come say hello to Mrs. MacCracken."

A dark-haired, pink-cheeked woman emerged from the bushes. "You are Mrs. MacCracken, aren't you?"

I nodded.

"I'm Mrs. Stone, and I'm sorry," she said, shaking my hand and then pointing toward the rhododendron bush. "He's not always this bad. I just can't get him out of those bushes."

I smiled. "I know what you mean. New experiences can be very exciting."

"Thank you for understanding and for seeing Joey," Mrs. Stone said. "We're at our wits' end. It's like somebody wound him up too tight before he was born. I've been waiting seven years for him to run down but ..."

Mrs. Stone screamed as Joey sped down the driveway toward the street. "Stop! You know you're not allowed!"

The small boy paused in the breakneck run, swerved gracefully toward the azaleas, performed a perfect pratfall on the lawn, picked himself up, and dashed down the driveway again.

"I'll get him," I said. Words obviously meant little to Joey.

A delivery truck lumbered down the street, and Joey braked at the end of the driveway to watch it pass. I took advantage of this brief pause in activity and crouched beside him, capturing his small dirty hand in mine. "Hi, Joey," I said. "I'm glad you're here."

Startled, he turned to face me, his blue eyes wide, head tipped to one side, sunlight ricocheting off his bright red hair, highlighting the freckles on the bridge of his nose and cheeks.

"Here we go," I announced, still holding his hand. I ran toward the azaleas, swerved back onto the driveway, up onto the low stone wall that ran beside it, lifting Joey with me. He laughed out loud as we made one fast turn through the parking lot, down the slate path along the other side of the building, running at top speed, Joey right beside me, back to the front door of the office building. Joey was smiling but was breathing hard, and I waved to Mrs. Stone with my free hand. "See you in about an hour," I called. Not stopping, I propelled Joey through the door and up the stairs to my office, hoping I'd used up some of his excess energy.

We watched from the window as his mother backed the station wagon out the driveway and onto the street.

"She'll be back," I promised. "Come see the rest."

Joey was immediately involved. He no longer raced madly, purposelessly; now he explored the shelves of books, the children's drawings that covered the walls. The same electricity that drove him to random motor movements could be used to divert him. Joey wandered from the bookshelves to the table of games. "Can we play one of these?"

A Safe Place for Joey

It was the first time that I had heard him speak a full sentence, and I was pleased that his speech was clear and well-articulated. "Sure. But first come over here and let me show you the stopwatch."

I settled Joey behind the big desk, handed him the stopwatch, and sat down beside him to show him how it worked.

He was obviously surprised and pleased to be holding the heavy silver watch by himself. "Is it s'pensive?" he asked.

"Yes," I said. "See, you push this to make it start, this to make it stop, this to take it back to the beginning. Let it run for one minute, and then open this drawer and put it in the box. I need to ask you some questions."

Joey sat perfectly still for a minute, immersed in the stopwatch. Then he carefully put it in the box, but he couldn't resist picking up a Magic Marker from the drawer. "Later," I said, putting the marker back and closing the drawer, and making a mental note that Joey had continually used his left hand so far. "Now," I said, "see if you can tell me your name, address, and telephone number."

Joey was getting happier all the time, and so was I. What did the school find so terrible about this little boy? There was energy and a contagious exuberance about him. He could speak; he could follow directions.

Joey had been referred to me by Dr. Grayson, his pediatrician, who disagreed with the Child Study Team at Joey's school, which felt he belonged in a special class. Dr. Grayson recommended that Joey be seen by a pediatric neurologist, who reported "a mild ADD (Attention Deficit Disorder) not severe enough to require medication at this time." Dr. Grayson then recommended that the Stones contact me for a diagnostic educational evaluation. I had been somewhat reluctant, feeling that Joey had already been tested by qualified people. But Dr. Grayson was eager for a second opinion, and because he was an old, respected friend, I agreed to see Joey at least once. Now I forgot my earlier reluctance to evaluate Joey – I wanted to know everything I could.

I spent the next hour concentrating hard on Joey, noting all the things that were right with him. First of all, he was an appealing boy – his thick shock of red hair plus freckles and a wide mouth and slightly asymmetrical face made him look like the kid on the cornflakes box. His movements were quick and graceful, and I liked the way he got interested and involved when I showed him how things worked. I liked his laugh. I liked the information he had stored up. He knew that his dad worked in a bank and that his dad's name was Al. His mother's name was Gail, and she ran computers. He knew his two older brothers' names and ages and that the reason he didn't have any pets was because his mother said he was "lergic."

I liked the way he understood about the chips, which I used as a reward system, immediately comprehending which colour was worth how much. I liked the independence with which he took over. "No. Don't tell me which colours I earned," Joey said halfway through our first session. "Just how much. I can figure it out."

Joey pulled the old cigar box that held the chips close to him and studied the list on the back cover of the box. "Oranges are five, blues ten," he said out loud, "reds are twenty, greens are twenty-five, yellows are fifty, and these silver ones are worth a hundred each, right?"

"Right."

"Are the silvers real?"

"Yes, they're fifty-cent pieces. My dad collected them. I put them in with the other chips to make it more interesting. All this testing can get to be pretty dull stuff, so at the end of our time you count up the chips I've paid you and then decide if you want to spend for something little or save for something bigger. You buy stuff from the basket – stickers, balls, pens – things like that. I'll show you when we're through."

I didn't say it out loud, but chips can also help keep a child from getting too discouraged. Most tests have "ceilings," and when a child misses three or four questions in a row, the test ends. So in the course of an hour's evaluation, a child may "fail" a dozen times or more – and most of the children I see are smart enough to know when they're wrong. Shoulders slump. Heads droop. But if I pay at the end of each test, counting up the answers by fives or tens, adding a fifty or so, and say something like "Pay yourself one hundred eighty-five," shoulders straighten and heads perk up like flowers after a summer rain. As the child's pile of chips grows, his confidence grows along with it. I may be skewing a few statistics, but I'm seeing the child at his optimum, and that's what's important to me.

Every once in a while I'd ask Joey a bonus question like "Why do you think you're here, Joey? I ask all the kids that."

"'Cause I've got a lot of problems." Joey's voice was barely audible.

"What kind of problems?"

Joey shrugged. "I don't know. I think maybe there's something wrong with my head."

And Joey was right, in a way. There was something wrong with his head. The federal government has defined "learning disabilities" in Public Law 94–142 (the Education of All Handicapped Act) as follows:

Specific learning disability means a disorder in one or more of the basic psychological processes involved in understanding or in using language, spoken or written, which may manifest itself in an imperfect ability to listen, think, speak, read, write, spell, or to do mathematical calculations. The term includes such conditions as perceptual handicaps, brain injury, minimal brain dysfunction, dyslexia, and developmental aphasia. The term does not include children who have learning problems which are primarily the result of visual, hearing or motor handicaps, of mental retardation, of emotional disturbance or of environmental, cultural, or economic disadvantage.

The Association for Children and Adults with Learning Disabilities states, "Each child with a learning disability is unique; each shows a different combination and severity of problems – each has one or more significant deficits in the essential learning processes and is considered to have near average or above average intelligence."

Most of the children I work with have a learning disability that is known as a specific language disability – dyslexia. The Orton Dyslexia Society, which promotes the understanding, treatment, and prevention of the problems of dyslexia, suggests that while some people have a natural talent for learning their native language and learn to read and write and express their thoughts clearly in the early years of school or even before, most of us must work much harder and need more teaching.

Some (the Orton Society says as many as 10 percent of us) find this learning exceptionally difficult – so difficult that it can get in the way of progress in personal growth.

A Safe Place for Joey

The dyslexic child can't learn and remember whole words, so he doesn't learn to read when he is taught by a whole-word or "see and say" approach. He often cannot even remember letters themselves and twists *b* and *d* around. He has difficulty retrieving the words he needs in order to say what he wants to say: "Can I borrow the … you know, the thing you cut with?" Or words come out wrong sometimes: "bermembered" for "remembered" or "basgetti" for "spaghetti." He may read "united" as "untied" and "nuclear" as "unclear."

Math difficulties, the Orton Society says, are now included as another part of dyslexia; math is another language that needs remembering and managing. A child with dyslexia has difficulty with overall organization – he loses his sneakers, his homework, and his sense of direction. Other members of the dyslexic's family through the generations probably had similar difficulties.

Dyslexia is not a disease but a kind of mind, often a very gifted mind. There have been many famous dyslexics – Thomas Edison, Woodrow Wilson, Albert Einstein, Leonardo da Vinci, Nelson Rockefeller, Cher, and Bruce Jenner among them. A child, or even an adult, with a dyslexic mind can learn. He or she (though four times more often he) just needs more help and must be taught in a systematic, sequential way, using strengths, minimizing weaknesses, and helping him or her achieve success. Experts agree this child can learn to read, to write legibly, to spell passably well, and to put his or her thoughts into clear, understandable spoken or written words.

Children with learning disabilities, or dyslexia, or learning differences, as some of my colleagues put it, have very real and important problems that deserve study, effort, and understanding. The labels don't really matter; the children do. We can help them – and we know how. These are children who can succeed if they are given the chance.

By the time I had finished my four diagnostic sessions I had found a lot more things to like about Joey. He had even more going for him than I had suspected. He was far, far brighter than the average seven-year-old. Mrs. Stone had given me a copy of the Child Study Team report, and there the school psychologist had written that Joey's "Full-Scale Intelligence Quotient on the Wechsler was in the average range." This was true; the full-scale score was average, but it didn't begin to tell the whole story. There were enormous differences in Joey's subtest scores, ranging from a high 98th percentile in Vocabulary to a low 2nd percentile in Block Design. When there are tremendous peaks and valleys of this kind, the child is almost always much brighter than his full-scale score shows. To average out subtest scores is like averaging the temperatures at Death Valley to seventy degrees when in actuality it's sometimes one hundred forty degrees during the day and zero degrees at night.

Unlike many learning disabled children, Joey's receptive and expressive word knowledge was large and rich. When asked what a nail was, he replied, "It's a construction material – you hammer it in like this." On another test Joey described elbows and knees as "joints," whereas most children his age answer, "Things that bend."

In contrast to his good vocabulary, verbal abilities, reasoning, practical judgment, and common sense, his abilities to understand spatial relationships, to put things in proper sequence, and to repeat from memory a series of digits or words were very poor.

A Safe Place for Joey

In the Block Design subtest of the Wechsler Intelligence Test, he pushed the blocks across the desk in frustration and banged his head with his hand, shouting, "Stupid kid!"

When he couldn't remember more than two numbers and none at all backward on the Digit Span subtest, he began bouncing up and down and finally out of his chair.

During the third testing session, Joey told me that he thought maybe he "saw things funny." He was right, or at least when he tried to reproduce what he saw with paper and pencil they came out "funny" and bore little resemblance to the original. Joey continued to use his left hand consistently, and some designs were drawn sideways, some upside down; angles looked like double dog ears.

Joey had other troubles. He read 41 as 14; the letters he meant to be *d*'s turned out as *b*'s. He had memorized twenty sight words, but when he came to a word he wasn't sure of, somehow the letters twisted around and he read "cliff" as "calf" and "felt" as "fleet." When he read out loud he skipped lines and made up words, but if I read to him, he could answer every comprehension question in detail.

Joey was not only smart, he was aware and sensitive. As we started a spelling test he said, "Okay. I'll do it, but could you please not put that big circle on the front that tells how many I got wrong, like they do in school." Joey demonstrated:

It wasn't only letters and numbers that Joey mixed up. He jumbled his own thoughts as well. I asked him to write a few sentences about whatever interested him. He thought hard and then took a long time to write. "I'm going to make this neat," he told me as he worked.

When I asked him to read out loud what he had written, he read, "I like to go fishing because we always win."

"Wait a minute here," he interrupted himself. "That's not right. See, I began about fishing, but then somewhere, about here" – Joey put a line after fishing, which was written "fsihign" – "I must've begun thinking about soccer."

I didn't have a test to measure the restlessness inside Joey. But observation made it clear that he was much more active, tense, and distractible than the usual seven-year-old. I even wondered if the neurologist's decision against medication was correct.

I had worked with other children who were labeled hyperactive or as having a "hyperkinetic syndrome" – and I had seen medication such as Ritalin work for some, although not for all. Originally, the thought of medication of any kind repelled me, but I learned that it did work for some children as long as it was carefully monitored by a pediatric neurologist or experienced pediatrician. Often hyperactivity and learning disabilities are considered one and the same, but they are actually two separate conditions. When they occur together I think of it as "dyslexia plus," the plus being hyperactivity. Both teaching and rearing these children takes a great deal of energy and love. Just to get them to tune in so that they can hear what you are saying is a big job in itself – to sustain their attention minute after minute so that they can learn is a tremendously difficult task. These are vulnerable children – their sensations heightened, their motors always running a little too fast, never quite in time with the rest of the world. They are exhausting children. They need more supervision than most. They need more loving. They also give it back in quantum measure.

The Stones arrived at the same time but in different cars, coming straight from work to my office. Mr. Stone was well over six feet tall, lean, with hair just slightly darker than Joey's.

"Did you get a sitter?" Mr. Stone asked his wife.

She shrugged, a small frown crinkling her forehead. "I tried three, but no luck. I think they were making excuses." She turned to me. "Ours isn't the easiest house to baby-sit. When I went back to work last year I tried to make arrangements to have someone there when the boys got home from school. Nobody lasted longer than a week. They all said they couldn't take Joey. They never knew where he was or what he was up to – and if he was there, he was into something he shouldn't have been into. So now the boys look after themselves. Joey, and Bill, he's our eleven-year-old, fight constantly, but Richard, the oldest, is thirteen and responsible, and he can handle Joey better than most. My parents live across town, so Rich can call them if anything serious comes up. My mother is ill, but my father can drive over."

"Which usually makes things worse rather than better," Mr. Stone added.

Mrs. Stone turned her head toward her husband. "Don't start," she warned.

"Shall we begin, then?" I asked, wanting to interrupt the tension that was building between them. "I've read everything you sent," I continued. "The Child Study Team reports, the teacher's comments, the neurologist's report, the background information form that I asked you to fill out. I've scored the dozen tests that I gave Joey, and I've reviewed them with Dr. Golden, the psychologist and learning disabilities professor I mentioned.

"Now, I'd like to go over it all with you and see if we can pull it together and come up with a plan of action. Let's begin at the beginning."

I began to summarize. "Joey was a full-term baby, born October twenty-ninth with a birth weight of six pounds, ten ounces. The pregnancy was a difficult one in contrast to earlier pregnancies with Joey's brothers. Toward the end of the third month staining was severe enough for the doctor to advise complete bed rest for several weeks …"

For the next hour we went over each of the tests. I read them Joey's intelligent, sophisticated answers, and they were surprised and pleased at how much he had learned about his world in spite of all his troubles. One by one I showed them the intelligence tests, academic tests, visual and auditory processing tests, puzzles, drawings, and Dr. Golden's comments.

I summed up Joey's strengths: his intelligence; his excellent verbal skills, including both word knowledge and speech; his love of people and ability to make friends; his excellent physical coordination; and his intelligent, supportive family.

I also went over Joey's weaknesses: the large gap between his intelligence and his achievement in academic areas; his difficulty in "sitting still"; the sleep disturbances that Mrs. Stone mentioned; his difficulties with spatial relationships; his reversals in both reading and writing; his left-right confusion; his inability to sequence digits, letters, days of the week, months of the year; his difficulty with all forms of writing; his lack of understanding of decoding skills, which resulted in wild guessing; his pattern of disorganization; his lack of confidence in his ability to learn; and an overriding factor of distractibility and frustration.

"Joey has various learning disabilities and also a certain amount of hyperactivity," I said. "It's possible to have either of these conditions without the other, but in Joey's case both are present, each compounding the other.

"From reading his report it seems there may have been some tiny damage to neurological pathways before Joey was born," I continued.

Mr. Stone looked at his watch and cleared his throat. "All right, I can accept that. The neurologist said the same thing, and also my brother claims he has dyslexia himself – but the main thing is, what are we going to do about it?" He looked directly at me.

"Tell me the two things about Joey that are causing the most trouble," I said.

They both spoke at once. Mrs. Stone said, "I don't want him to go to a special school. Everyone will think he's retarded."

"I don't care what other people think," Mr. Stone said. "But Joey is sure to get even more down on himself than he already is if he isn't allowed to go to the school where his brothers went."

"How about his teacher? What do you think she finds most difficult about Joey?" I asked.

"He disrupts the class. She also said he acts like he's not aware of what's going on," Mrs. Stone replied. "I think what started the talk about a special class is that he falls out of his chair all the time now. She thinks maybe he's having fits."

"He's not having fits," I said. "You've already had him examined by a neurologist who found no sign of convulsive activity.

I'd be willing to bet that Joey is falling out of his chair because he's not successful when he's in it.

"What he needs to know," I continued, "is that he's smart and can learn and doesn't have to act like a fool. I think Joey would rather have the kids in his class think he's a clown than think he's dumb. Joey himself is pretty sure he actually is stupid, but at the same time he's smart enough not to want anyone else to think so."

"How can Joey ever feel good about himself when he has so many problems?" Mrs. Stone asked. "His teacher says he can't read or write like the others – now a special class ..."

"I'll tell you honestly that I don't think that Joey belongs in special education," I said. "I taught in special ed for many years, and it's the right answer for some children. But I don't think Joey's problems are that severe, and his intelligence and social abilities outside of school say to me that he belongs in a regular classroom. I think he's smart enough to learn to use his strengths to bring his academic skills up to grade level. You've had top medical advice that his hyperactivity is not severe enough to warrant medication at this time, and I think maybe Joey can learn to control his impulsive behavior if it doesn't pay off. We just have to try to convince the school to let him have a little more time, in a regular class."

"That will be a miracle in itself," Mrs. Stone said. "I think they've already made up their minds."

"There's one thing I want to get straight before we go any further," Mr. Stone said. "Are you going to help? Are you going to work with Joey? Or are you just telling us this so we'll tell somebody else?"

It was a fair question, and I knew what my answer should be. There were so many children now who needed help that I often didn't finish in my office until seven thirty or eight o'clock; understandably, Cal would not be eager for me to take on another child. Still, there was something about Joey …

I returned Mr. Stone's steady gaze and then turned to Mrs. Stone as well. "Yes. I want to help. I'd like to work with Joey, but I can't do it alone. I'll need a lot of help from both of you and from Joey and his school. I'd like to talk with his teacher every week or so. It's important to know how he's doing in the classroom, because no matter how well he does here with me, if there isn't carryover into his classroom it isn't going to help Joey stay in a regular class.

"I have two things I'd like you to do. I'd like you to have a pediatric audiologist check Joey – just to cover all bases and make sure there is no physical cause for the low scores in auditory processing. Second, I'd like you to try to see that he eats well, with an emphasis on fruits and vegetables rather than sweets and junk food. I don't think there's a diet in the world that will teach him to read, but it may cut down the hyperactivity.

"The main thing will be to get Joey to believe in himself and take responsibility for his learning and behavior.

"I tell you what. Let me try over the summer – and also talk to the Child Study Team and see if they will agree to take another look at Joey at the end of August. If there's been enough improvement, maybe they'll let him start in second grade."

We went over schedules – Joey's and mine. School closed for summer vacation the following week, so Joey and I would both have more time. Somehow we'd have to work it out in the fall, but for now I'd see him from a quarter past nine to ten o'clock on Tuesday and Thursday mornings.

Joey arrived Tuesday morning still steeped in sleep. Hair uncombed, eyes half shut, shirttail out, shoes untied. He plopped himself onto the chair behind the desk.

"Well," he began, laying his head on the desk, "the good news is that school's over. The bad news is that I had to get up to come here."

"Would you rather come in the afternoon?"

"No. I got to swim in the afternoon. That's how come we're not going up to the lake till August. I got to be in about a hundred dozen swim meets." Joey had opened the middle desk drawer and was fiddling around inside.

"Close the drawer, please, Joey." He had already explored it several times on other visits. I wanted his complete attention now.

Some part of Joey was always in motion, touching this and opening that. He did it unconsciously, not really aware of what he was doing. He had no real concept of what belonged to him and what didn't. Whatever was in reach was fair game. Before he could change, he would have to become aware of what he was doing.

Joey replaced the box of rubber bands he'd been playing with, and I said, "Good. Pay yourself twenty, that's two blues or one red chip, for following directions so quickly.

"Now let me show you what we're going to do today. This is your notebook; this is your bin. This is where we'll keep the things you're working on. Would you please write your name on the notebook?"

"Can I use the Magic Marker you got in the drawer?"

I laughed. This was the child that was reported to be unaware of his surroundings? "Sure," I said. "It doesn't erase, though."

A Safe Place for Joey

Joey got out the pen and then looked through the black and white marbleized notebook, blank except for the first page, where I'd made out our schedule for the day. He turned back to the cover.

"Maybe I'll just do it in pencil first. In case. You know?"

"Good thinking, Joey – pay another twenty."

Joey's turn to laugh. "Twenty for just thinking? Thinking's easy."

"Maybe," I said, "but it's the most important part. You're lucky you're good at it."

"Yeah," Joey answered, writing his *J* backward with his left hand and then scrubbing it out with his eraser and making it correctly. The *o* came out fine, but somehow when he made the *e* it overlapped the *o*. Joey attacked it with the eraser again.

As he rubbed away, Joey looked over at me, grinned, and said, "This old eraser sure does have a hard life, doesn't it?"

How could I have missed having Joey in my life?

After Joey had written his name in pencil and gone over it with the black marker, I took his folder from his bin and showed him how he'd done on each test.

Joey was only mildly interested, and I decided to be clearer. "The main thing is," I said, "I want you to know you're smart, so you don't have to go around shouting 'bout how dumb you are and falling out of your chair."

"I can't help that."

"Maybe."

"And I am dumb. I'm the only one in my reading group. There's the Eagles and the Robins and the Bluebirds. And then there's me, all by myself. I don't even got the name of any old kind of a bird."

"I didn't say you could read well. I said you were smart. There's a difference."

"What?"

"If you're smart, you can learn to read better – if I can teach you the right way and if you work hard enough."

Joey was going to be a difficult child to help, because testing had not shown either his visual or his auditory processing to be an area of strength. I had a suspicion that Joey's auditory skills were better than the tests had shown and that the low scores in this area were more than likely due to lack of attending. His spoken language was so clear and he had picked up so much information that I felt his auditory reception couldn't be that bad, even if he couldn't repeat a string of numbers. Anxiety could also have interfered; it's hard to remember anything when you're scared. Later, the audiologist confirmed that there was no physical impairment in his auditory channels.

I decided to use a combination of methods to teach Joey to read until I discovered which one worked best. The biggest thing Joey had going for him was his intelligence. If he could see that reading was like a code, the letters standing for certain sounds depending on their position, then he could learn to crack the code.

It was important for Joey to understand that 85 percent of reading is made up of decodable words; the other 15 percent would be designated *red words*. I would print these *red words* on index cards in red ink and ask Joey to memorize them. But that was the only memorization I would ask for; the rest of the words he could figure out by using the rules. The books that I gave Joey to read would have a carefully controlled vocabulary, using words that followed the rules he had already learned. I was counting on the fact that someone as independent as Joey would love being able to figure it all out himself.

The spelling and writing would go hand in hand with the reading. Once a child has learned to read "hat," he can also learn to write it, if he is taught how to match graphemes (letters) to phonemes (sounds). We would incorporate Orton-Gillingham methods, and I would have Joey visualize the word – saying it out loud, writing it on the desk, sand tray, or paper.

I would be careful not to ask him to spell words that were not phonetically regular, and I would also be careful not to present too much new information at one time. I felt that much of Joey's trouble was that when he was given too much at one time he became overwhelmed. I suspected that this was when he fell out of his chair.

That first morning I simply told Joey the sound of each letter and showed him how to write both the lowercase and capitals. "See it, hear it, say it, write it, Joey. Take your time." This wasn't easy for Joey. He confused the sounds for *b* and *p* and, of course, reversed many letters. Still, his writing improved enormously in that one short session as he learned how to form each letter correctly and to say its sound as he wrote it.

I knew I was beginning at the beginning and that I was running the risk of boring him since all this had been presented in first grade and probably earlier, but I also knew the risk was slight.

Few learning disabled children are bored. They may pretend they are or their parents may like to think they are, but most are scared instead. Neither they nor their parents can understand how they can know something one day and not the next. Usually this is because they haven't learned the beginning steps of a task thoroughly enough to use them spontaneously and "on demand," and particularly when they're under pressure to perform.

In any event, we both got so involved with what we were doing that we ran five minutes into the next child's session. Still, we took the time to count up Joey's chips and to enter the total, 840, in his notebook and then subtract 600 for the sugarless, all-natural-ingredient lollipop that he bought from the "goody basket." I kept a small supply of treats in a wicker basket on top of the file cabinet, and at the end of each session the children had one minute to decide if they wanted to spend their chips or save them up.

Twice a week through June and July, Joey and I read and wrote and spelled together. We added and subtracted.

We also talked and played a few games. There were no miracles. I just taught and retaught and let Joey practice and end with success each time. His ability to decode and his sight vocabulary both improved; his writing became more legible and computation more accurate. I assigned small amounts of homework, which Joey did on his own and, even more important, remembered to bring back.

He still twisted in his chair and fiddled with paper clips, but he learned how to breathe to consciously relax his body and to live with the three breaks I allowed him each session.

By the end of July we had both learned a number of things. Joey had learned to read, although he was still below grade level, and I had learned that Joey's disorganizational problems were not his alone. They seemed to be part of the family lifestyle. My phone messages rarely got delivered, and Joey often arrived on the wrong day or ten minutes early or not at all.

Still, we all felt encouraged. It had been a month and a half since Joey had fallen out of his chair or said he was dumb. But then again, it was summer and Joey always did well in the summer.

I sent him off on his August vacation with two books to read and a workbook I knew he could handle. We'd just have to see what happened in the fall.

The Stones came back from their vacation a week early to give Joey a chance to review with me before he was retested by the school. The Child Study Team tested him the day after Labor Day and said that while he was still "deficient," there had been "significant improvement," and they agreed to let Joey go on to second grade in his own school.

None of us anticipated that Joey would end up in Mrs. Madden's class. It was nobody's fault. The second-grade teacher Joey was slated to have became pregnant over the summer and on the first day of school decided she didn't feel well enough to handle both her first pregnancy and a second-grade class. She opted for a year's leave of absence. The principal, Mr. Templar, thought the new teacher he hired was too inexperienced to handle Joey, so he transferred Joey to Mrs. Madden's class.

Mrs. Madden was certainly experienced. Thirty years of experience – most of it in the same school system. When I called her during the first week of school to tell her about Joey's evaluation and what we had done over the summer, and to ask if I could check in with her every week or so, Mrs. Madden made it clear that conferences or phone calls with me were not necessary. She said she had discussed Joseph's case with the Child Study Team. She understood they were giving him a trial in second grade. She assured me that she had known plenty of other children with problems and that Joseph would not cause any trouble in her class. She also said she thought she should be honest with me and tell me that in her opinion tutors were a waste of time – worse than a waste if they let the child become dependent on them. Of course, if the Stones wanted to throw their money away it was up to them.

When I called the Child Study Team to say that it appeared that I was going to have some difficulty communicating with Mrs. Madden, they said they understood, they had difficulty themselves, but that in many ways she was a very good teacher.

Joey dragged himself up to my office at a quarter to six the Tuesday after school started. He stood in the middle of the floor and raised his arms and then let them drop. "The bad news is, I got Madden. The next bad news is, I'm still not in a group – there's the Yankees, the Red Sox, the Orioles, and me. The next bad news is, she made me miss gym and stay after school, too! I'm never going to make it through second, Mary!"

"Sit down, Joey. I'm glad to see you. Pay yourself forty. That's a lot of bad news."

I'd been thinking about Mrs. Madden ever since our phone call. I had silently hoped against hope that somehow she and Joey would communicate even though she and I hadn't been able to. Evidently that hadn't happened.

I looked at Joey. "Okay. I hear you. So you got a tough teacher. You're a tough kid. You can figure out how to get through second grade."

Joey rolled slowly to one side and then silently toppled from his chair to the floor. He sprawled across the grey carpet – eyes closed, body limp as a rag doll. I sat watching. After a full minute had passed, Joey opened one eye and squinted up at me. I looked benignly back, waiting for the full show. There was no question that Joey knew how to put on a wonderful act.

Sure now that I was watching, Joey rolled his eyes up into his head so that white, pupil-less eyes stared out at me, and his legs and arms flailed up and down. The kids in school must have loved it.

"Okay now, Joey. That's enough." I reached down and hoisted him back up beside me. "We've only got forty-five minutes. We don't have time for any of that stuff. Besides, I don't like it. The next time you hit the floor it costs you one hundred."

"One hundred!" Joey howled. "Cripes! You wouldn't do that!" He put his hand protectively over the red plastic dish that held his chips.

"You know I would. But I'll tell you what. This first month of school, every day of September that you make it through with Mrs. Madden I'll pay you a hundred."

"What do you mean, like … like if I don't have to stay after school?"

"Right. And don't get sent to the principal or have to miss gym. Things like that. You're going to have to be so good, Joe. Not just a little good, but one hundred percent good every day. Never mind about the Red Sox – I know you can read and you'll learn to read better. But you have to hand in whatever work Mrs. Madden gives you. Always remember your homework, keep your desk clean, keep yourself in your seat, raise your hand before you say anything, stay in line and a whole lot more."

"I don't know. It sounds like a pretty terrible life."

"Well, Joey, consider the alternatives."

"What's alternatives?"

"Other choices. Like failing second and having to stay back and have Mrs. Madden all over again."

"Oh, boy."

During the fourth week of school I decided to drop in on Mrs. Madden. If my phone calls didn't work, I had to find some other way to discover what was going on in school.

At ten after three I walked down the hall to second grade, nodding to the janitor. I'd been in the school many times to talk to other children's teachers, but I'd never encountered Mrs. Madden before.

She was seated at her desk going over papers when I tapped on the window. Her grey hair was neatly and tightly curled against her head. The bow of her blouse hung in two perfect loops between the lapels of a maroon suit. Mrs. Madden got up and walked slowly across the room.

She opened the door and stood without smiling.

"Mrs. Madden? I'm Mary MacCracken," I said.

"Yes. I thought as much." She made no move to invite me inside.

"May I talk to you for ten minutes?" I knew all teachers were expected to stay until three thirty.

She looked at the clock over the door. "Three twelve. All right. Come in."

I followed her to the front of the room, and she motioned me to a chair beside her desk. I sat facing Mrs. Madden, aware that the room was much more pleasant than I had expected. The large, sunny windows to my left were filled with leafy green plants of all sizes. A fish tank hummed on the window sill. The blackboard had the day's homework assignment printed neatly in the left-hand corner, and five short sentences about a trip to the police station were lettered in the middle. Had Mrs. Madden actually taken her class to the police station?

I held two of Joey's folders on my lap. One contained the written report of the testing I had done (I had asked the Stones' permission to bring it), the other some of his recent work. But I didn't open either. I was there to try to find out how Mrs.

Madden and Joey were getting on. Did she realize the potential he had? Was he working? Was he learning?

"May I ask how Joey is doing?"

Mrs. Madden reached for her grade book. "You have the parents' permission, I assume." I nodded, and she read from the book: "Arithmetic: 68, 75, 90, incomplete, incomplete, 80. Reading workbook: 55, 72, incomplete, incomplete, incomplete, 84, incomplete, incomplete. Spelling: 45, 25, 60, 50. There are no incompletes in spelling because everyone takes the test on Friday, ready or not. Phonics: 60, 50, incomplete, incomplete, incomplete, incomplete, 60."

Mrs. Madden snapped her grade book shut. "You will have to consult with the specials about gym, art, library, and remedial."

"Thank you," I said, putting my notebook back in my purse. "There seem to be a lot of incompletes."

"Yes. Joseph often doesn't complete his work. This is partly due to his not paying attention, so he doesn't understand what to do. He always wants me to go over it again with him. I do not believe in this. He must learn to listen.

"The other reason he gets behind is that he's out of the room so much," Mrs. Madden continued. "Out with the reading teacher, out for some program or other. Out for this. Out for that. No wonder he gets behind in his class work."

I got the strong impression that Mrs. Madden didn't believe in remedial help any more than she did in tutors. Well, at least she didn't seem overly anxious to get Joey out of her room, and that was a positive sign.

The clock ticked its way toward three twenty-five, and I stood up, to reassure Mrs. Madden that I would not linger.

"One last question. Would it be possible to borrow an extra copy of any of Joey's books? Spelling, arithmetic, phonics?"

Mrs. Madden shrugged, stood up, smoothed out her unwrinkled maroon skirt. "Call Mr. Templar, our principal. That's up to him."

"Thank you," I said as I walked toward the door. "I appreciate your time and your interest in Joe."

Mrs. Madden accepted my appreciation with a nod as she eased me out the door. "I will tell you one thing," Mrs. Madden said magnanimously. "It doesn't show in the grade book, but that boy is a lot smarter than those Child Study Team tests show. A lot smarter!"

I stared at Mrs. Madden, restraining a nearly overwhelming impulse to hug her. "I agree," I almost shouted. "But how did you find out? Did you give Joey some tests of your own?"

Mrs. Madden turned back to her classroom. Like a queen in her kingdom she pronounced, "After thirty years, I don't need tests."

Joey dragged the heavy plastic bag across my office floor. "Mr. Templar said to bring you these." He dumped the contents onto the carpet beside the desk and moaned out loud as his reading, math, spelling, and phonics books fell out. "Oh, no. It's horrible to have to do them in school. It'll be even horribler to have to do them all over again here."

We didn't, of course, "do" the books, but Joey could show me where he was and what he didn't understand. It was much easier for him than trying to explain it. Also, since Mrs. Madden proceeded page by page, chapter by chapter, I could look ahead and see what was coming up next, and let Joey become a little familiar with it before Mrs. Madden introduced it in class.

Mrs. Madden was still curt, but she was doing her part. She now answered my phone calls if I timed them right and sent Joey's test papers in a sealed envelope on Fridays. She hadn't complained or called the Stones in, except for the scheduled fall conference. All she told them then was that Joey still needed a lot of work, but that he was making progress. The main thing was what she didn't say. There had been no mention of a special class.

My phone rang around noon one day in February. It was snowing hard and I had gone down to pick up the mail, so it took me five or six rings to get back to the phone.

"Mrs. MacCracken? This is Mrs. Madden. I almost hung up. I thought you must be out." Disapproval edged her voice.

"Sorry." I was so glad she'd initiated the call that it was worth sounding penitent.

"Yes. Well. Joseph is getting further and further behind in his B book. Phonics book, that is. He always has to go out when it's time for phonics. Now he's twenty pages behind – hasn't even touched the magic *e* rule. I'd like him to do pages ninety-eight, one hundred one, one hundred five, and one hundred seven with you. That will give him an idea of what the others have covered. Don't do the work for him. I want to see his own work. Send it in so I can check it. I'd have the specials do it with him, but they say they have too much work of their own."

"All right," I said, writing on the telephone book. "Page ninety-eight ... could you give me those other pages again?"

I knew how the specials felt. This would take time that I would much rather spend on other things, but what mattered was that Mrs. Madden was becoming a member of our team. And that was a top priority.

There was no doubt about it. In spite of missed pages in the B book, Joey was flourishing. He added, he subtracted, he even multiplied a little. His facts still weren't totally automatic and he sometimes got mixed up during subtraction and regrouping (another word for borrowing and carrying), but he understood what he was doing and he was one of the best in the class at problem solving.

With our combined efforts on phonics, word attack skills, and sight vocabulary, Joey's reading was improving steadily. One of the things that helped most was that the Stones took turns reading to Joey every night. After Joey was washed and brushed and in bed, either Mr. or Mrs. Stone read to him for a half hour. To their joy, not only was he enjoying reading more, he was also sleeping better.

But only one thing was important to Joey. "Do you think she'll let me be a Red Sox now?"

Not a Red Sox and not till April.

"Da-de-ah-da-dah!" Joey blew an imaginary trumpet in the doorway of my office. "The good news is, I'm a goddamn Oriole!"

"Joe – cool it. No swearing."

"Well, I am. I got moved up yesterday. I'm in a group!"

A cause for celebration. Joey was no longer alone, isolated, different. Now he, like the others in his class, belonged.

In June Joey graduated from second grade and was promoted to third. On my testing he had moved up to the 54th percentile in silent reading vocabulary and to the 69th percentile in comprehension. His math was on grade level, spelling slightly below.

On the school tests, Joey was on grade level in all areas, and Mrs. Madden wrote on his report card, "Marked improvement in behavior and academic skills." High praise indeed from Mrs. Madden.

One unexpected piece of news was that Mrs. Madden was retiring. I couldn't imagine her classroom without her – or the other way around. She had believed in Joey and given him a safe, structured place where he could learn. Mr. Templar assured me that it was her choice. She'd always wanted to travel and was looking forward to retirement. Maybe. But it would take an awful lot of lakes and mountains to make up for Joey.

If it was sad to hear that Mrs. Madden was retiring, it was good to hear that Mrs. Stone had decided to freelance and use her computer skills at home rather than in an office.

"It's funny," she told me on the phone. "I actually like being home now; I don't know whether it's because Joey's better or because I don't feel so guilty anymore. Even though I never even realized that I felt guilty. All I know is that now I want to be around the kids as much as I can. I never would've believed I'd ever say that. I'm taking the summer off and then come fall I'm going to start working at home.

"Al feels the same. He hardly ever works weekends anymore. In fact, he's the one who bought me the home computer."

I was happy for them and for Joey. But I was also glad that Joey remained himself. I loved the slightly lopsided, ebullient, dramatic part of him as much as or more than the part that had made it into the Orioles.

He came for one last visit before summer vacation and we picked out some books and workbooks that would review the skills he'd learned in second grade. He promised to keep the study sheet I gave him that would show how he spent his twenty minutes of work each day while he was at the lake.

"How does it feel, Joey?" I asked. "Do you feel good about this year?"

He shrugged. "Yeah. I guess so. I mean, I know I'm pretty good at reading now, and I can add and even subtract pretty good. I don't fall out of my chair or get in as much trouble. But multiplication's hard and you got to be able to do two digits in third. I'll never get that."

He shook his head and stood up. "See, Mary. It's like this with me. If it's not one thing, it's another."

I laughed. "You'll get it in the fall, Joey," I said.

Joey's taxi was late, but Joey was my last appointment for the day and I was glad to have a few extra minutes with him before he left for vacation. We munched on nuts and raisins and the popcorn I always kept in the office as we chatted and waited for the taxi.

A horn beeped and Joey picked up his books, workbooks, and papers. He grabbed an extra handful of popcorn and ran through the door and down the steps.

Halfway to the cab he turned back to wave, and as he did, his feet somehow slid out from under him and he fell flat, face down in the driveway, surrounded by books, papers, and popcorn.

"Oh, Joey …" I started toward him, but before I was down the steps, Joey was back on his feet, shrugging his shoulders in my direction, grinning, waving one last time.

By the next day the squirrels had eaten the popcorn, and I'll never be quite sure whether Joey's fall was an accident or his idea of a perfect exit.

Second grade had gone so well that Joey and I both took the whole summer off. Joey was at his cottage at Lake Champlain; I was at our summer house in Connecticut. We were also both late getting back in gear, so Joey had been in school for over a week before I saw him for the first time.

Obviously, something had happened since I'd last seen Joey, and whatever it was, it wasn't good. Joey was a wreck. He sat behind my office desk opening drawers, shuffling papers, bending paper clips. His nails were bitten down to the quick. His old-time nervous restlessness was running high, but there was also a new listless quality that bothered me even more.

"What's wrong, Joey?"

He hunched his shoulders. "I don't know."

"Do you like your teacher?"

"Not much. She's new."

"It's okay to be new. Everybody's new sometime. What don't you like?"

"I don't know. I can't explain it. She gets me all mixed up."

I didn't press further. If Joey was forced to continue to struggle, trying to put emotions he didn't understand into words, it would only make him more anxious.

I switched to something more concrete. "Did you bring your notebook?"

Joey dragged his book bag onto the desk. One look confirmed that things were not going well. Already, covers were coming off books and scraps of papers and pencils mingled with gum wrappers and an odd sock in the bottom of the bag.

I lifted out the notebook. There was no assignment pad in the front; in fact, there was nothing at all in the notebook except blank paper.

"Do you have homework for tomorrow?" I asked.

Again Joey shrugged. "I don't know."

"Joe ..." I began.

But Joey interrupted. "I mean it," he said. "I don't know what's going on. She reads out the homework so fast I can't even hear it, and I sure can't write it down. She never puts it on the board. It doesn't matter anyway, because even if I do it she never collects it.

"Then like in spelling, she hands out these purple dittos with the spelling words all scrambled up. She says it's a game to help us learn our spelling words, but I never even know what the spelling words are 'cause I can't get them unscrambled. Everything's like that – English, math, social studies – everything's all mixed up."

Poor Joey. The last thing he needed was a disorganized classroom and an inexperienced teacher. He had to work hard enough to keep things straight inside his own head without having outside confusion heaped on top of it. What was Mr. Templar thinking of? He knew the kind of classroom Joey needed. But the way it was now, Joey was going to have to muster up his own skills in order to survive.

"Listen, Joey. I hear you, but I don't want to see all you've learned go down the tube just because you have a new teacher. You have to get your assignments down – and you have to clean up your act. If you don't hear what your teacher says, then you have to go up after school and ask her again."

"Sure. And by the time I get out all the other guys will be gone."

"Then go in early and get it before school starts. I'll talk to her, Joe, but you've got to do your part."

We talked about this and Joey softened a little. "Yeah – okay. Anyway, what's expanded notation? See, I did write my math homework here on my book cover, but I don't get it."

A Safe Place for Joey

We discussed expanded notation for the rest of his time, and Joey was doing it easily by the end of the hour. But somehow this didn't make me feel much better, and I watched uneasily from my office window as Joey unlocked his bike from a tree. Before he got on he took a pair of headphones from the pocket of his jacket and clamped them on his head, as if to seal off the rest of the world.

I called Joey's mother at home the next day. No answer. On impulse, I called her old office number; she picked up on the first ring. "I know you can't talk now," I said, "but I was wondering if we could get together sometime. Your husband, too. I'm worried about Joey."

"I was going to call you," Mrs. Stone replied. "He's been terrible at home. One thing Joey always had was a sense of humor. Not anymore. Everything anybody does is wrong. Listen, I know Al wants to talk to you too – but he got this new promotion and he's working late every night. Actually, I'm back at work too, as you can see," she giggled nervously. "Or hear." There was a slight pause. "I guess we both changed our minds. Anyway, I hate to ask it, but do you think you could come over on Saturday afternoon? Rich has early football practice, and Joey and Bill always go and hang around to watch him, so we'll be able to talk."

I hesitated. I tried to save the weekends for my own family. But I was worried about Joey. I had the feeling that he was getting in deeper every day.

"How's two o'clock?" I asked. "I'll check in with his teacher before Saturday. Ms. Ansara, is it?"

"I guess so," Mrs. Stone said. "At least that's what it sounds like. Back-to-school night isn't until October. Uh-oh. I gotta go. See you Saturday."

I stopped by Mr. Templar's office the next day to return Joey's second-grade books and to try to get the ones for third grade. I also needed to find out about Joey's teacher. Mr. Templar was a good principal – fair and caring, about both the children and his staff – and putting Joey in with an inexperienced teacher wasn't consistent with what I knew about him.

"Ms. Answera, you mean. Third grade. Yes, she's new, but she got good grades at college." Mr. Templar made a wry face. "Whatever that's worth. How they expect us to teach children when they don't teach the teachers is beyond me.

"Look, I know it must be hard for Joey, but it's equally hard for Ms. Answera. And me. Do you know how many of my teachers left this year? Over a third of my staff, including both third-grade teachers, are new. Do you have any idea how many parents are calling me? Well, I do the best I can. What more can I say? I can't even blame the teachers. They can get a lot more money as well as more respect someplace else. Anyway, come on, I'll take you down and introduce you."

The third-grade class was pouring in from gym. They'd been out in the yard in the warm, sunny September weather and now, hot and sweaty, they pushed and shoved one another through the classroom door. Ms. Answera adjusted the strap of her blue sundress as she teetered back and forth on high-heeled sandals, cautioning the class to quiet down.

I looked around for Joey. Situations like this could set him off like a Roman candle. But not this time. Joey walked by, shoulders hunched, hands in his pockets, oblivious to everything that was going on; even his red hair seemed dull and lifeless. I could not believe he was allowed to wear headphones in school, but he had them on and no one seemed to notice.

"Ms. Answera," Mr. Templar said, "I know this isn't the best timing, but Mrs. MacCracken isn't in our school very often, and I wanted you two to have the chance to meet. Mrs. MacCracken works with Joey Stone."

Ms. Answera peered at me through violet-tinted glasses, big as saucers. "Pleased to meet you," she said.

"Listen, I'll come back tomorrow before school, if that's all right? You don't need interruptions on a day like this."

"Sure thing," Ms. Answera answered amiably. "That'd be fine."

I waved to Joey before I left, but if he saw me he gave no sign. He slouched against the coat closet, headphones in place, eyes focused on something out of sight.

I was more concerned than ever after my visit to the school. I didn't blame Mr. Templar or Ms. Answera, and besides, blaming the system wouldn't help Joey. Maybe I'd been wrong. Maybe I shouldn't have fought so hard to keep him in a regular class. If Joey was in special ed now, there would be fewer kids and less confusion, and probably the same teacher as the year before.

Mrs. Stone was watering the lawn when I pulled up in front of her house.

"Thank you for taking time on a Saturday," she said, as we walked down the front walk.

She smiled, but before she could open the door, her smile disappeared. A loud, angry, male voice shouted, "Get out of here! Right now! Damn it! I told you a hundred times! No food in the den! I don't care if that's where the television is. This place is a mess! Now get that plate back to the kitchen, you little pig."

"That's Grandpa." Gail Stone sighed. "The boys drive him crazy, especially Joey. Mom died early this summer, and with his blood pressure I didn't dare leave him alone. So we sold their house and he moved in here. It seemed like a good idea at the time."

"Anyway," she said, "let's go out back. Al will be right down."

There was a small terrace at the far end of the yard, and Mrs. Stone motioned me to a canvas chair and handed me a glass of iced tea.

Al Stone came out from the house and across the backyard. He looked tired, thinner than I remembered. Something in his hair glinted in the sunlight, and I stared in disbelief. The metal sidepieces of headphones identical to those Joey wore reflected the afternoon sun.

Al slipped the headphones off as he approached and shook my hand. "Good to see you. How've you been?"

"Fine," I replied, still riveted to the headphones.

"Oh," he said, following my eyes. "These? Only way to survive around here."

"Gailllll? Where are you? Gailllll?" Grandpa stood in the back doorway, calling plaintively.

"Excuse me. I'll just be a minute," Gail Stone said apologetically, as she scurried across the yard.

Although the sun shone and the birds sang, I shivered in the canvas chair. It was clear that Joey's world was coming apart, both at home and in school.

Al Stone said nothing all afternoon. It was as though he too had turned off the world. Although his headphones were off, he was still listening to something else. He was pleasant but quiet, and either resisted or ignored every attempt I made to draw him into the conversation. Mrs. Stone and I talked, but all the important things went unsaid.

Gail Stone did not mention that she was torn between her obligations to her father and the resentment of her husband.

A Safe Place for Joey

All afternoon she ran back and forth between them, trying to keep the peace, while we talked in snatches about what was happening to Joey.

Al Stone did not talk about the anger he felt at having his home invaded by a querulous, demanding old man – he just tuned out. He stayed at work as late as he could and put on his headphones when he got home. When I commented on the inappropriateness of Joey wearing headphones in school, Al Stone smiled pleasantly and said that he hadn't realized Joey wore them in school.

But I never did point out to Al Stone that his actions spoke more strongly than his words. Joey, like his father, was shutting out the confusion of his world by putting on his headphones. In fact, Gail Stone murmured as she walked me to my car that both father and son often fell asleep with headphones in place, music blasting into their eardrums. Who knew what effect this had on Joey's auditory processing? How was Joey ever going to make it? His world at school was a jumble of confusion; his world at home was filled with anger, resentment, guilt, and noise. I didn't see how things could be any worse for Joey.

But I was wrong. Grandpa dropped dead from a heart attack two months later, just before Thanksgiving, and instead of improving, things got even worse. Now Joey stopped talking almost completely. He did no homework and, according to his mother, "didn't eat enough to keep a bird alive." Gail Stone and I talked by phone once or twice a week. She was as troubled as I was and just as confused. None of us could figure it out. As far as we knew, Joey had been frightened of Grandpa, and it would certainly be expected that Joey would be relieved not to have Grandpa after him all the time.

I tried to talk to Joey, but he tuned me out as effectively as if his headphones were in place. He worked while he was in my office and most of his skills were still there, but he handed in absolutely no homework and Ms. Answera reported that he did not "contribute" in class. Mr. Templar called to say that Ms. Answera had told him she didn't think Joey belonged in a regular class.

I strongly recommended that the Stones arrange for Joey to see a psychologist, but Al Stone wouldn't hear of it.

"Joey's not crazy," he said. "Grandpa was the crazy one. Joey'll be all right now that Grandpa's not around. Just give him time. It's only been a few weeks."

I wondered if Al Stone had taken off his headphones yet. I knew that Joey hadn't.

It was almost Christmas, a month since Grandpa had died. I put a little tree at one end of my office and decorated it with paper chains and ornaments that the children brought in. There was a small wrapped gift for each of them beneath the tree to take home after their last visit before the holidays. My other children were all thriving. Only Joey remained cold and silent, nervously chewing his fingernails.

Just before Joey arrived for his last session before the holidays, I impulsively scratched out the lesson I had planned and decided to read to Joey instead. If he couldn't tell me what was wrong, maybe we could at least share a story. It was a gentle tale, and the boy in the story had small worries of his own. There was no fireplace or chimney in his house, and he was certain that Santa wouldn't know how to find him. Finally his mother persuaded him to hang his stocking from a post at the foot of his bed and to go to sleep thinking loving thoughts. Santa, of course, found the stocking, and in the morning the boy woke to find it fat and overflowing with toys and candy.

In the center of one page there was a black line drawing of a narrow bed with four spool posts; a bulging striped stocking dangled from the post at the bottom of the bed.

I started to close the book, but Joey, sitting beside me, pushed it open. Silently he traced the bed with his finger. I moved my hand to cover his, but he shoved me away impatiently. Over and over he traced the drawing of the bed from head to foot.

I thought I heard him say something and I leaned closer.

"The bed," Joey mumbled.

"What did you say, Joey?" I asked softly.

Joey didn't hear me, or if he did he gave no indication of it. But he was surely talking, if only to himself. "On the bed. On the bed."

"On the bed," I repeated. "Something was on the bed."

Now Joey responded, nodding his head. "On the bed. He was on the bed."

I willed myself to tune to Joey, to understand what he was saying.

I repeated, "He was on the bed." I took a chance, adding a little more. "He was lying on the bed."

Joey continued nodding, almost frenzied now. "Lying on the bed. Lying on the bed. Grandpa."

Grandpa?

Suddenly Joey turned his body so that he faced me squarely. His voice was flat and cold, but he was talking directly to me, not to himself or the book. "Grandpa was on my bed when he died. I killed him."

"No," I said. "No, of course not. You didn't kill him."

"Yes," Joey insisted. "Yes, I did. I even listened to him die."

My eyes stayed locked with Joey's, and he went on talking in the same flat voice.

"See, he chased me," Joey said. "I didn't know he was going to. I just ran out of the TV room 'cause he got so mad when I imitated the way he yells. I ran up to my room and hid under my bed so he couldn't get me.

"But then I heard him coming after me, running all the way up the stairs and sort of bumping along the wall. Then all of a sudden he came crashing into my room and fell down on my bed real hard and began making these choking noises."

The way Joey told it made it so clear. Joey's facility for imitating and dramatizing must have infuriated Grandpa. No wonder he'd charged after the boy, forgetting his own high blood pressure.

"Then after a while he stopped and it was real quiet ... and that was even worse," Joey went on, "because then it began to get dark and I knew I had to get out of there before Rich and Bill got home and found me under that bed. If they found me there, they'd know for sure I'd done it."

There were three loud knocks on my office door. My next child had arrived. "Just a minute," I called as softly as I could, never moving my eyes from Joey's. "Go on, Joey. Don't stop."

"I got out," he said, his voice just above a whisper, "but it was hard 'cause the bed was way on top of me 'cause Grandpa was so fat, but I squeezed out and ran downstairs and turned on all the lights. The TV was already on, and so I just stayed there in front of it, real quiet.

"When Mom found him ... see, Grandpa didn't come to supper like usual, so they started calling him and then they went looking for him, and after a while Mom found him in my room. And she began to scream and cry and yell that he was dead. That's when I knew I'd killed him for sure. I'd been thinking he was maybe just sick. But he wasn't, he was dead."

The knocks sounded on the door again. "One more minute," I called back.

"Don't tell," Joey said, panicking, pulling at my sleeve. "I didn't mean to tell you."

"Joey, listen. Grandpa was very old and very sick. He had a heart attack. Your mom told me he did. That happens to lots of old people."

"I don't even know when he died," Joey said. "Maybe he was still alive when I left. Maybe if I'd called a doctor, he would've been all right. Besides, I wanted him to die. Sometimes I even prayed that he would. Maybe my praying made it come true."

No wonder Joey hadn't told anyone. He must have been terrified, lying there alone trapped underneath Grandpa while he died, later convinced that he had killed him.

Joey put his head down on the desk. I put my arms around him for a second and then I phoned his mother.

Joey stayed in my office through my next two appointments. He lay curled under a woolen afghan on the couch and either slept or pretended to, until his mother arrived.

In the waiting room, I asked Gail Stone if it was true that she had found Grandpa in Joey's room.

She nodded. "Why?"

"Why didn't you say something at the time?" I asked in return.

Tears gathered in Mrs. Stone's eyes. "I don't know. Joey was taking it so hard I thought it would just make it worse if he realized that I'd found Grandpa in his bed. Joey was downstairs watching TV the whole time it was going on. I think Dad must have been on his way to the bathroom just across the hall from Joey's room. All I can think is that maybe he felt sick or dizzy or had a spell and thought he'd go in and lie down on Joey's bed for a minute. Nobody will ever know for sure. What does this have to do with Joey, anyway? Why'd you call me? Is anything wrong?"

The next day Gail Stone and I met in my office during her lunch hour.

"Al and I talked for hours last night after the boys were in bed," she said. "It really shook Al up to realize what had been going on in Joey's head and he – Al, I mean – had never suspected it.

"Al's a good man. He works hard, he's smart, he loves his family. He's been true to me through thick and thin. It was my fault – bringing Grandpa home. I know that now. I think I was still trying to please him, like I did when I was little. It never worked then either. I should have just hired somebody to stay with him, seeing that his house was so close by.

"Well, never mind," Gail continued. "It's over now. We'll mend. But will Joey? That's what we want to know. I know you probably think we should all go into therapy, but Al's dead set against it. He says we at least ought to give ourselves a chance first. He says he'll talk to me, he'll talk to the boys, but he doesn't want to have to start talking to some stranger – at least not now. I understand that. But I have to know that we won't lose Joey again."

"I know," I said, struggling for words. I did believe family therapy would help, but not if it were forced. "How do you feel about it?" I asked.

"I've been thinking all night," Gail replied. "I didn't sleep much. I guess none of us did, except Joey. He slept the clock around, and this morning he seemed the best I'd seen him in months. Ate two bowls of oatmeal – told his dad all about Grandpa, when I would have thought he wouldn't mention a word. I let him stay home from school today, and Al took the day off, too. When I left, Joey was watching TV and Al was reading the paper, peaceful as could be.

"I think we can do it. Al and I go back a long way, and we've seen a lot of troubles along with the good times. Besides, Al's a determined one. Once he puts his mind to something, he sticks to it."

I thought about Joey as she talked. He had made such progress the year before. He had turned his high level of energy toward active learning. He had stopped playing the fool, although he still liked to joke and kid around. He loved people; he was intelligent and well-coordinated; he had a good ear for music and an unusual flair for the dramatic. His strengths were all still there. They just couldn't get through in the confusion of school and the tension at home.

"Will it be any different at your house now? Because with Ms. Answera in the classroom, I don't think there is going to be any big change at school. And you know Joey. He thrives when things are structured and safe and organized – and he falls apart when there's change and confusion or he's scared."

Gail nodded. "And so do I. I'm not very organized myself. I know that, but what I'm saying is we're going to try. You told me once that everyone could grow – not just children. Remember?"

"I remember," I said.

"And you still believe it's true?" she asked.

"Yes," I nodded. "It's still true."

"Well, for starters," Gail said, "I'm giving up my job. I have that computer Al got me a year ago, and we almost made it that time.

"I guess what I'm telling you is, I'm ready to be the best wife and mother I can."

I smiled at her and stood up. "It sounds to me as though you and Al have thought it through and that your minds are pretty well made up. You know I believe parents know their children better than anyone else. Anyway, if it feels right to you and Al, I'd talk to the boys and go ahead and give it a try."

Who says wishes don't come true? Ms. Answera went home to Florida for Christmas vacation and never returned. And even more wonderful for Joey, Mr. Templar was able to persuade Mrs. Madden to come back and teach Joey's third-grade class for the remainder of the year.

"Portugal has been around for quite some time," Mrs. Madden said when I went over to school to talk to her. "It's likely it'll still be there six months from now."

Once again I had to stick my hands in my pockets to keep from hugging her. Joey would be all right now – at least for this year, with Mrs. Madden back in charge at school and Joey's mom and dad a team again at home.

I continued seeing Joey twice a week through third and fourth grades and worked closely with his teachers. He accumulated a solid foundation of knowledge on which he could build and a growing confidence in his ability to learn. He was also the star of every class play. His tremendous natural energy projected out from the stage, and within minutes he held the audience in the palm of his hand.

We cut our sessions to once a week halfway through fifth grade and ended completely in sixth.

A Safe Place for Joey

I was there for Joey's graduation in an aisle seat. He shone like a burnished penny – dressed in a new blue suit, his red hair washed and neatly combed. He managed to sit still through the graduation exercises and receive his diploma without incident, but he caught my eye on the way out. The lopsided grin lit his face, and he did a perfect miniature imitation pratfall as he passed my seat.

As I said earlier, there was always something about Joey …

Eric

Nobody was in the waiting room the night that I met Eric. In fact, the lights weren't even on.

It had been a long day, and once the last child had left and I had cleaned up and put away books and toys, I was eager to be off. It was a good forty-five-minute drive from my office to our apartment, and the commuting traffic was heavy on the highways.

I shrugged on my jacket, turned out the lights, pulled shut my heavy office door, and almost stepped on Eric.

I rocked back away from him in surprise. "Hey, now! What's this? Are you okay?" As my eyes grew more accustomed to the dim light, I could make out a small boy sitting on the waiting-room floor just outside my door, examining the contents of a woman's purse.

The janitor had evidently already turned down the lights in the waiting room, so the only illumination was from the over-head light in the hall. I groped my way toward one of the reading lamps, and the little boy gave a whimper as light flooded over us.

A woman's voice came from one edge of the room. "Mrs. MacCracken? Is that you?"

She pushed herself up from the sofa with effort, at the same time pulling her worn black coat more closely around her. She must have once been a handsome woman, but now as she came closer I could see that her face was gaunt and deeply lined and there were dark circles beneath her eyes.

She spoke to me, but she was looking at the boy. She walked past me toward where he huddled against the wall, hands across his eyes. She pulled him toward her, gently cradling his head against her thigh, crooning, "Shhh, Errol. Shhh. It's all right now."

She turned to me and said, "He doesn't like the light."

They made a strange picture here in the lamplight – the black-cloaked figure bending over the tiny boy, her knobby fingers entangled in his limp brown hair, his face buried in her coat.

I glanced at my watch. Almost eight o'clock. More than a half-hour drive back home. I cleared my throat. "I'm sorry," I said. "It's very –"

"Please," the woman interrupted. "Don't go." She moved closer to me, her dark eyes searching my face, the boy clinging to her leg. She looked too old to be the mother of such a young child, but her next sentence implied she was.

"Mrs. Tortoni told me to come. You helped her Frank. She said you'd help us, too."

I felt a small rush of pleasure. When I'd begun my private practice as a learning disability consultant, Frank was one of my first students. Frank was dirt-poor, streetwise, smart as a whip. His father was a mechanic at the garage I used. Frank had been easy to help, mainly because there was nothing really wrong with him. No signs of any learning disability, no serious emotional problems. He'd just fallen through the cracks of the huge, inefficient school system in the economically bankrupt city where he lived. Someone had equated poor with dumb and placed him in the lowest track of skills classes. Each year he was passed on to the next grade in the same slow, dull track. But given a chance and a little outside help, Frank was off and running, eager to show what he could do, his parents cheering him on.

"I get it," he'd shout. "That stupid factoring! Ain't nothin' but doin' times and matchin' 'em up. Whyn't they just say so?"

I coached Frank before the state competency tests and called the school to see how he'd done.

The next year he was in the second-highest track in the middle school and flourishing.

Seduced by my thoughts of Frank and how little it had taken to help him, I hesitated.

"Please," the woman said. "Please just let me talk to you for a few minutes."

"Do you live near the Tortonis?" I asked, knowing they lived almost an hour away.

She nodded. "Two blocks down."

"How did you get here?"

"Bus," she said, matter-of-factly. "We changed at Grover."

A long, cold bus ride, particularly at this hour of day. This worn, weary woman must care a great deal about this strange boy or she would never have bothered.

I unlocked my office door, and they followed me back inside.

Now she sat silently. The effort of getting them both to my office seemed to have used up all her strength. I walked around the room collecting toys for the boy who sat on the floor by her feet. He was tiny, the size of a four-year-old, although his pale, pointed face seemed older. He turned away when I leaned down to place the cars and trucks and dolls beside him, and hid his face against the couch. I was tempted to stay on the floor myself, but then decided that right now I needed to talk to his mother – if indeed that was who this woman was.

I pulled a chair beside her and reached for a pad and pencil. "Why don't you begin by telling me both your names?"

"Kroner," she said. "I'm Blanche Kroner and this is Errol. Well, his name's really Eric. I just give him the name Errol, like a nickname. You know – like the movie star. Handsome and all."

I watched as Eric began to push one of the cars back and forth across the rug, never looking up, his little peaked face serious and intent. Did she really think him handsome?

Gradually Eric's story emerged bit by bit. Eric had one older sister, Bella, now fourteen. She had been born on the Kroners' first anniversary. Mrs. Kroner had vomited every day of her pregnancy with Bella, and after a labor of eighteen hours she'd sworn she'd never have another child. And she hadn't for eight years, although she said she had "lost two when she was two or three months along."

The summer after Bella's seventh birthday, Mrs. Kroner began to feel sick, and when the vomiting started she knew she was pregnant again. She thought about having an abortion, but somehow she couldn't bring herself to do it. She counted the days until the baby would be born, not because she wanted it, but to get relief from the pain and exhaustion. Then, to make matters worse, the baby was two weeks late, and when he did finally come he weighed only five pounds – so little and weak he couldn't even suck right.

Mrs. Kroner sighed. "I had to get him a bottle with a hole in the nipple so big I could practically pour the milk down him."

Unexpectedly, her face lit up, and for a few seconds there was a radiance that eliminated the weariness. "Even so, he was a sweet little tyke. The nurses were all crazy about him," she smiled, remembering.

As she talked I glanced at Eric from time to time. If he understood any of what was being said, he gave no sign. He was moving around a little now, lining up the cars and trucks in a straight row. He turned each car over and over, inspecting it carefully. Then, evidently having made a decision based on some standards of his own, he placed it in a certain spot in the row. There was something enormously appealing in his serious concentration. Sometimes he used his right hand, sometimes his left. When the cars were all properly aligned, he began lifting the dolls out of their carton, which was designed to look like a dollhouse.

There were five small figures made of soft, bendable plastic – their felt clothes somewhat torn (they had been with me a long time), but still completely recognizable – father, mother, girl, boy, and a diapered baby. Eric took them all out and laid them on the rug.

The bottom of the box was divided into compartments, representing rooms. I watched as Eric picked up the father doll and sat him in a room at the back end of the box. Next Eric placed the girl beside the father. Now he put the mother standing up in a room at the opposite end. Only the boy and the baby remained. He picked them up – holding one in each hand – and then put the baby next to the mother, but only for an instant, replacing the baby with the boy. He tried the boy doll in several different positions – standing, sitting, lying down – but evidently none was to his satisfaction. Finally he stashed the boy doll under one of the cushions of the couch and put the baby back beside the mother.

I had become so absorbed in Eric's play that I missed some of Mrs. Kroner's words. Now her voice reached me again, saying, "… never was one to say much, but he didn't get into things or talk back the way Bella did."

She hadn't sent Eric to nursery school. It had seemed like a waste of money, and besides, she liked having him around. Bella and her didn't get along, and Mr. Kroner slept days and worked nights at the factory, so it was kind of nice to have some company.

Eric had started kindergarten a year ago, when he was five, and everything seemed to be going along all right, although he was smaller than the other children and he was sick a lot. Just colds, earaches – nothing serious.

He didn't want to go back to school after summer vacation, but Mrs. Kroner had taken a job in a cosmetic factory a few blocks from their home, knowing Eric was going to be in first grade and in school all day. So she had to insist that he go, and after the first week or so he got used to it and stopped "crying his head off. But he still doesn't like school. He doesn't act up, but he can't wait to get out."

Neither she nor Mr. Kroner had ever gone for a parent conference, until last week. His first-grade teacher, Miss Selby, was "just real pushy" and said if they didn't come in, she'd come see them.

"So last Thursday I went, but now I wish I hadn't. All she did was say Eric didn't know this, didn't know that, didn't do show and tell, didn't follow directions, didn't talk right, couldn't learn his sounds. Said she wanted him tested. Well. I don't want any tests. I've had plenty of tests myself over the years, and if there isn't something wrong with you when they start, there is by the time they're done. So now I make Errol do his sounds at home with me every night."

It was not a happy picture. Mrs. Kroner had been in her late thirties during her pregnancy with Eric. She had a history of a difficult earlier pregnancy and subsequent spontaneous abortions. During Eric's gestational period she had severe nausea and vomiting. Eric was a low birth-weight baby with a weak sucking reflex, and he was colicky. He lacked the stimulation of nursery school. There was a history of ear infections, and Eric had disliked school from the beginning. Besides, there were intimations from Eric's play and Mrs. Kroner's comments that there was something odd about the family configuration. And yet there was a magnetism – I could feel myself being drawn to him almost against my will.

"What does Mr. Kroner think about all this?" I asked. She shrugged. "He leaves Eric to me. Says he has enough trouble keeping bread on the table. Says the school is probably making a fuss over nothing." Mrs. Kroner sighed. "But I don't know," she said. "I got to thinking about Mrs. Tortoni and Frankie, and I got thinking maybe you could help Eric with his schoolwork. You know, help him sound it out. Like I do at night."

I looked over at the little boy. He was holding the baby in the palm of his hand, stroking it rhythmically as he rocked back and forth, his eyes closed. It was my turn to sigh. Whatever it was that Eric needed, it was a lot more than sounding it out. Suddenly Eric opened his eyes, and I could see that they were filled with tears, his long dark eyelashes wet and clumped together. Why was he crying silently to himself?

"Suppose I go over to Eric's school and talk to his teacher. Miss Selby? Is that her name? Maybe she can give me some more information about the kind of help Eric needs."

"No!" Mrs. Kroner spoke sharply. "I don't want the school to know I'm here. Then they'll be even surer there's something wrong with him. Or else they'll say it's the tutor what's doing the work, not Eric."

"Mrs. Kroner, I'm sorry." And I really was. Despite the hour, despite the obvious problems, there was something about this little boy and his mother that drew me to them, and I was moved by how much she obviously loved her son and how desperately she wanted to help him. Still, I couldn't work behind a cloud of pretense. I tried to explain. "I can't work that way. I need your help and Eric's teacher's, too. We all have to work together, be a team, if we're going to help Eric."

"What would you say to her?" Mrs. Kroner asked. "I wouldn't want you talking behind Eric's back – or mine neither."

"I would ask about the kind of things Eric does in school – where he does well and where he has trouble. I would ask about the other children and how he gets along with them."

"No," Mrs. Kroner said again.

I sighed – half weariness, half exasperation.

"Then I don't see how I can …"

I stopped speaking as something touched my right foot. I looked down and saw that Eric had put the baby in one of the trucks and was crouched beside his mother's legs, pushing the truck back and forth. The truck had bumped against my shoe. An accident, or was this Eric's way of asking for help? He was as pale and silent as before, but now he looked steadily up at me and pointed at the truck. My heart capitulated.

"What is it, Eric?" I asked, bending down. But the moment was gone. I had lost him. He buried his head back against the couch. But during that one brief instance of eye contact I could feel the intelligence behind those eyes, and I knew without a shadow of a doubt that if I could reach this little boy, I could teach him.

Mrs. Kroner interrupted my thoughts. "Could you call her instead – his teacher?" she almost whispered. "Instead of going over there?"

"Yes," I said. "I guess I could. If you would feel better about that."

"If you did call her, would you tell her what I told you? You know – about how I didn't even really want Eric at first?"

"No," I said. "I don't think there's any need to talk about that. In fact, I'm not even sure it's true."

I wished Mrs. Kroner had given me permission to visit the school. I could have gathered so much information by observing Eric's interaction with the other children and his response to his teacher. And I certainly needed all the information I could get, particularly since there was to be no formalized testing. I had compromised because I didn't want to lose Eric, and now I had to stick to my agreement. I could only hope his teacher was a good communicator.

Miss Selby spoke clearly and matter-of-factly. "I'm very concerned," she said at once. "I'm new. This is my first year here and it's a big school. There's a lot I don't understand – I'm the first to admit it. But I really don't see why Eric's in our school at all. He just doesn't fit in with the other children. Why they ever promoted him from kindergarten is beyond me.

"He doesn't do anything. Good or bad. And he isn't getting any help. Not even from me, and I want to help. But I don't know where to begin. I'm not even sure he hears me."

"Does he talk to the other children?" I asked.

"Well, yes and no. I can't make any sense of it. But they somehow like him, and somebody or other always seems to be watching over him."

We discussed the testing she'd suggested to Mrs. Kroner and her refusal to consider it. "I told her," Miss Selby said, "that I thought Eric had some kind of language disability and that he should be referred to the Child Study Team for a workup. But she just acted as if I were the one who needs help. She said there wasn't anything wrong with Eric and that nobody had complained about him last year.

"Well, in spite of that, I did talk to the psychologist the other day – and asked him to just stop by my room sometime for a kind of informal observation. He agreed, but he didn't say when."

I pressed on, asking more questions. Does Eric play? Does he colour? Does he eat at snack time?

"I told you," Miss Selby replied. "The others keep him with them, but he doesn't actually do anything."

I thanked Miss Selby. She was certainly interested and trying to do all she could. But somehow Eric and school were still a blur to me.

I called Mrs. Kroner to tell her that I had talked to Eric's teacher and felt she genuinely wanted to help him – and that it might be a good thing to have the Child Study Team do an evaluation. Again, Mrs. Kroner was adamant – no testing.

I also asked again if she couldn't find someone closer to where she lived who could help Eric, trying not to admit, even to myself, how much I wanted the chance. But when she insisted that there was no one and that she was determined to bring Eric to me after she got home from work, I couldn't hold back my unabashed delight. I cut my fee in half, and we set up an appointment for half past six on the coming Wednesday.

Eric surprised me by leaving his mother's side and coming slowly but without complaint into my office.

He stood in the middle of the room as I again gathered up some toys, but this time I sat down on the floor myself, putting the toys in front of me. I needed to be on eye level with Eric if I was to have a chance of making contact again. There was so much I had to know. Mrs. Kroner had said Eric wasn't one to talk much, although she was unable to supply any details. His teacher had said she suspected a language problem. But what kind? Was it a receptive problem? Was he unable to hear or if he did hear, unable to understand what was said? Could he hear the sounds of the world around him? Could he decipher words? Did he understand a sentence, or a group of sentences?

Listening comes before speaking. The first thing I had to find out was if Eric could hear me, and then if he understood what he had heard.

I had promised not to do any testing, but nobody had said anything about playing.

I piled some blocks together, talking to myself. "I guess I'll make a garage for this truck. Here are the walls – and this will be the door. It just swings open like this. Now here comes the truck. Rummm-rummm …"

Out of the corner of my eye I could see Eric turning, taking a step toward where I sat by the couch.

"Rummm-rummm, I'll drive it right into the good old garage. Rummm. Rummm. Rummm. Oh-oh! Oh, boy. I didn't mean to do that. Knock down the wall. I guess I drove too fast."

A Safe Place for Joey

I reached to put the block upright, but Eric's hand was there before mine. Caroom! I had him! At least he was down on the floor with me. Now we could begin.

A siren wailed as an ambulance drove by on the street outside my front window. Eric turned, distracted for a moment. Had he heard the sound or was it happenstance? Too soon to tell.

I went back to my play. "Thanks, Eric, for fixing that wall. Now I guess I'll build a store over here." I began to make a two-tiered square building. "No, I know," I said, making it up as I went along, "not a store. I'll make a farm. That's better. That's more fun. I'll get the animals."

I got up, taking a chance, hoping he'd stay. I brought back some small plastic animals, moving quickly, watching Eric. He stayed crouched beside the garage, eyes on the truck.

"All right. Now. This is the barn, and I'll put some of these cows in there – and this part is a field. That's where the horses go. That's enough." I left the pigs and chickens and ducks in a pile.

"Okay. Now I'm going to drive my truck over to the farm. Rummm. Rummm. Backing out now. Careful. Want to come?" I paused, looking at Eric, but he kept his eyes fastened on the blue truck. "Guess not," I said cheerfully. "Well, here I go. Rummm. Rummm. This sure is a loud old truck. I'm going to drive it right up to the barn." I pushed the truck in front of me, moving on my knees perhaps a foot or so away from Eric.

"Well, here I am. Mmm. Nobody here but the cows. I wonder if anybody else is around."

And what do you know. Here comes Eric, creeping right along beside me. Not only creeping, touching me now. His hand on my knee. Not only touching – talking!

"Da," he says.

"Da?" I repeat. Make me understand. Don't lose him now.

"Da." He pointed to the closet at the side of the room. "Da – 'fore."

"Four da?" Come on. Come on. What's the matter with me?

Eric shook his head. "Da – wi 'fo."

Yes! Of course. The dolls.

"Dolls," I repeated, getting it, blood pumping hard. "Like you played with before when you were here. Good idea."

Eric heard. He understood. He talked. He communicated. Maybe not clearly. Maybe not in sentences. But that was okay. That could be fixed.

I lifted the box containing the doll family down from the closet shelf and handed it to Eric.

"Da," he nodded affirmatively and headed back to our primitive farm.

I followed, quiet now, letting Eric take the lead.

He took off the cover and lifted out the mother doll. "Hou?" he said, pointing to the floor.

"How what?" I was certainly out of practice in this kind of communication.

Eric shook his head, pointing again. "Hou." He put the mother doll on the floor and picked up a block, putting it near the barn I had built. Carefully he placed another on top. "Hou," he said positively. "Bill hou."

I placed a block alongside his. "I see now. We need to build a house for the people, right?"

Eric nodded without answering, busily piling block on top of block, colour in his cheeks, eyes bright.

There certainly didn't seem to be anything wrong with his eye-hand coordination. His movements were swift and accurate. He lined up the edges of the blocks with ease and soon had built a house three blocks high, with both a front and a back door.

"Ma," he said, placing the mother inside the walls and nodding.

I joined him again, pushing the blue truck over from the barn. "Guess I better go on over to the house. Doesn't seem to be anybody here at the barn. Rummm. Rummm. Just back her up and go on down the road. Rummm."

I let my little finger knock down a brown and white plastic cow. "Oops. I guess I scared the cow. A little too noisy."

"Cow," Eric said clearly, placing it back on its feet.

Well, no trouble with the *k* sound, or *ow* either.

I tapped on the door. "Hello, there. Anybody home?"

Eric maneuvered the mother to the front door; the baby followed in his other hand.

"Hello there, ma'am. How're you today? That's a fine-looking baby you have there."

Eric bobbed the mother up and down.

"Is your husband home? I need to talk to him."

Eric shook the mother and his own head as well.

"Mmm. Well, that's too bad. I'll come back another day. Rummm. Rummm." I drove my truck back to the garage.

It was clear that Eric could hear and understand what was said to him. He could also process the information, match it with what he had learned before, and make it meaningful. His difficulty lay with expressive language – his words were unfinished and unclear. Both his vocabulary and sentence formation were limited, and he had trouble articulating the *l*, *r*, and *s* sounds.

Now that I had a general feel for Eric's language, I wanted to get to the blackboard. I wondered about his graphomotor skills. Could he draw, write? Did he know the letters of the alphabet?

It was difficult to contain my eagerness to find out. But I knew myself well enough to know that my excitement could carry me away. I had to watch myself – not go too quickly. I must remember to move to Eric's rhythm.

Eric put the mother and the baby back in the house. He laid the father down on the bottom of the box in the same place he'd had him before. He took out the girl and boy dolls and looked around for me.

"Thcu?"

"I haven't a glimmer," I said.

He laid down the dolls and picked up more blocks. I sighed. We obviously weren't going to get to the blackboard today. Eric was much too involved with his play – to interrupt would be unfair and pointless. The thing to do was to stay tuned in to him right where he was.

I moved back to his side and placed another block alongside his. He nodded his approval, "Thcu," he said again. "Big thcu."

B and *g* sounds are intact, and he sometimes uses descriptive words, I thought, still building. But what could "thcu" be?

The building was now twice as big as the barn, and Eric put the boy and girl inside it. "Go thcu," he informed me.

"Right again, Eric. You're way ahead of me. That's where they should be. In school."

Our eyes met across the school. Could he sense my pleasure? I wondered. He knew so much – so much information inside this little boy. Why didn't it show in school? Maybe there were too many children, or maybe his kind of information wasn't valuable in school if he couldn't communicate it verbally.

"Listen, Eric," I said. "We have to stop in just a few minutes, but you'll be back next week. Shall I help put the dolls away? Or would you rather do it?"

Eric spread his hands protectively over the dolls. "Okay," I said. "I'll work on the blocks. You do the dolls."

I began fitting the blocks back into their wooden box, and Eric took the boy and girl out of the school and put them in the house with the mother and baby. Then he reluctantly transferred them to the doll box, laying them in a row – mother, baby, boy, girl, father.

"Thank you, Eric. Let's go find your mom now."

Mrs. Kroner almost fell into the office when I opened the door. She'd obviously had her ear pressed tight against it, which was fine with me. Who had a better right to know about Eric?

She steadied herself and then asked defensively, "Did you sound out?"

"We began," I said. "Look. I really need to talk to you. We need to make plans for helping Eric. Could you call me during your lunch hour tomorrow?"

The phone rang at exactly twelve o'clock the next day.

"Mrs. MacCracken? This is Blanche Kroner. You wanted me to call you."

"Yes. Thank you. I wanted to tell you how pleased I was to find out how much Eric knows and understands. And I also wanted you to work with him yourself, if you'd be willing."

How much parents can or should work with their children is always a tricky thing. Sometimes it is just an exercise in frustration, with more being lost than gained. In this case, Mrs. Kroner was already working with Eric – but on the wrong things. Eric's teacher was right – he couldn't "sound it out" – but he also wasn't ready to do it. Learning proceeds along a continuum. It's like building a wall – each brick carefully placed, each skill carefully sequenced. My guess was that Eric couldn't sound it out because he didn't know any sounds. That would come. In fact, we'd begin next time. But right now he needed to hear as many meaningful complete sentences as he could so he would have a model for language.

"All right," Mrs. Kroner said. "Wait. I'll get a pencil."

"No, you don't need …" But in her eagerness she was already gone.

"All right. Go ahead now. I'm back."

"Well, all I was really going to suggest for right now is that you go over to your library and go down to the children's room. If you don't already have a card, ask them to show you what to do to get one. Then tell the children's librarian that you'd like some picture books for young children – say, age four to six – and have her show you where they're kept, and then just pick out a half dozen different books that you think Eric would like."

"Yes. All right. I can do that. Then what?"

"Then every night before Eric goes to bed read to him for a half hour. Don't feel you have to read all the words on the page. Just read as much as you can, but if he starts to lose interest then just look at the pictures and talk about them – talk about concepts like over and under. The sun is over the house. The flowers are under the tree. Point to some of the pictures and ask him to name them. We want to build his vocabulary as fast as we can.

"Don't worry about how his speech sounds. We'll talk about that later. For now, just teach him all the words you can. Try to keep your own sentences short and clear and ask questions to get him talking."

Eric was through the door before I had it all the way open. "Book," he said, holding two out in front of him.

I paused for a minute in the doorway and smiled at Mrs. Kroner. "You're a fast worker."

She smiled back, and again I was struck by the radiance in her face when she spoke of Eric. "He loves it," she said. "Can't get enough. We read every night, and he carries his books around with him the rest of the time. And they were real nice over at the library. I'm going to take Eric with me this time when I go on Saturday."

"Good. I'll see you in a little while."

Eric was sitting on the floor in front of the couch, same spot as before, except now he leaned back against the couch, one of the books open in his lap. I sat beside him, leaning back myself.

"Bawne," he said, pointing to a large bear, standing behind a chair.

"Yes," I agreed. "I think that's the mother bear and I think somebody's been sitting in her chair." I put a slight emphasis on the *r* in both bear and chair.

Eric nodded emphatically as I retold Goldilocks's story, and he pointed to pictures in answer to my questions.

"Who is Goldilocks, anyway? What did she do when she got tired?"

At our next session I'd try to get him to tell me the story, or at least part of it.

We looked at his other book briefly, and then I walked to the large blackboard that was fastened to the wall on the far side of the room. I said, "Come on over here. I want to show you something. See this chalk? Did you ever see chalk that fat? We have yellow, blue, pink, white. I like it 'cause it doesn't break."

I drew a circle, the size of a saucer. "Can you make a circle like that?" I asked Eric.

He produced a wobbly looking oval with overshooting lines and shrugged his shoulders.

"Not too bad." I smiled at him and added smaller circles to both, some ears, eyes, mouth, whiskers, and tails. "A fat cat and a skinny cat. Okay, Eric," I said, handing him an eraser. "Get rid of the cats. Rub them out. Now, how about a square?" This time I did not draw first. Eric made a figure recognizable as a rectangle, although two comers were open and one rounded. He also drew a cross – when I showed him what it was I wanted – but couldn't do a triangle, diamond, or star.

I drew two parallel lines on the board, about three inches apart, and a half dozen straight lines between them. "This will be a fence. Can you finish it?"

Eric tried, but he had difficulty controlling the chalk, and his lines straggled down the blackboard.

He obviously had trouble with his graphomotor skills – and yet it wasn't just eye-hand coordination, because he had moved the blocks so easily. I made a mental note to get out the pegboard and puzzles as soon as we left the blackboard. Would he have the same difficulty controlling pegs and judging the spatial relationships, or was it primarily a lack of strength in his fingers?

Before we left the board, I asked, "Can you write your name, Eric?"

He picked up the chalk and made an uneven *E*.

"Okay. Good. That's the first letter. Can you do any more?" Silently, Eric shook his head.

A Safe Place for Joey

"Watch me. First I'll do an *E* like you did – a tall, straight line down – now three arms stick out. One at the top, one in the middle, and one at the bottom. Now a small *r* – short, straight line down, half as tall as the line in *E*, and a little curve here at the top. Next is *i*, a cinch – again, a short straight line and dot it; there, like that. And now the last letter, *c* – to make it, just start drawing a backward circle and stop before it's done. Here, now – take this blue chalk and trace over my letters."

As Eric wrote I made a mental note to talk about this with his mom at the end of the session. There were lots of things they could do to improve his drawing and writing.

Eric put down the chalk and headed for the closet. "Da," he said, nodding positively.

"Whoa. Come on back here. We're not quite through. See, Eric, I want to teach you how to read, so you can read books yourself." I immediately had his attention. And, of course, it was his attention I really wanted. I couldn't teach him anything without that. Everyone in first grade was learning to read, so, of course, this fascinated Eric. And I could continue working on his language while throwing in a few basic skills.

"Book," Eric said, trotting off to the books he'd left on the couch. If he couldn't have the dolls, his books were the next best thing.

"Right," I agreed, steering him back to the board. "We'll put the books right here by the blackboard. Now see," I said, opening to a page at random, "books are made of words – like your name Eric is a word – and words are made of letters. Each letter has its own sound, and when you've learned the sounds you can read the words.

"Stay with me, Eric. We'll do just one letter so you can practice it this week with your mom.

78

"Okay, now. We'll do it together." I put chalk between his fingers and my own fingers over his. "We'll make a *B*," I said. "Now tall, straight line down. Good. Now one fat stomach – out like a ball – at the top, now another fat stomach at the bottom. There. That's a capital *B*. And right beside it we'll make a small *b*. Again, straight line down – now just a small ball at the bottom. Good. *B* is the letter that begins the word ball." I drew a quick ball on the board.

"Can you say that, Eric? Ball?"

"Bow."

"Yes. Good." I'd forgotten he couldn't or didn't make the final *l* sound. "Here's another." I drew quickly. "That's a *B* for boy."

"Boy," Eric repeated.

"Terrific. Okay, let's get the dolls."

Much as I wanted to get out the pegboard and puzzles, I had to play fair. Eric had worked hard for me; it was my turn to follow him.

I handed Eric the box of dolls, and I carried the wooden box of blocks. We both went instinctively to the spot in front of the couch where we had played before.

Eric opened the doll box and lifted out each doll carefully. His actions were precise. He did not dump and jumble as some children did.

After he had inspected each doll, he lined them up and then proceeded with his plan for each one. He put the father doll in the back bedroom, laying him down on his stomach. "Slee," Eric said.

He put the mother in the kitchen and then held the boy and baby side by side, this time putting the boy beside the mother and the baby under the couch cushion. He made eating noises with his mother, and I said, "The father is sleeping and the mother and boy are eating. I wonder what time it is. Are they eating supper?"

Eric shook his head. "Bref."

"I see. They're eating breakfast."

Now Eric put the mother and boy outside the house. "Co thcu."

I remembered that one. "They're going to school. Where's the girl?"

Again Eric shook his head. Evidently the girl did not walk to school with them, but Eric had not yet put her in the house.

Eric pulled a cushion from the couch. "Thcu," he announced. He wasn't going to take time to build a school today. I wondered if somehow he sensed that we were already running late.

In front of the cushion the mother and boy kissed, then both waved as the mother walked away. "Ma go wer," he said sadly as he placed the boy on the cushion.

His longest speech so far – a real sentence! "Yes," I agreed, "the mother goes to work and the boy goes to school."

Tap. Tap. Tap. I got up and opened the door. Mrs. Kroner said apologetically, "I don't mean to rush you – but the buses don't run too often out of Grover at night, so we have to hurry to make the eight o'clock. That first night we came we didn't get back till almost midnight, and I don't like Errol out that late as a rule."

"Of course. I understand. I'm sorry. Could you call me, then, like last week, so we can talk?"

Mrs. Kroner was putting Eric's arms into the sleeves of his jacket, zipping it up. I wanted to say, "Please don't. Let him do it himself." But criticism is not the way to end a session.

Instead I dug an empty scrapbook from the bookcase and pressed it into Mrs. Kroner's hands. "Here. Take this. I'll explain when we talk."

Mrs. Kroner's call again came just after twelve the next day. "Did you get home all right?" I asked.

"Fine. Made it right on time. No trouble at all. I've got my paper ready."

She was going to need it this time. I was pleased that she and Eric were working well together, and I felt that she was happy about helping him. I just had to be careful not to overwhelm her and to go over very carefully just how to do the things I asked. I wanted Eric to work where daily practice would increase his skills. I wanted him to improve. And most of all I wanted both of them to be successful.

I explained how to help Eric write both the upper- and lower-case b (B, b) on the top of two pages of the scrapbook, and then to cut out as many things as they could find in newspapers, ads, or magazines that began with the sound of b and paste them on those two pages. Next I explained that Eric needed to learn to write his name. I told her, as I had Eric, how each letter was formed, and asked her to write "Eric" along the bottom of the scrapbook pages and to ask him to trace the letters every day.

I asked Mrs. Kroner to get some clay and snap clothespins, and to encourage Eric to roll and pummel and pinch to increase the strength in his fingers. I asked her to have Eric trace pot covers, bottle caps, and playing cards.

I asked her to write the letters B and b on index cards or blank pieces of paper and let Eric search through the house till he found two things beginning with the sound of b – any two (bed, bathtub, ball, bureau), whatever he found – and then have him tape the letters there and leave them.

81

A Safe Place for Joey

I suggested she help Eric lay out his clothes for school the night before and let him dress himself by himself as much as possible.

I asked her to keep on reading to him, to occasionally underline the words with her fingers as she read, to show him how the words ran from left to right across the page. Eric should be encouraged to use words as much as possible. If he wanted milk or a cookie, have him ask for it.

I told her how well Eric had done at this last session and that I could already see improvement in his speech.

Mrs. Kroner carefully read back her notes to me, and it was clear that she really understood. I cautioned her to keep their practice sessions to no more than a half hour at a time and to end each one with a task that Eric could do well. I also told her not to worry if something came up and they missed a day – and most of all to have fun.

Mrs. Kroner proved to be a talented teacher. During the following weeks she not only did the things I suggested, she went further and played games based on the same ideas. When she unpacked the groceries, she had Eric hunt for items beginning with the letters we were working on.

Consequently, well before the month was out Eric had learned the *b*, *p*, *t*, *k*, and *d* sounds, and could also write the letters. He was still having difficulty with *l* and *r*, but his speech was clearer and he rarely used single words to express his thoughts. Now he spoke two, three, sometimes four words at a time, arranging them in meaningful order.

Best of all, there was carryover in school. Each week I reported to Miss Selby what he was doing at home and with me, and I suggested the kinds of things he might be able to do in school, such as matching some of the upper- and lowercase letters, circling pictures to go with sounds, tracing templates, colouring. I ran off some worksheets of visual motor skills (increasingly difficult paths to trace, mazes to follow) and sent them in with Eric.

And bless Miss Selby, before I knew it she had cajoled some readiness workbooks from the kindergarten teacher, and Eric was actually working along with the other children every day. She was careful to remind me that the work he was doing was "certainly not on grade level, but at least he was doing something."

Easter came early that year, and the day before Eric's sixth visit I set up an Easter egg tree on a table by the window. Not really a tree, just a bare branch sprayed white and hung with decorated eggshells. A friend had shown me how to make a little pinhole at the end of each egg, put a straw to one hole and blow the insides out the other. This way the egg could last forever. And each year I managed to get through this messy job and make a special egg for each child who came to my office.

Actually, I made six for Eric. They were easy – just dipped in primary colours, a different letter on each one. I couldn't wait for him to come and pick his eggs and tell me the names and sounds of each letter, his eyes shining with excitement, his head nodding up and down with pleasure.

Six forty-five. I checked my watch again. Mrs. Kroner had never been late before. They had to leave promptly at the end of each session to make the bus back home, so she and Eric were always in the waiting room well in advance of their appointment.

At seven o'clock I called the Kroners' house. A female voice answered on the third ring.

"Hello," I said. "This is Eric's tutor, Mary MacCracken. I was –"

There was a click on the other end. I dialed back immediately. The phone rang a dozen times. At seven thirty I dialed again. Nobody home – or at least nobody who wanted to answer the telephone.

I called again the next morning, only to reach a busy signal. A busy signal that lasted all day long.

I searched the Yellow Pages, trying to find the name of a cosmetic factory in the Kroners' part of the city, without success.

At noon I called Miss Selby, and she said Eric wasn't there; in fact, he hadn't been in all week. She didn't know what was the matter, but that this wasn't unusual. The school nurse rarely had time to track down the absentees.

"Could you give me Mrs. Kroner's work number?" I asked.

"No. Sorry. That would be down in the file in the main office. I can try to transfer you," Miss Selby offered. "Let me know if you find out anything."

The phone disconnected, and I called back and eventually got Mr. Kroner's work number. Mrs. Kroner's wasn't listed.

I knew he worked the night shift, but I wasn't sure when that began. I decided to call early and leave a message so I wouldn't interrupt his work. By nine o'clock I'd stopped caring about interrupting him and dialed Gare Manufacturing again. I had no idea what kind of work Mr. Kroner did there or how big the business was.

A man's voice answered the phone, and I asked to speak to Mr. Kroner. I could hear the heavy rhythmic thud of machines in the background.

"Who's calling?" the man asked.

I hesitated. Would Mr. Kroner know my name? I wasn't sure. Yet he might not like me to identify myself as Eric's tutor.

"One of his children's teachers," I compromised.

"Well, is it urgent?"

"Yes," I answered, not knowing.

"Jack," the man called. "Telephone."

There was the sound of the phone against a table or desk. The machines thudded on.

"Hello." The man's voice was softer than I'd expected.

"Mr. Kroner. This is Mary MacCracken. We've never met, but I've been working with Eric the last few months, helping him with …" I hesitated. What had I been helping Eric with? Why was I finding it so difficult to speak?

"Uh, with some of his school work. He didn't come for his appointment yesterday, and they say he hasn't been in school all week. I was worried about him. I … uh … couldn't reach anyone at your house."

"That so?" I pressed a hand over my other ear, as if that would help me hear him above the machines. "Well, could be. Mrs. Kroner's taking a little trip – took the boy along with her."

"A trip? She didn't mention anything about a trip or cancel any of Eric's appointments. Where did they go?" I realized too late that my question sounded abrupt.

But Mr. Kroner continued to talk in the same soft voice. "I don't know where they went. No idea. When she decides to go, she goes and takes the runt along. When she decides to come back, she comes back."

The runt? Did he mean Eric? But his voice was so soft, so sweet; perhaps I'd misunderstood. No one at school had mentioned previous absences – but then, I hadn't talked to his kindergarten teacher and Miss Selby was new.

"But Eric's all right? I mean he's always been all right before?"

"All right? You said you knew him." Even the sarcasm came so sweetly and softly off his tongue that I didn't recognize it immediately. "I gotta go now, lady," he continued. "But he'll be back. Always has. It's just his mama's got this little drinkin' problem. Gets worse around the holidays and off she goes." The phone clicked. The dial tone hummed, and I replaced the receiver.

A drinking problem? I couldn't believe it. Mrs. Kroner was always so responsible, so in control. She did look much older than her years, but I assumed that came from work and worry. I had never seen or heard anything to make me suspect she drank. But if she did have a problem, how bad was it? Was she capable of caring for Eric? Mr. Kroner certainly hadn't sounded concerned, but then Mr. Kroner also referred to Eric as "the runt."

Nine thirty. I got out the telephone book again, knowing it was late, but maybe not too late.

I searched through the half-dozen Tortonis, found a Frank, dialed, apologized when a woman answered.

"Mrs. Tortoni?"

"Yes. Who is this?"

"Mary MacCracken. I'm sorry to call this late, but, well, it's a long story. I've been working with a friend of yours – little Eric Kroner – and … I guess I was just worried about him and called to see if you knew anything."

"Well, Mrs. MacCracken, I'd like to help you. I really would, after all you did for us. Frankie's still doin' real well. But I'm afraid I can't tell you anything, and I really can't talk more now. Good-bye."

Mrs. Tortoni had sounded guarded. Not her usual self. She hadn't even asked why I was worried about Eric. I had the feeling she knew more than she'd said. But there was no point in calling her back, at least not until tomorrow morning.

By ten o'clock the Tortoni kids would be in school and Frank Senior at the garage. If Mrs. Tortoni was ever going to talk to me, this seemed the most likely time.

"Hello." Mrs. Tortoni's voice seemed a little friendlier.

I identified myself, and then without actually repeating what Mr. Kroner had said, I implied that I was concerned about Mrs. Kroner as well as Eric.

"Well, now, look. It's really kind of you to be thinking about them," Mrs. Tortoni said. "I know they'd appreciate it and all, but there isn't anything you can do. Believe me. Now I'll let you know if something comes up. And Frankie said to be sure and say hello."

Late Friday afternoon the phone in my office rang, and I handed the boy I was working with the stopwatch (I always pay a chip for each second I'm on the phone) and picked up the receiver.

"Mrs. MacCracken. This is Blanche Kroner. I'm sorry to interrupt you." She spoke in a strained whisper, but her words were clear.

"That's all right. I've been trying to reach you. How's Eric?"

"That's why I'm calling. He's all right, but I need some work for him. I can't talk over the phone." Her voice had dropped so I could barely hear her. "What I wondered was if you could come to Grover tomorrow morning and bring work for Eric. I can't talk anymore. Will you meet me at the Main Street Diner at ten o'clock?"

She hung up before I could answer.

That night, when I'd finished work I went through my shelves and closets collecting materials that I thought might be helpful to Eric. I wasn't quite sure what kind of work Mrs. Kroner wanted – or for how long a period – and I couldn't find a great deal. I made up most of what I used out of my head, but I found a scope and sequence chart, a few readiness workbooks, and a teacher's manual, and put them in a large manila envelope and took it home with me.

The next morning I followed the map to Grover, and Main Street was easy to find. The diner was at the far west end of the run-down street.

Mrs. Kroner had obviously been watching for me, and she came forward and led me to a back booth in the almost empty diner.

I ordered coffee for both of us and waited for Mrs. Kroner to explain. She wore her usual black cloth coat. She looked thin and tense, certainly not drunk, but I wasn't exactly sure what to look for.

The waitress set our coffee on the red Formica tabletop, and as soon as she left Mrs. Kroner leaned across, reaching out, almost touching my arm.

"I need work for Eric, like I said. See, I'm leaving this afternoon, and I want him to keep on learning like he's been doing and you're the only one I can talk to." There was a tremendous urgency behind her words, although she spoke in a hoarse whisper.

"Where are you thinking of going?"

"I don't want to talk about that – just going, that's all."

"What about Eric?"

"He's going with me. That's why I need the work."

"Mrs. Kroner," I said. "I think you ought to think about this more. Eric's been doing so well, making such progress, I don't think it's a good idea to take him out of school now. He's already missed a week. I talked to Miss Selby."

Mrs. Kroner leaned toward me, immediately alert. "What did she say?"

"Nothing. She didn't know any more than I did."

Mrs. Kroner relaxed, but only for a minute.

"Did you bring the work?" she insisted.

"Yes." I put the envelope on the table. "But I think I need to tell you that I talked to Mr. Kroner and –"

"When?" she interrupted. "What did he say?"

"I'm trying to tell you," I said as gently as I could. "He said that you often went off on trips, particularly around the holidays."

"That's not true. Where would I go?"

"He said," I continued, "that you take Eric with you and that you go on these trips because you have a drinking problem. Now if this is true, please don't leave. Stay and get help – think about Eric."

Mrs. Kroner's mouth was tight with anger. "I don't drink. He tells everybody that, speaking so sweet, so nice. He does it so that if I ever – never mind. Thanks for the books."

She stood up and reached for the envelope, and I put my hand on her arm.

"Why, then? Why do you have to go? You just said you didn't have any place to go."

"I meant for trips. I'm going for good now." She sat down heavily, and her untouched coffee sloshed into the saucer.

"Do you know how hard it will be for Eric to start in a new school in the middle of the year?" I asked. "More than the

89

middle – there are only a little over two months left. For Eric's sake, couldn't you wait that long?"

"It's for Eric's sake I'm going," she said quietly, but no longer whispering.

I waited for her to say more, but she sat without speaking although she made no move to leave. Finally I said, "What do you mean, for Eric's sake?"

She put down the paper napkin with which she had been wiping up the spilled coffee.

"All right," she said. "I didn't know for sure until this year. I had my ideas, but, see, Jack works the night shift – I told you that – and when Eric started school full time I began working days at the cosmetic factory.

"I liked it. I liked the company. I liked the money. But then one of the girls got some kind of bug or virus, and we all got it one after the other – headache, fever. Didn't last long, but it came on fast.

"When it hit me, I tried to keep on working. I didn't want to go home. To tell the truth, I didn't like being around him, Jack, any more than he liked being around me. We just stayed out of each other's way.

"But then I began to heave, so I decided I had to go home. It's only about six blocks, and I made it all right. I let myself in – didn't even stop to take off my coat, just wanted to get off my feet. Our bedroom door was closed, which was queer, because Jack usually sleeps on the cot in the back room – says its quieter there during the day – but I felt so sick I didn't stop to think about it. I just opened the door – and there were Jack and Bella in the bed, both of them stark naked.

"'Get out of here, the both of you,' I yelled at them. But Jack picked up a towel by the side of the bed and wrapped it around him. He told Bella to take her clothes and go on down to the drugstore for a while, and Bella did like he said. Then he comes over to me and puts his hands around my neck. He's strong, Jack is, even though he doesn't look it. And he says if I ever tell he'll kill me. Not only me – Eric, too. Says it's my fault anyway 'cause I'm such a dried-up old crone."

I didn't want to hear this. It belonged in some scandal sheet or maybe a textbook. Not in Eric's life. I wanted to think Mrs. Kroner was lying or making it up. But it was too real. I waited for her to cry, but she looked at me steadily and dry-eyed.

"So we made a deal," she said. "I wouldn't tell, and he wouldn't bother me and Eric."

"What about Bella?"

"She's a born slut. She'd do it – and does – with any Tom, Dick, or Harry. She doesn't care he's her father. She likes the presents he brings her and all that pretty talk. I can hear them sometimes up in Bella's room in the attic. I try to cover Eric's ears."

I looked hard at Mrs. Kroner. Bella was her daughter, still a child, no matter what else. Shouldn't she have tried to protect Bella instead of making a deal? I started to say this to Mrs. Kroner but she interrupted.

"I know it wasn't right. That's why I didn't want anybody testing Eric. I was afraid somebody would find out something. But life's not easy, you know. You make do. You get through. A lot of it isn't pretty. And I had Errol – Jack kept to his word and left us alone."

I thought about Eric. How had he done as well as he had? Not only serious learning disabilities, but all this as well. But Mrs. Kroner was still talking.

A Safe Place for Joey

"That is, he kept his word until last Wednesday. I came home from work in the late afternoon. Errol was watching TV in the kitchen, Jack was asleep in the back room, and Bella was out. Everything seemed like usual.

"I washed up like I always do before bringing Errol over to you. Then I called to Errol to come get his bath, like always. But he didn't want to. Fussed and cried and carried on. I didn't know what to make of it. Usually he wants to look clean and nice for you. So finally I just took his clothes off him, but before I got him in the tub I saw how his bottom was bright red and splotchy. Some kind of rash, I thought. Now what's he coming down with.

"But then Errol started to cry, and I shut the door tight so he wouldn't wake Jack, and Errol shows me, acting it out, how Jack made him take down his pants. And then when Errol wouldn't get under the covers with him, Jack smacked him across the bottom with an old curtain rod. And when I looked close I could see the welts – the red wasn't from any rash.

"I put Errol's clothes back on him as quick as I could and went out the door calling that we were going to your place – just in case Jack had heard and was starting after us. Then I didn't know where to go, so we took the bus here to Grover. But I couldn't go on to you 'cause that's where he thought we were going. So finally we just came here and waited till I was sure Jack would be at work.

"Since then we've been at the Tortonis' – you know her, she said you'd called. I had to stay till I could get back in the house when both Jack and Bella were out and get the money I had hid. I had to get bus fare.

"I don't want to say exactly where we're going, but it's upstate New York, where I grew up. My mother's still there, and she'll take us in. But I gotta put Errol in school as soon as we get there. I know that. That's why I had to talk to you. To find out what's best for him.

"Well, I got the money late yesterday. That's when I called you. And now I'm going back to get Errol from the Tortonis, and we're leaving this afternoon."

I left the diner a half hour later. I went over the books I'd brought and urged Mrs. Kroner to enter Eric in kindergarten when they arrived. He was so small, I was sure he'd fit in – and he'd have a better chance of handling first grade next year. I also urged her to contact a mental health clinic for support and help for both of them. All she really wanted was the books, as if they were some magic talisman. That was the last time I saw Mrs. Kroner, and I've never again seen or heard from Eric.

I did call Family Services about Bella, but by the time they got over to the house both she and Mr. Kroner had disappeared.

I saw Eric for only a few sessions, a fraction of the time I spend with most children, yet he is the one who haunts my dreams.

If our time together hadn't been interrupted, could he have continued his growth? Over and over I ask myself why I didn't realize what was going on. Eric tried to show me with his play – always the girl doll beside the father, always the struggle to decide whether he was a boy or a baby. Why hadn't I asked Mrs. Kroner more questions? Did I think I shouldn't intrude? If I had, could I have made a difference?

I'll never know. But I'll always wonder and hope that Eric got the help he needed and deserved. There are still six eggshells in a carton somewhere in my attic. The colours have faded, but you can see that each is marked with a different letter. I take this to be a good omen.

Changes

"You are squandering your most precious asset," the lawyer said in a voice that was mildly accusing.

"What is that?" I asked. "What do you mean?"

"Time, of course. Time. You are throwing away almost two hours every day in commuting. You should find office space closer to your home or move closer to your office."

I listened carefully. I'd come to this highly recommended, successful man for advice. My days had become too crowded, too full. There was never enough time, and yet I loved my work. Instinctively, I trusted this man and knew that what he said was right. Without the long commute each day there would be more time for both my family and the children.

Cal and I talked. Cal – inventor, engineer, entrepreneur, manufacturer, and my friend and husband – had operated his manufacturing plant for over twenty years in the same city where I had been born. We now rented an apartment almost an hour away from both our offices, and it made a great deal of sense to buy a house that would eliminate commuting for both of us.

We found a house that had been built by an architect as both his office and his home – low and quiet, surrounded by woods.

The office, two rooms and a bathroom above the garage, would be mine, with only a five-minute drive to work for Cal.

I said good-bye to Rea Oldenburg with sorrow. I would miss our conversations and shared lunches.

"No, no," she said. "The lawyer is right. It is a waste for you to be in the car so long. We will still meet, and now the children will drive to you."

I moved my file cabinets and the secondhand desk and chairs (they had been lucky and I had no wish to change). I carpeted the stairs and the floors of the two rooms in blue, painted the walls a creamy white, and bought some new towels and a rug for the bathroom, a five-foot blackboard for one wall of the office, and a secondhand copy machine. The ceiling sloped down low from the roof, and the back window looked out over the woods. Two walls held deep cabinets, designed for architectural drawings but equally good for children's games, books, toys, and testing material. I left the walls bare, except for the blackboard, waiting to fill them with the children's pictures and stories.

Rea Oldenburg was right. Most of the children I had been seeing did drive to me; others were ready to graduate, and old friends sent new children to take their place. My practice seemed like a kind of garden, with children growing in place of flowers – always new ones shooting up as the older ones matured.

I bloomed along with the children. If I'd been happy before, I was even happier now working out of our home. I loved wearing my sneakers and blue jeans. I loved not having to spend hours on the crowded highways. And, to my surprise, I loved having the time to do more diagnostic educational evaluations than I'd ever done before.

A Safe Place for Joey

Some of the evaluations were done simply because parents wanted to know as much as possible about their children – whether they were in the right school, what their interests and aptitudes were – and these evaluations were always a delight. No problems to uncover, no painful disclosures to parents – just the fresh, wonderful responses of the children. "What does the stomach do?" I asked. (This is a standard question on the Wechsler Intelligence Scale.) Seven-year-old Eva, bright as a dollar, looked at me with confidence. "That's easy," she said. "It digests the food." Then, before I had finished writing the first word, she added with authority, "And from there it goes straight to the vagina where it's excavated."

But most of the evaluations I did were requested because a child was doing poorly in school and parents and/or schools wanted to know why.

The heart of my practice remained remediation, which is exactly the way I wanted it. The word "remediation" is derived from the Latin *remederi*, which means "to heal." I believed in this. I did not think it possible to take a slice of a child's head and merely try to fix up the reading part. I felt and still feel that the reading, or lack of it, must be helped and then integrated into the child's whole being. My job, as I saw it, was not just to shore up reading, writing, or arithmetic skills, nor to ameliorate dyslexia, dysgraphia, or dyscalculia, but to try to help children become successful in their place of work – school – and to improve the quality of their lives.

But I was becoming more and more convinced that the first step in the successful remediation of a child with a learning disability is a thorough diagnostic evaluation. How much easier to teach and heal when areas of strength and weakness were clearly defined. I became supersleuth, tracking strengths, ferreting out weaknesses, drawing hypotheses, translating to parents. I also found that the hour or two that parents and I spent together in conference, going over the tests I had given as well as discussing their deeper knowledge of the child, usually formed a bond of understanding between us that made it easier to help the child.

Yet, ironically, I could remember how I had once loathed testers and their testing. When I was teaching emotionally disturbed children, the children were required to undergo a kind of cursory testing once a year – and on this superficial testing, judgments were passed.

I hated these testers, and I hated their tests. Perhaps hate is too strong a word, but I certainly didn't welcome them. Who were these people to tell us about our children? We teachers had only four children each. We were with them six hours a day, five days a week – teaching, playing, eating – intensely involved all day long. The testers were certified psychologists, but they came to our school for only a few hours a week, observing the children from doorways, discussing them at staff conferences, never really interacting with them. And then "testing" them – taking the children out to another room, the children protesting, hating to go; I had a strong sense that the feeling was mutual. I doubted that the testers had any more desire to be close to the children than the children had to be with them.

But test they did, and they reported back weeks later that our children were "subnormal." What did these people know about the real child, I raged silently, when most of the time the children were frozen with fear and couldn't have answered the questions even if they had known the answers? I regarded the results of this testing with suspicion and disdain.

A Safe Place for Joey

Then in graduate school I learned that the fault was not in the tests themselves, but in the way they were used. In a course entitled Individual Psychological Testing taught by Dr. George Kennedy – a tall, gentle man with a fringe of white hair – I learned how valuable testing could be.

"Each week I will test a child," Dr. Kennedy told us. "You will observe the child and myself through this one-way window. The child and I will sit here at the table behind the glass." He tapped the window with his fingers. "And you," he gestured at the twenty graduate students his class was composed of, "will sit here in this classroom and watch and record the child's answers. At our next session we will go over the answers and your scoring and observations."

He smiled at us benignly. "It will be my job to furnish the tests. It will be yours to furnish the children."

So each week, sometimes twice a week, we took turns bringing our own or a neighbor's child to Dr. Kennedy and watched as he talked and tested and revealed to us the amazing amount of information that he discovered about each. If Dr. Kennedy had been at the school for emotionally disturbed children, I would have trusted his tests. He didn't give one single test and make broad pronouncements. He gave a battery of tests, each one revealing a different facet of the child. He didn't rely solely on the number of rights and wrongs for the final answer. His tests were covered with notes, and from these he taught us that observations were even more important than numbered scores.

Most important of all, the children loved him and opened up easily to him. This was not a painful ordeal for them, but rather a special time spent with a person who cared about them. The children sensed his genuine interest and responded to it.

I loved every minute of that course and the magical way Dr. Kennedy drew out the children, as well as his meticulous, careful scoring of each test and the conversion of the scores into meaningful statements and recommendations. It was then that I began thinking that maybe, someday, I might have an office of my own and do individualized testing that would form a solid base for remediation.

I got an A in Individual Psychological Testing, and I immediately signed up for the same course again the next semester, knowing I must learn as much as possible about evaluations from this sensitive, intelligent man. A proper evaluation is more than just a test. It should clear up questions, point out the kind of remediation that is needed, forge a team to work together to help the child, and bring about changes in the climate and patterns of family life and school.

It is the beginning of the turnabout. At least, it was for Ben.

Ben

Benjamin Bradford Aylesworth stood on the low stone porch that runs across the front of our house. Benjamin Bradford Aylesworth was his given name. "Banana Brain" was what the kids at school called him. They just took his first two initials and fashioned him a nickname. Dr. Golden, the psychologist who had referred Ben to me, had heard this from Ben's teacher. He wasn't sure if they called Ben "Banana Brain" to his face; he wasn't even sure if Ben knew about it at all.

One look at Ben and I knew he knew. He not only knew, he believed it was true. If ever a child projected defeat, it was Ben. He was tall for twelve, with pale gold hair falling down over his forehead, hiding his eyes. His features were even, almost handsome, but his whole body drooped forward in sullen, melancholy dejection.

"Hello," I said, stretching out my hand.

Ben's eyes remained fixed on the toes of his Adidas.

"Ben!" His mother's voice rose slightly as she spoke. "Say hello to Mrs. MacCracken."

"'Lo," Ben muttered without raising his eyes.

There had been a request, almost an order, behind his mother's words that meant Ben was supposed to extend his hand and say he was glad to meet me. I knew Ben heard this as clearly as I did. I also knew nothing in the world would make him do it. He had somehow allowed himself to be dragged to my office, but he certainly wasn't going to shake my hand. I quickly put my hands inside my pockets to show that shaking was not a top priority with me.

I moved my eyes away from Ben and focused on his mother. This was the first time we had met, although we had spoken on the phone several times. She was slim, her hair only a shade darker than Ben's, and she rolled the thin gold chain at the base of her neck back and forth between her thumb and forefinger, her fingers trembling slightly. She was obviously very nervous. I longed to reassure her that I would be gentle, careful with her son, but this was not the time. Later we would spend hours together, but now belonged to Ben. I needed every ounce of concentration, observation, all antennas tuned only to Ben if I were to fathom him. I could only hope she sensed this and understood.

"Ben and I will be about an hour," I said. "Here is the background information form I mentioned on the phone. If you could just fill it in and drop it off sometime in the next week or two, I'd appreciate it. Now, would you like to wait here in our den or would you rather come back?"

She hesitated, looking at Ben, then cleared her throat. "Well … uh, Ben, do you want me to stay? Uh … what do you think?"

Ben shrugged without turning his head or raising his eyes.

Mrs. Aylesworth began backing down the front path toward the driveway, the form fluttering in her hand. "Well … uh, then I'll be back. Just do a few errands, and be back at … uh." She stared at her watch, blond straight hair swinging across her face. "What time should I come back?" she asked helplessly.

"A little after two," I said.

Ben and I watched together as the white Mercedes backed down the driveway.

"We go this way," I said to Ben, stepping inside, leading the way to my office.

As we passed the sliding glass doors that look out on the terrace, Ben suddenly stopped. Two chickadees and a tufted titmouse perched on the clear cylindrical bird feeders that hung just outside the doors. Ben stood perfectly still, his eyes riveted on the birds, which were only inches away. His head was up and with his hair back he was far more handsome than I had first thought. His eyes were greyish violet-blue, the pupils rimmed in black, his nose straight, mouth wide. Only his skin seemed out of place – milk white, almost transparent, without a trace of colour, except at his temples where little purple veins clustered and beat like a tiny heart on the side of his head. His skin made him seem vulnerable, without enough protective colouring.

"Look at that one!" Ben said, pointing to a tufted titmouse. "Look at him g-g-go!" His voice was high and excited, with just a trace of a stutter, and his light-boned, skinny shoulders trembled under the Norwegian patterned hand-knit sweater. The excitement in his voice was in such contrast to his initial behavior that I stood beside him for a moment or two, watching as the birds zoomed out of the woods behind the terrace, braked to an instant stop on the metal perches that extended from the feeders, plucked out a sunflower seed, and were instantly off again.

"I like the chickadees and the titmouse," I said, making conversation, giving Ben time, "but not the purple finches. They come in bunches, fill up all four feeders, and sit forever stuffing themselves. If a chickadee comes along, they squawk and peck at it, until I finally have to open the doors and shoo the finches away so the chickadees can get another chance. Anyway, let's go on up and I'll show you my office."

Actually, there's not an awful lot to show. Maybe that's why I like it. Clearly no decorator has ever been near the room. It belongs to the kids and me, and I try to make it a place where people don't have to pretend to be something they're not.

I pointed out the bathroom, the eccentricities of the bathroom light, and the window in the small adjoining room from which the driveway and front lawn were visible. I knew that Ben was both angry and scared, and I wanted him to have a chance to get familiar with the space around him. Then I motioned him to the chair behind the desk and pulled another one beside it.

"The first thing I want to do is just ask you some general questions – name, age, address, that kind of thing. What's your full name and what do you want me to call you?"

"Benjamin Bradford Aylesworth."

"Yes?"

"What?"

"Should I call you Ben?"

"D-d-doesn't matter. It's a stupid name anyway." Ben's voice was high, almost whiny now.

"Address?"

"One twenty-five Mountain View Road. South M-M-Millwood."

"Phone?"

"Which one? We got three. Two regulars and I g-g-got one in my room."

"That's pretty nice. I guess you better give me all three." Obviously, Ben did not lack the material things in life.

A Safe Place for Joey

"How old are you, Ben?"

"Twelve."

"Birthday?"

"November twenty-third."

"Do you have any brothers or sisters?"

"Yeah, one sister. J-J-Jessie."

"How old is she?"

"Seven."

"How do you two get along?"

"Jessie's okay."

"How about pets?"

"Yeah. I got a dog."

"What kind?"

"A black Lab. MacArthur. I call him M-M-Mac for short."

Ben's voice seemed slightly friendlier, and the occasional stutter did not seem to be connected to the subject matter. I decided that this was a good time to see if he would be interested in the chips.

"Pull that box over, Ben, and open it up," I said.

Ben stared at the chips without speaking.

"If you want, you can pay yourself for everything you do here. If it's too much trouble, that's okay, too." I wanted to give him an out if the chips seemed babyish. But Ben was fingering the chips, letting them slide through his fingers.

"What do you mean?"

"Each colour is worth a different amount. Like yellow is fifty and green is twenty-five. It's written there on the inside cover."

I explained about the chips and prizes.

"You can buy things when you're done. Nothing much. A sticker is worth a hundred, a Matchbox car seven thousand."

"Seven thousand. That's a rip-off."

104

I shrugged and counted up the brief information Ben had given me so far. "Okay. Pay yourself sixty-five so far. A yellow, a blue, and an orange. Now, what grade are you in?"

Ben picked out the chips quickly. "Sixth."

"And your teacher?"

"Mrs. Holber."

"Who did you have for fifth?"

"Mrs. Andrews."

I asked and Ben told me the names of each of his teachers back through nursery school.

"Which one did you like the best?"

Without hesitation, Ben named his kindergarten teacher.

"Why? What was good about her?"

"She didn't yell."

It was a familiar answer. So many learning disabled children remember kindergarten as their happiest year in school. Things were okay until it was time to learn to read.

"How about subjects? What do you like best in school?"

"Nothing."

I decided to change the subject myself. "What's your dad's name?"

"Ralph."

"What does he do?"

"Zyloc Corporation. He's p-p-president."

"Your mom's name?"

"Carol."

"And what does she do?"

"Nothing. Well – she d-d-drives us around and she goes shopping and stuff."

"Okay, Ben. Two more questions. What do you like to do best when you're not in school?"

"Sail." The answer came quick and fast.

"Where do you sail?"

"At the river. In the summer." For the first time his blue eyes met mine, and I thought, Okay, all right, we're going to get there.

I smiled at him. "Sounds good. Last question. Why do you think you're here? I ask everyone that."

Ben looked straight at me, every trace of friendliness gone. "Because they s-s-said I had to. D-D-Dad and M-M-Mom and Dr. Crazy all said I had to c-c-come."

"All right. Thank you, Ben. Let's see." I counted up. "Pay yourself one hundred and thirty-five. That would be a silver …"

"I know, I know," Ben interrupted, picking out the chips. "You don't have to tell me. I can figure it out."

I moved from the chair beside Ben to the opposite side of the desk, sat down, and picked up a brown envelope from a briefcase on the other chair. I took a small pack of 4-by-6-inch white cards out of the envelope and placed them upside down in the center of the desk. I gave Ben a pencil and piece of paper (the pencil a number two, the paper 8½ by 12 inches).

"This is called the Bender Gestalt, and what I'd like you to do first is just copy these designs. Each of these cards has a different design on it. I'll turn them over one at a time, and you copy it."

Ben picked up the pencil, holding it in an awkward, hooked, right-handed grip – three fingers on top, close to the point. He copied the circle with a diamond beside it, but somehow he couldn't get the two figures to touch and the diamond looked more like a rectangle. At his age this should have been an easy task, and his struggles immediately set off warning signals of the possibility of difficulties with perceptual organization.

He erased and began again, glaring at me across the desk. "What's the point of this d-d-dumb test? I can't draw these kinds of things anyway."

"Just do it the best you can."

Ben begrudgingly finished the design and I turned over the next card.

Ben counted the dots on the card with his finger, counting backward from right to left. He drew three tiny circles and counted again, this time from left to right. It was obvious that Ben had a great deal of left-right confusion. Inwardly I wondered if he also reversed or had once reversed letters and words, a condition that often accompanies confused directionality.

As a teacher or tutor I would never have let Ben struggle so, but during these four evaluation sessions it was necessary for me to test and learn what Ben could do on his own – to discover his strengths and also his weaknesses.

The Bender Gestalt is primarily a test of visual motor perception, but it also gives clues to the child's work style, his organizational skills, a sense of how he feels about himself. Ben's left-right confusion and difficulty drawing angles were obvious, but underneath his sullenness was a surprising determination. He continued to work hard, although silently now, at a task that was clearly very difficult for him.

"Okay. That's fine," I said as he finished copying the last design. "Now take this new piece of paper and draw as many designs as you can remember."

"Oh jeez," Ben whined. "That's not fair." I understood – always I wish the test instructions included the fact that the child will be asked to reproduce the designs later. Somehow it seems so much fairer, but while I may fudge the rules a little with chips, I'm strict with myself about administering tests the way they are written.

Ben began to draw immediately, despite his complaints, and produced six of the nine designs, although one was upside down and all six were only one-tenth the size of the original. A recall of five designs is considered average.

"Pay yourself twenty-five for each design you remembered, plus ten for each of the nine you copied."

Ben was counting and figuring and paying himself. He wasn't willing to become involved with me as a person yet, but he was certainly into the chips.

Most children dump their chips any old which way into one of the empty containers on the desk, but Ben sorted his by colour and lined them up in even rows.

"Whadda we do now?" he asked, avarice overcoming anxiety.

"Well, we'll begin the WISC-R. The first part has to do with information – facts about the world. The questions are easy in the beginning. They get harder, up to high school, so I don't expect you to know all of them. Here's the first one. How many pennies in a nickel?"

"Jeez. Whadda you think? A hundred? Five, naturally."

The questions became increasingly difficult, and Ben's answers became increasingly inaudible, a stutter in almost every sentence now. Still, he worked with concentration, and we finished four more subtests of the WISC-R – Picture Completion, Similarities, Picture Arrangement, and Arithmetic.

Finally, I leaned back and said, "That's it for today, Ben. Count up."

I helped him separate his chips into piles equal to a hundred, talking to him as we worked together. "I don't know if your mother told you or not, but you'll be coming three more times for testing. If you'll open that middle drawer and hand me the black book, I'll tell you when your next appointment is."

Ben opened the drawer and rummaged around, taking his time, fingering the Mickey Mouse watch and letter opener. There was no hyperactivity in his actions. He was just doing what I'd asked and taking his time about it. That was okay. If I was going to prowl around in his head, he could at least investigate my desk drawer.

He handed me the book, and I opened it to March. "Here. Next Friday at one o'clock – is that going to be all right with you?"

He gave me the same shrug we'd started with. "I guess so. Doesn't matter. Anyway, they say I have to. One hundred, two hundred … nine hundred. And then I have these left over. Fifty, sixty, seventy. Nine hundred and seventy."

I wrote 970 in the back of his folder, walked to the filing cabinet, and lifted down the wicker basket and "menu." The "menu" consists of a list of ten or twelve items and the amount of chips each one costs. I print each item in a different colour to heighten its appeal. I try to change the menu a little each week to keep things interesting.

This week's choice
stickers – 100 each
sugarless gum – 200 a piece
raisins – 500
Snoopy pencil – 1,000
erasers – 1,200
animal crackers – 1,400
ruler – 3,800

click erasers – 4,000
automatic pencil – 4,100
scissors – 4,200
coloured note paper – 6,000
Matchbox car of choice – 7,000

Ben studied the list. "What does 'of choice' mean?"

"That you can order the one you want from this catalog," I answered.

Ben nodded. "Anyone ever get seven thousand?"

"Sure. The kids who come after school for extra help save up all the time. It takes them a while though, because that's not as hard as testing."

Ben nodded. "Yeah. Uh. Can I see the catalog?"

"Yes. You always have one minute to decide whether to spend or save. Would you start the stopwatch?"

I wanted him to use the stopwatch as much as possible, because the more familiar he was with it the less anxiety it would create during the timed subtests. After thirty seconds of glancing through the catalog and the basket, Ben turned off the stopwatch and put it back in the case. "I'm saving."

After Ben left, I collected his papers and made notes about his performance on the WISC-R. I considered all intelligence tests somewhat suspect, because I knew from experience that scores can and do change on different days or with different testers. Still, the WISC-R (Wechsler Intelligence Scale for Children-Revised) is the best of the intelligence tests. I liked the fact that there are two sections to the test: the Verbal section, where all six subtests require verbal answers; and the Performance section (puzzles, blocks, and so forth), where the six subtests require nonverbal answers. So, as I watched a child taking the test I could see where he felt comfortable and sure of himself and where confidence faded. The WISC-R is far from perfect. I wish there were more "right-brain" tests, such as measurement of ability in music and rhythm. (The renowned neurologist Dr. Norman Geschwind claimed that if the WISC-R contained a subtest that measured musical ability, he would be classified as having dysmusia, in contrast to dyslexia – and I'm sure I would, too.)

I also wish there were less emphasis on the Full-Scale IQ score and much more on the individual subtest scores, which point up the areas of strength and weakness.

Because the children I evaluate are usually suspected of having some type of learning disability, the WISC-R is almost always a pleasant experience. Nearly every child scores far above his academic grades in at least some of the subtests, and he knows it. You can't fool these kids when they're failing, and it's just as true when they're succeeding. They love to find that they are good in some things and not the overall "stupid head" that their academic grades suggest. Of course, the low subtest scores are valuable, too – they yield clues to areas of weakness, which is necessary for planning remediation.

On the Information subtest of the WISC-R, Ben missed relatively easy items, such as "Where does the sun set?" Yet he was able to answer in detail a question about hieroglyphics.

He didn't know which month comes after March and had difficulty saying the months of the year; he knew there were twelve but was able to think of only ten in scrambled order. Yet, on Similarities, which measures the ability to think and reason abstractly, he scored in the superior range, even if he stumbled in expression.

111

A Safe Place for Joey

On the Picture Completion subtest, Ben spotted the missing detail of a picture instantly, but then fumbled for the word to describe it, calling the knob on a bureau a "button thing" and pointing to the missing strap of a watch and calling it "the thing … uh … I mean the watch's belt is missing." Because Picture Completion is not a test of verbal ability, the child only needs to point to the missing detail for the item to be scored as correct. Consequently, this did not lower Ben's score. But difficulty with word retrieval is another indicator of learning disabilities and points up the importance of observation rather than just the numbered scores.

Picture Arrangement was more difficult for Ben. In this test he was supposed to place cut-up picture sequences in order so that they told a logical story. Ben had trouble partly because he was confused about directionality and so couldn't tell whether trucks were coming or going, and partly because he rushed. Also, he was very innocent and insecure about social situations, and this subtest requires social awareness, the knowledge of what to do when, as well as sequencing ability.

The Arithmetic subtest of the WISC-R was also hard for Ben, not because he didn't know how to do the problems, but because they were given orally and he couldn't remember what was said long enough to hold the facts in his head so that he could figure out the solutions.

I tucked the papers back into Ben's file and then turned to the notes I had made during phone calls with Phil Golden, the clinical psychologist who had referred Ben to me. Phil and I had known each other for years. We had both been on the second floor of Rea Oldenburg's office building, and we often shared discussions of our cases. He was a big, kind, intelligent man, and I respected his work. We both believed that emotional and learning problems are usually linked in one way or another, and he referred children to me for what he called "educational therapy." We both believed that if one person in a family is troubled or hurting, the other members will also be affected. Phil was an accomplished family therapist, and so I, too, referred cases to him.

Phil had been working with the Aylesworths for about two months at the time of my first meeting with Ben. They had contacted him because Ben's pediatrician had insisted upon it. Ben had become increasingly withdrawn during the fall months, keeping almost entirely to himself. His grades had slipped from C's to D's and lower. Then one day just before Christmas, Phil told me, Jessie – Ben's sister – had gone out into their yard and looked up to see Ben standing barefoot on the roof. She called to him, but he didn't answer, and she ran to tell her mother.

So far, no one was sure what Ben was doing on the roof. He wouldn't talk about it, but it was the precipitating incident that made Ben's pediatrician insist that the Aylesworths contact Phil Golden.

The Aylesworths had planned to send only Ben, but Phil insisted that the whole family come in. They did so reluctantly, except for Jessie, a sunny seven-year-old, and Phil said that things were now moving very slowly. Ben still refused to say what he was doing on the roof. His father complained incessantly about Ben's grades and behavior, but found one reason after another why he couldn't keep appointments. So to Phil's frustration he was presently seeing only Mrs. Aylesworth and the two children.

Phil said he suspected that some of Ben's troubles in school might be due to some type of learning disability and suggested to the Aylesworths that they bring Ben to me for a diagnostic evaluation.

Mrs. Aylesworth had immediately picked up on the suggestion and called for an appointment. She had been anxious to talk and I listened to her carefully.

"Ben was fine," she said, "till it came time for him to go to school. Everybody in the family loved him. He was his grandmother's favourite – 'the brightest and the best,' she always said. Even now she thinks he's wonderful, but that's because she only sees him in the summer.

"Still, even though he's never liked school, he's never been like this before. He's failing everything and then lying about it. Saying he's studied when I know he's never opened a book. Ben's not like Jessie, his sister. She's in second grade now, and I sometimes think she can read better than Ben."

I was not pleased by the comparison, but this was not the time to discuss it. Instead I asked if Ben had had any previous evaluations. It seemed odd, with his continuing history of school difficulty, that someone hadn't picked up on it.

There was a short silence, and then Mrs. Aylesworth said, "Well, actually, his third-grade teacher wanted the Child Study Team to do what she called a workup. But Ralph wouldn't hear of it – and Ben wasn't all that bad until this year, sixth, you know. Now he says – Ralph, I mean – he says since you're private and not connected with the school it's all right to go ahead. Ralph feels strongly about Ben staying in public school and getting to know all classes of people."

I wondered if he knew "the people" called his son "Banana Brain."

I explained in detail to Mrs. Aylesworth what I looked for in a diagnostic evaluation – the child's intellectual potential, his levels of academic performance, styles of learning, any indication of learning disabilities, strengths, weaknesses, and how the child views himself and his world. I was surprised when she called back the next day to say that Ralph wanted to know exactly what tests I would give Ben.

I had recently composed an evaluation sheet listing the usual battery of tests I gave when there was reason to suspect some type of learning disability (see the Appendix). I mentioned this to Mrs. Aylesworth, and she immediately asked if she could stop by later in the day to pick it up.

I put the sheet in an envelope, wrote her name on the outside, and put the envelope in our mailbox. Before the day was over, she had called again to say that Ralph had looked over the test sheet and had agreed to the evaluation. And so we set up the four appointments for Ben.

Ben arrived at the side door at exactly five minutes before one o'clock on Friday. The Mercedes was already at the bottom of the driveway when I opened the door.

"I'm early," Ben announced. He still wasn't looking at me, but at least his gaze was up from his feet.

"Not much," I said. "Come in."

I closed the door and immediately realized that Ben was looking beyond me to the birds. It had snowed lightly the night before and the feeders were full, every perch taken; even the suet box had an energetic woodpecker tapping away.

Ben walked past me. "Since I'm early I'll wait here," he said, standing in front of the glass doors.

"All right. You can leave your jacket on the back of the chair."

He shrugged off the navy down vest, and simultaneously the birds, sensing unfamiliar action, rose in a feather cloud and disappeared.

"Jeezus cripes," Ben said. "What'd you tell me to do that for? Look at what happened."

"Don't worry. They'll be back. Just stand still."

Before I had finished speaking a chickadee landed.

"They have to be quick on a day like this – before the finches take over," I said.

"What k-kind are those?" Ben whispered, pointing to three yellow-green birds that arrived together.

"Goldfinches, I think. But I'm no expert. So far, they're not as mean as the purple ones, but I'm reserving my opinion. This is the first year they've come."

Unexpectedly, Ben crouched down on the white wool carpet in front of the glass doors. Then he stretched out full length, hands behind his head, lying quietly, looking up at the birds. Suddenly, he clapped his hands together, and again the birds rose up and flew into the woods.

I frowned as Ben stood up. "Why did you do that? You scared them on purpose."

Ben shrugged, eyes down. "I just wanted to see their wings from underneath. That's all."

"Well, next time please just wait for them to fly by themselves. They have to get used to enough going on around here without someone scaring them on purpose. Let's go up."

Ben sat down behind the desk without being asked.

"How many points do I have again?" Ben asked, fingering the chips.

I checked the back cover of his folder. "Nine hundred and seventy. Okay now. Has anything good happened since I saw you? I ask everyone that." (I can never quite give up the Best and the Worst – I just modify it a little for the older kids. When

I was first teaching seriously emotionally disturbed children, we didn't start our day with show and tell. Those children had little to show and nothing to tell. But I found that if I intensified the questions to "What was the best thing that happened since I saw you – or the worst thing?" not only did they talk, but I had to set time limits. Often what they talked of was fantasy – garbage truck's eyes, or playing with a neon sign or vacuum cleaner, whom they considered their best friend. But what was important was their desire to communicate and the willingness to use language to do it. Now, in my office, I still had to know what the children were doing, thinking, feeling before I began either testing or teaching.)

"No." Ben's voice was cool. "What could happen that's good?"

My turn to shrug. "I don't know. Maybe you went for a walk with MacArthur, maybe a good TV show, maybe something at home. Sometimes you have to learn to look for the good things."

"Yeah. Sure."

"All right. What was so bad?"

Ben hesitated. "School. Mom. Dad. They found out I was supposed to hand in a stupid book report. I just forgot. How'd I know the d-d-dumb teacher was gonna call Mom?"

"I can see where that would mean trouble. Pay yourself twenty-five."

Ben registered surprise and quickly picked out a green chip. "Then D-Dad started yelling about how all I do is s-s-sit on my b-b-butt and think the world owes me a living and on and on. I don't even know what he was t-t-talking about. Then Mom began crying while he was yelling. It was d-d-disgusting. And now I'm grounded for the weekend." Ben folded his arms and slouched across the desk. "Not that it m-m-matters. I wasn't g-g-going anywhere, anyway."

"I don't have any instant answers, Ben, but it does sound like a mess. I'm sorry."

"How much of a mess?"

"What? Oh. About a sixty-chip mess, I'd say."

Ben wasn't smiling, and neither was I. But something better was happening between us, and he was using the chips to initiate communication.

"Now," I said, "we're up to the WISC-R Block Design in the testing, and we've still got a ways to go, so we need to begin. Here." I dumped the blocks on the desk. "They're all the same – red on some sides, white on others, and half-red, half-white on the other sides. Here's the first card. The idea is to make the design on the card by using the blocks. Here. Watch me first."

Ben was wonderful with the blocks. Where his fingers curled around a pencil had been awkward and unsure as he copied the Bender designs, now they moved quickly and gracefully, arranging first four and then nine blocks into the required patterns.

With each successfully completed design, Ben became a little looser and a little happier. The pulse at his temple was barely visible. Obviously, it felt good to him to be doing something well.

"Pay yourself two hundred twenty, Ben," I said. "The next test is Vocabulary. I'll say a word. You just tell me what it means."

"I hate that kind of stuff. I lots of times know the word, but I d-d-don't know how to say it. I mean I know it in my head, b-b-but when I go to say what it means … oh, I don't know."

"Well, just try. Remember, the words start easy and get harder, but I don't expect you to know them all. Hat. What is a hat?"

"Thing you wear."

I waited, but Ben didn't elaborate.

"What is ..."

"Here," Ben said, patting his head. "You wear it here."

Ben's answers were all terse, and the rhythm and content of his speech were that of a much younger child. And he was right. He did get mixed up.

"What does 'brave' mean?"

"It's like when you're scared. Well, not like that. Like the opposite. You know?"

I nodded and leaned back to look at Ben, sensing that he had something more to say.

"Do you think those birds are brave?" he asked. "Like are they scared flying around up there or do they like it?"

"I think they like it," I said. "The landing looks like the hard part." What was it with Ben and birds? Why did he watch them with such fascination? Why did he want to see their wings from underneath?

I shook my head, both to clear it and to get back to work. To stay completely with a child like Ben, who often went off track, took concentration. Ben continued to struggle to express himself. He knew a lot more than he could put into words. When asked to define "gamble," he replied, "Bet over money." Then he shrugged. "Oh ... I don't know. I mean I know, but I don't. Just forget it."

Object Assembly, another subtest of the WISC-R, consisted of four puzzles and for Ben was as easy as or easier than Block Design. He immediately knew what the puzzle was supposed to be. He saw the gestalt, the unified whole, and efficiently put the pieces in the proper places. Ben could build from a design. He could also put isolated pieces into a meaningful whole without copying. Both of these tasks require visual awareness. Block Design is also considered to be an excellent indicator of general intelligence. Ben's understanding of spatial relationships far exceeded his ability to express himself verbally.

Ben did only fairly well on the Comprehension subtest, which measures practical judgment and common sense. His judgment was adequate, but he often failed to gain extra points because his answers showed a lack of independence. When asked what he should do if a much smaller boy started to fight with him, his answer was, "Tell somebody – like tell your mother," instead of thinking of a way to handle the problem himself.

Both Coding (in which the child is asked to match and copy symbols, testing the ability to learn combinations of symbols and shapes and then to reproduce them with paper and pencil) and Digit Span (which consists of repeating an increasing number of digits both forward and backward) were near disasters for Ben. He copied only a few symbols during the two-minute span – his pencil moving slowly and awkwardly – and he could repeat only four digits correctly. After that he would have the right numbers, but in the wrong sequence – or else forget them altogether. Ben's spirits wilted as quickly as they had risen earlier; only the chips sustained him.

I put the WISC-R away and handed Ben the WRAT (Wide Range Achievement Test). "This is a short test of spelling, reading, and arithmetic," I said. "The questions all begin easy and get harder. Try not to get down on yourself if you don't know some. Remember, I don't expect you to know them all. We'll start with spelling."

Ben held the pencil in his right hand in the now familiar cramped, hooked grip more usually seen on lefties. He printed the words in pale, uneven letters, reversing the *b* in "boy" and the *d* in "dress," and erasing letters over and over again, usually making the spelling worse than before.

In the reading (word recognition) section, he skipped lines, lost his place, read "sour" as "sore" and "plot" as "pilot."

We finished the session with arithmetic. This time it was a written arithmetic test, in contrast to the oral arithmetic on the WISC-R. This was much easier for Ben because he could actually see the problems, rather than just hear them. He worked quickly and with concentration, adding, subtracting, multiplying, dividing. He understood measurement and fractions, and although much of his computation was done on his fingers or by counting under his breath, he still scored well. He knew this stuff, and we both smiled when I said, "Okay, Ben. We're done for the day. Pay yourself three hundred eighty and count up."

I try to end each session with a test on which I think the child will do well. It makes it easier for them to come back next time. I don't always guess right, so I'm pleased when I do.

Ben had large piles of chips in front of him, and he counted carefully: "One hundred, two hundred ..." then his voice gradually faded and his fingers rested on the chips without moving.

"Can I ask you something?"

"Of course."

"What kind of doctor are you, anyway?"

"I'm not a doctor, Ben. More like a teacher."

"Well, why did they say I had to come? What do they want you to do?"

"I'm trying to find out how you learn best so I can show you how to use your strengths to help in the areas where you have trouble."

A Safe Place for Joey

Outside a car honked, and Ben stood up.

"That's not true, you know," Ben said. "You're lying to me just like everybody else. What you're trying to find out is whether I'm retarded or crazy or both. Right?"

"No. I don't lie, Ben. And I don't expect you to lie to me either. I don't think you're retarded or crazy. I do think school is hard for you and getting harder, and I'm trying to find out why. I hope you'll help me. I promise you that when the tests are finished I'll show you how you scored, and we'll figure out what it means and what to do about it."

Beep. Beep. Beep. The honk was more insistent.

"I guess you'd better go," I said. "It sounds as though your mom is in a hurry. I'll finish counting up and add it to the rest."

Reluctantly, Ben came out from behind the desk. "That's not Mom. That's Dad's honk."

From downstairs a child's voice called. My next appointment had arrived. We'd run out of time.

"Okay. Good-bye for now, Ben. Do you mind letting yourself out? I'll see you on Tuesday."

I walked to the lookout window in the front room as my next child climbed the stairs. I had never met Ben's father, and I could not restrain my curiosity. A Jaguar waited in the upper part of our driveway. A black-haired man wearing dark glasses sat alone in the front seat, leaning intently over the wheel. As I watched, Ben opened the right rear door, climbed in and huddled against the window. As far as I could tell, neither the man nor the boy spoke.

"This will be a long, hard session, Ben. I've asked your mother to give us two hours for this one. Lots of academic things – more reading, writing. But at least each test is worth a lot of

122

points. And let's see." I turned to the back cover of the folder. "You had fourteen hundred thirty-five last time, plus the first nine hundred and seventy, so you're up to two thousand four hundred and five already."

Ben nodded, but didn't say anything. I handed him a small book. "Would you just read these words – there, where it says Word List Two?"

I turned to the same page in the examiner's copy of the Spache Oral Diagnostic Reading Test so I could write down Ben's responses. It's of little help to know that a child made six or sixteen errors. It's of tremendous value to know the kind of errors he made. Reading "was" as "saw" is very different from reading "was" as "were" or "house" as "home." Each type of error has a different cause, and once you know what causes a problem, you have a much better chance of fixing it. So I tracked errors carefully.

"I thought you said you always asked," Ben said, interrupting my thoughts,

"Pardon?"

"Last time you said you always asked about good things that happened."

I put the examiner's book on the desk and leaned back, feeling the little kick of excitement that comes when the child takes the initiative, but keeping my voice low to cover it. "You're right, Ben. Pay yourself twenty-five. It's a much better way to start."

"Well, if it doesn't have to have just happened, I figured I could tell you about the river."

I nodded agreement.

"We've been going there ever since I was little, before I was even a year old, I think. And Mom and Dad went before that.

Mom's been going since she was born. It's really Granny's place. We stay there all summer, and it's really cool."

"That's where you sail?"

"Yeah. We've got a Lightning. That's a kind of sailboat, but you need two people to sail it. And then …" Ben stopped. "Well, we've got a lot of boats – the Sun-fish, a big old Garwood, and then a fiberglass speedboat and a little alinum … alminium, however you say it, boat, and a couple of canoes."

"Sounds like there's more boats than people," I replied, thinking to myself that he had stumbled over "aluminum," but he hadn't stuttered once so far this session.

Ben almost smiled, and the whiny quality was completely gone from his voice. "No. See, there's Granny's big house, and then Uncle Joe uses the boathouse cottage, and we have the little house over on the other side."

"Does Uncle Joe have kids?"

"Danny and Melissa. Danny's almost as old as I am. He has a Lab, too – MacArthur's brother. They get along real good."

Ben was having no trouble talking now. We could have spent an hour just on the river, but I was supposed to be doing a diagnostic educational evaluation. I had to get on to the educational part.

"It sounds wonderful, Ben. Do you have any pictures of the river? Or maybe you could draw one and bring it next time? Anyway, pay yourself one hundred. And now, please just read the words on this page."

Ben reluctantly picked up the book and read through the forty words. He read rapidly, stuttering toward the end, but thirty out of the forty words were correct. The errors were mainly substitutions – "far" for "fair," "itch" for "inch," "ether" for "either." When he got to "guard," he said, "I know what it is – like someone who watches prisoners – but I can't pronounce it." Ben had missed the last five words, which meant that he did not continue on to Word List III.

Reading the thirty words on Word List II correctly entitled him to try a fourth-grade reading selection. He substituted, omitted, and lost his place time after time, stuttering on almost every other word. But even so, he was able to answer eight out of eight comprehension questions correctly.

Just for my own interest, I had him read the fifth- and sixth-grade selections. He was way over the error limit for substitutions and omissions on both, but he still could answer six or seven of the eight comprehension questions correctly. I suspected that if I read out loud to him his understanding would far surpass his grade level.

On the Phonetic Analysis section of the reading test, Ben was unsure of vowel sounds and could not decode isolated syllables. In order to read the nonsense syllable "ock," he said "clock" and then separated out "ock."

He struggled through the five-minute section of the Speed and Accuracy part of the Gates MacGinitie Silent Reading Test, completing only thirteen short passages – about the amount expected of beginning fourth graders. But he did answer twelve of the thirteen comprehension questions correctly. Conversely, on the longer, more difficult Vocabulary and Comprehension sections, he raced along, obviously not reading, just guessing at answers. It was as if he felt he wasn't going to be able to do it no matter how hard he tried, so why bother.

Written expression was painfully difficult. On the first section – dictation of a fourth-grade paragraph (I didn't expect him to be able to write at a higher level than he could read) – his trouble with spelling and transcoding words that he heard into written symbols was even more apparent than it had been on the WRAT spelling section. He spelled circus as "cirs." He left out many words and phrases, even though I had told him that he could have a sentence repeated as often as he wanted. But at least he wasn't complaining, and he wasn't giving up. Ben was struggling, but struggling gallantly, and I paid out chips generously. I wondered if anyone had any idea what it must cost Ben to go to school each day – aware, intelligent, but nowhere near the academic level of his class, "Banana Brain," "Banana Brain" echoing in the corridors. I wondered that he went to school at all.

Halfway through the session, Ben had earned over a thousand chips. I went over to a sack in the file cabinet and brought back ten more fifty-cent pieces. Ben was pleased. "Did anybody ever get all ten silvers before?"

"A few. A few others that worked as hard as you're working. I've had these fifty-cent pieces a long time. My dad collected coins, and he let me play with them when I was sick and had to stay in bed. I loved the way they looked and felt, and I decided the kids who come here might like them, too. So I mixed some in with the chips. Now, please just write a paragraph about anything you want – just a few sentences."

Ben hesitated. "I can't think of anything."

"Well, try. If you don't come up with something, I'll give you a topic."

Two more minutes of silence and then Ben began writing. He wrote for several minutes, and then pushed the paper toward me.

I pushed it back. "Read it to me first, okay?"

"One day I went sailing with Danny and a big storm came up …"

Ben read on. The ten or so sentences sounded coherent, but after he'd counted the words and was paying himself ten for each, I looked at the paper and could see that almost a third of the words he'd read to me were left out. Punctuation was nonexistent and spacing irregular. Some words collided with others, some ran off the paper, some wandered up from the line and would have been indecipherable if Ben had not first read them.

While he figured out the correct amount of chips, I got out the Detroit Test of Learning Aptitude. This is not designed to measure either intellectual potential or academic achievement, but rather to assess various categories of learning, such as visual attentive ability, auditory attentive ability, motor ability, and so forth – in other words, to discover through which modalities a child learns best.

I started with the test for Auditory Attention Span for Unrelated Words. Here the child is asked to repeat the words the examiner says. First, "cat, ice." Each sequence becomes longer until eight unrelated words are given at one time. Ben sped along in fine shape until we reached a four-word sequence; here he became confused and repeated "cart" as "kite." In a five-word sequence, he could repeat only three of the words correctly, and by the time we reached eight words he could repeat only two. His chin had sunk low on his chest and he muttered, "See. I g-g-guess I really am s-s-stupid."

I counted the words he had said correctly. "You had forty-one right, Ben. Pay yourself five for each. Besides, this test doesn't measure how smart you are – only auditory memory."

"Audi … what? What do you mean?" Ben asked. "What's that, anyway?"

"Auditory memory. Just a fancy way of saying 'remembering what you hear,'" I answered.

Although Ben perked up slightly as he piled up two more silvers, from experience I knew this was indeed a rather low score. "Now try this," I said. "See if you think it's harder or easier than the test we just did."

I turned to Visual Attention Span for Objects. "This time I'm going to show you some pictures. First, there'll be two pictures, then three – more each time, and I'll leave them out a little longer each time, too. Again, remember nobody's ever gotten them all right."

The first picture showed a house and a girl. Ben remembered them perfectly. He also remembered a three-picture sequence and a four and a five. He was becoming increasingly pleased with himself. Even in an eight-picture sequence, he could recall six of the eight correctly.

He piled up his earned silvers and remarked, "That was much easier than saying the words." What he meant, of course, was that it was easier to remember what he saw than what he heard.

Ben, as well as the test, was telling me that he could process information better through visual than through auditory channels.

I was not surprised. There had been lots of indications of difficulty with auditory processing – the Digit Span of the WISC-R, dictation, and Auditory Memory for Unrelated Syllables on the Detroit. It was as if Ben's head went on overload when too much material was presented at one time through his auditory channels. If the material was organized and meaningful, he did better, and he scored somewhat higher in Auditory Memory for Related Syllables, in which he was asked to repeat sentences. It was interesting that the overload factor was not apparent with visual stimuli.

We did five more tests on the Detroit – Motor Speed, Free Association, Memory for Designs, Oral Directions, and Visual Attention Span for Letters. These tests, too, indicated that visual memory was a strength for Ben, and auditory processing weaker. However, when he had to use a pencil to copy designs or draw them from memory, he once again had difficulty.

As so often happens, a mixed pattern of difficulties was starting to appear. Much as parents, teachers, and I myself long for one simple answer, it is always more complicated. And as I often remind myself, considering the complexities of our brains this is not surprising.

The last test of the day was my own variation of the Harris Test of Lateral Dominance. I always include this, although there is controversy about the importance of its results. It simply shows which hand, eye, and foot the child prefers to use for different tasks. The majority of the world is right-handed, right-footed, and right-eyed. For whatever reason, a large percentage of the children I see have what is known as mixed or crossed dominance: that is, they are right-handed and left-eyed or left-handed and right-eyed. Footedness (the foot used for kicking, stamping, and so forth), if there is such a word, is also noted. Research has not shown this to be a cause of learning disabilities, but still I always check it out. One more piece to the puzzle.

The trick in identifying which eye, hand, or foot a child uses is to have the child focus on the task.

"Okay, Ben. Take this piece of paper. Roll it up and then look through it and tell me how many fingers I have up. I'm going to try and fool you."

I twined six fingers together and held them out in front of me.

Ben put the paper scope to his left eye. "Six."

"All right. Fine. Take it down. Now once more. How many?"

Again the scroll went directly to his left eye. "Eight," Ben said with confidence.

"Now scrunch the paper up into a ball and bring it over here." I motioned to a spot between the two green chairs on the far side of the desk. A mural of prancing horses made of different-coloured cloth, a present from a former student, ran across the far wall. "See the orange horse at the end. Try to hit it with that paper ball."

Ben pegged it hard with his right hand, missed, threw again with his right hand, and got the tail.

"Okay. Now put the paper right here and kick it out the door."

Right foot. "Pick it up and hop back and put the paper in the wastebasket." Left foot. "Now skip to the bathroom and open the door." Ben turned the knob with his left hand. I handed him the kaleidoscope. "Quickly – how many patterns can you see before I count to three?" Left eye. "Write your full initials on the rug with your toe." Left foot. "What do you see in this microscope?" Left eye. "Make a cross on this paper with this marker." Right hand. "Wind the stopwatch four times." Left hand.

Ben and I stood facing each other in the middle of the floor. Ben was actually grinning at me. "Touch your right eye." Ben hesitated, then took his right hand and pretended to write – so he could figure out his right side – then touched his right eye. "Touch your left ear." Hesitation, but he did it.

"Okay." I stretched out my hands. "Touch my left hand."

Ben did just what I would have done. He turned around so he was facing the same way I was, found which was his own left, turned back, and touched my left hand.

"Okay. That's fine. Pay yourself two hundred seventy-five."

Whatever mixed dominance means or doesn't mean, children enjoy moving around and it's a good way to wind up a session. Ben looked happier and more relaxed than I'd ever seen him.

He counted his chips carefully, and when he added them to the ones he'd saved he had 6,070.

He asked to see the Matchbox catalog and perused its pages carefully, setting the stopwatch when he started.

I watched Ben as he turned the pages with concentration, wondering, as usual, at the magic of chips. I was sure Ben had enough money stashed away somewhere to buy everything in the catalog, but somehow earning the chips to buy the car or truck or plane made it special. My guess was that the value of the chips was that each one in essence said, "You're okay," "You're good," "You're terrific," and my kids don't hear that kind of thing very often.

"Hey, Mary," Ben said, bringing me back. "Do you think the wings on this thing move?" he asked, pointing to a small green and white plane.

"I know they do." It was the first time he'd used my name. I wanted to savor it, but there wasn't time. "I got one for somebody else last week." Then, suddenly, I took a breath and asked quickly, quietly, "Why, Ben? Why does it matter if the wings move? Is it like the birds?"

Ben was silent. Had I gone too far too soon? Ben turned the catalog over and over in his hands. Finally, he said, "Yeah. Sort of." There was another long pause, and then he added, "That's what I was doing up there on the roof that day. I couldn't use the porch anymore – well, I'll tell you about that later – anyway, see, I sneaked out this old pajama top of Dad's and I took off my shoes to get lighter, and I figured if I could flap the right way, kind of like the birds, maybe I could fly. I never did get to try it, though. Ole Jessie came out in the yard and saw me and started yelling, and then Mom called Dad and he came home from the office." Ben shrugged. "Everybody made such a big deal out of it. That's why I have to go to that Dr. Golden and come here. They both – Mom and Dad – think I'm crazy, but I bet it would've worked."

"Suppose it hadn't, Ben?"

Ben shrugged. "Well, at least I wouldn't have had to go to school for a while."

The car honked.

"I'll check out the airplane," I said to Ben, thinking, How can we end now? How can I send this child out and away? And yet another child was waiting downstairs, and there would be four more after her.

"Listen, Ben, maybe you could draw me a picture of what you think it would be like – flying, I mean. Why don't you borrow these?" I said, nodding toward a box of Magic Markers. "There are sixteen different colours," I added, as if quantity would help.

I woke early the next morning, thinking about Ben, and went up to my office and scored and reviewed as many of the tests as I could.

I studied the scores and my notes when I'd finished, and even though all the test scores weren't in yet, it was easy to see that there was a large gap between Ben's intellectual potential and his academic achievement. He scored far above the average range of intelligence, but his academic achievements were far below the average. This was related to his difficulties with auditory processing and memory, poor graphomotor skills, difficulty with verbal expression, and the fact that he had very little confidence in his own abilities. However, he was beginning to open up a little, and I was sure Ben's understanding exceeded far more than he could explain in words.

I decided to add the Peabody Picture Vocabulary Test, a test of verbal receptive intelligence, to our last session, even though it would mean extending his time and rescheduling my following appointments. None of that mattered now. I was hot on the trail, tracking down clue after clue, trying to solve the mystery of Ben.

I had thought about calling Phil Golden for backup information and support, but our usual arrangement was for me to talk with him after I had finished all four evaluation sessions, scored the tests, and reached my own conclusions. This was partly because Phil did not want to impose his opinions before I had formed my own, and also because he liked to see everything all at once rather than piecemeal.

Also, I liked to acquire as much information as possible directly from the child himself. I knew other people could give me their impressions of Ben. I also knew that only Ben could give me the truth.

Still, the thought of Ben barefoot, in his father's pajama top, haunted me. Had he been suicidal?

Certainly he was depressed and discouraged, but then, who wouldn't be if he were Ben? And, I told myself, Ben had seemed more open and relaxed during his last visit than he ever had before.

I decided to wait.

I was watching for Ben when he came for his fourth and last appointment and went outside to greet him.

A Safe Place for Joey

Mrs. Aylesworth lowered the front window of the Mercedes. "Is something wrong? Did I come at the wrong time?"

"No." I smiled, wanting to reassure her. "I just came out to remind you that we'll be about an hour and a half today."

"Yes. All right. How is Ben doing? Have you found out anything? And oh, I'm sorry I haven't returned that form. I'll drop it by tomorrow. It's just that it's so … uh … difficult."

"Just fill in as much as you can. We can complete the rest when you and Mr. Aylesworth come for your conference. Ben is working very hard, but I'd rather not try to talk about it in pieces. Besides, I'd better get to work. We'll go over everything when you come."

Ben had already gone in through the side door that I'd left open and was lying on the floor watching the birds, his head propped on one hand, the markers in the other. There was only one titmouse and a woodpecker on the feeders.

But there were numerous sparrows and one bright red cardinal on the stone steps.

"How come that red one doesn't fly up?" Ben asked.

"I don't know. The bird book says that cardinals are ground feeders; it doesn't say why."

"Maybe he's scared."

"Yes. Maybe he is."

Ben got up slowly and carefully. Not a bird moved. I smiled to thank him; he smiled back and went up the stairs first, leading the way.

He sat behind the desk, and I pulled the other chair over beside him. He put the box of markers on the desk and then lifted the top off the box and took out a packet of snapshots held together with a rubber band. Ben didn't mention the markers or having drawn anything.

134

"Look," Ben said, his voice high and excited. "I brought some pictures of the river, but don't tell Mom. I had to take them out of this p-p-picture al-albin-albinum, uh … whadda you call it … picture book, and she'd have a p-p-purple fit if she knew. She keeps it real neat with everything written underneath – the names of the p-p-people and the dates, like. But I can put them b-b-back okay. I know where they go.

"See, this is Granny's house and part of the boathouse and dock. You can see the flagpole out on the rocks – the whole place is mostly rock. I put the flag up every morning when I'm there and take it down before sunset. Granny says it's my job 'cause I'm responsible."

"That's nice, Ben." And it was – both what she said and the place itself. The house was big and rambling with weathered grey shingles and a wide porch that wrapped around three sides. There were wicker chairs and a glider on the porch, and the steps and railing were lined with window boxes filled with red geraniums.

"This is me and Jessie and Danny. I told you about him, remember."

The picture showed three handsome blond kids in their bathing suits, fishing off the boathouse.

"And this is me and MacArthur."

It was a wonderful picture. The dog sat beside Ben on the front seat of a boat looking straight ahead, with Ben relaxed and confident behind the wheel.

"What kind of boat did you say it was, Ben?"

"A Garwood. Granny's had it a long time, but I wasn't allowed to take it out myself till last year. See. The sides are mahogany, and the hinges and stuff are real brass. It's a really special boat to her, so you have to have a pretty good idea where the shoals are and how to use all the gears and get it back in the boathouse right before she trusts you with it."

"I can see why you like it there," I said.

"This is the last picture. See, this is the new speedboat. Dad got it last summer, and that's him driving."

The same dark intense man I had seen in the car was again leaning intently over a wheel.

"I didn't bring a picture of Mom because I knew you'd seen her."

I still held the picture of Ben's father. "Does your dad like the river, too?"

Ben shrugged. "Some. He doesn't come up that much. He says he can only take so much of it at a time. Besides, he's real busy – he says we couldn't afford the river and stuff if he spent his summers loafing around like us."

I handed the picture back and waited.

Ben piled the snapshots together, making sure he got them in a certain order, probably so he could put them back in the album correctly. He put a rubber band around them and tucked them in the back pocket of his jeans.

"Would you like an envelope?" I asked.

Ben shook his head. "Mom gets nervous if anybody g-g-gets into her stuff. I'll just keep them in my p-p-pocket till I put 'em b-b-back."

It hadn't been easy for Ben to bring the pictures, and I also knew it had been important to him to show me that part of his life. I thanked him for it.

"Pay yourself fifty for each picture," I said. "Now let's get back to the testing. I know some of it's hard and boring. But it really helps later on.

"Now please take a look at this."

I laid the Peabody Picture Vocabulary book in front of Ben. The Peabody is a test of receptive, not expressive, language. It measures how much you understand rather than how well you say it. It consists of a book of black and white pictures, four to a page. The examiner simply says a word, and the child points to the picture described by the word. I did not intend to use it as a global intelligence test, but I did want to see if there was a difference between Ben's score on this test and his rather low vocabulary score on the WISC-R, which involves expression and also retrieval of information to a much greater extent. The Peabody takes only about ten minutes, and I had a feeling Ben would enjoy it.

If anything, I underestimated. Ben whizzed through the test, readily identifying such words as rodent, salutation, patriarch, ingenious. I felt sure that when I scored it, Ben would place well above his chronological age.

"Pay three hundred seventy-five. Let's see what we have left now. Some drawings, Raven Progressive Matrices, and sentence completion."

I handed Ben a piece of paper and a pencil. "Now I want you to do a bunch of different drawings. First, please draw your best picture of a house."

"I told you, remember? That I'm not so good at drawing."

"I remember. I'm not too great myself. Just make it the best you can."

I have taken several courses, read many books, and had supervised training by a psychologist in both the administration of the WISC-R and the interpretation of drawings. But still, I use great caution in my interpretations, particularly of drawings. I do believe that they are necessary pieces of the puzzle, and in my conferences with Phil Golden he examines the pictures carefully and I value what he tells me. But drawings should be considered in context with all else that is known about the child. Some children love to draw and can communicate ideas and feelings through drawings that they would never be able to express otherwise. Other children are uncomfortable with paper and pencil, and this should also be taken into account.

Ben's drawings reflected his constricted emotions. The house he drew was approximately one square inch in all, resting on the bottom of the paper, surrounded by white emptiness. The windows were few and barred, and the door was tightly locked. There was an attached garage with three cars and a motorcycle.

"Now, please draw a tree – the best you can," I said.

Ben drew quickly, producing a small, faintly drawn tree with sketchy sticks for branches. He shaded in the tree trunk, anxiety growing, while the pulse in his temple beat at a rapid pace.

"Now draw a person doing something."

"I can't do p-p-people, p-p-p-par-par-tic … you know what I mean – doing things."

"I know. That's okay. My people don't come out the way I want them to, either."

Quickly, almost as if to get it over with, Ben sketched a figure a half-inch tall perched on a line, hands over his head. "He's diving," Ben volunteered.

"Good," I said. "Now draw a picture of a woman doing something."

Ben had given up complaining. He drew a seated figure with something that looked like a balloon instead of a head. "She's getting her hair done," Ben explained.

"Last picture, Ben. Draw a picture of your family doing something."

"Oh, jeez." Ben's pain was real. "I don't know anything they can be doing." He stared grimly and silently at the paper, and then finally picked it up, folded it in half, and then folded it again. Then he spread it out on the desk, smoothing the paper till it lay flat, divided it into quarters, and then carefully penciled in the crease marks. He numbered the squares – 1, 2, 3, 4. "Well, I'll put D-D-Dad up here," he said, drawing what for Ben was a large figure. But he erased it before it was half done. "No, I know. I'll make him driving his car." And Ben drew a long, low car with a figure hunched over the wheel, and then blacked in both car and man.

"Mom can be reading," he said, and drew a small figure with long, perfectly even hair, holding a book, perched on the edge of a chair.

"Now Jess can be down here. I'll make her jumping rope." Ben drew a girl with a big smile and ribbons in her hair, holding a jump rope.

"Now there's just me left. I'll be at the river." He drew two parallel lines across box 4. "The river's a lot b-b-bigger than that, you know." I nodded as Ben added a tiny sailboat near the edge of the page. He added a circle on the top edge of the boat and blacked it again. "You can't see the rest of me," he said. "It's inside the b-b-boat. There's just my head there, my s-s-stupid head." Then he carefully added a bird above the boat. "There's always at least one gull out there," he said.

"All right. Thank you, Ben. Pay yourself six hundred, and then I'll ask you some questions about the pictures."

Ben's answers were short and the stutter was there, but he was obviously trying to tell me all that he could.

When we got to the last picture, he lingered over it, touching the picture of the boat with his finger. "I wish I could draw it b-better, so you could see what it's like. I don't know why it is, but you feel good up there, out on the water. I mean all the time you just feel happy." Ben smiled at me – and I wished I had a picture of him just like that.

I stood up and got my Polaroid and said, "Tell me some more," and snapped a picture as he talked. I always take a picture of each child I see, to help me remember. Many children come back years later for help in choosing the right boarding school or college. Without a picture, I often have difficulty placing a child. But when I can see their faces, I remember each one in detail.

I'd put the picture-taking off with Ben; somehow it had seemed too intimate a gesture until now. The picture showed a smiling, handsome, seemingly untroubled boy – one that I had rarely seen in person.

We were almost done. Only the Raven Standard Progressive Matrices Test and the Freeman Sentence Completion Test were left.

Ben enjoyed the Raven, as I had thought he would. The Raven Standard Progressive Matrices is an untimed test of designs, each of which has a missing segment. The test is used to measure conceptual thoughts in a perceptual field. The pictures are somewhat like visual analogies and range from clear perceptual problems to those of an abstract nature. Ben scored in the 95th percentile, again confirming his intelligence and good visual perception but leaving other questions unanswered.

I had the Freeman Sentence Completion on the clipboard, ready to write down Ben's endings to the sentences I read. But before I could start, Ben suddenly pushed the box of markers almost roughly across the desk.

"I couldn't d-d-draw it – that picture you wanted me to draw. I tried, but I didn't really know what to d-draw. See, the b-birds, and being sc-sc-scared, kind of got all mixed up in my mind. I don't know. It got worse at school this year – the k-k-kids made fun of me and I couldn't talk about it to anyone and everybody was always so m-mad. I began to dream about the river. At first I had to make myself do it on purpose, but then it began to come just b-b-by itself. All I had to do was just close my eyes for a second and I'd be at the river. I mean I could open my eyes and still be there. When they started to yell at me, or if I was supposed to take a t-t-t … like an exam, I'd just close my eyes for that one second and then I wasn't in school anymore. Instead I'd be out sailing, or swimming with Danny, or taking Mac out for a ride. I'd be doing something different all the time, but the birds were always there. Like they really are in the summer. Way up there, gliding along – just a few flaps – and then they'd just sail along. It looked so easy.

"That's how it began. And then I b-b-began to think how maybe flying and not being scared went together. How if you could fly you wouldn't ever be scared. And I didn't think it would be so b-b-bad if I couldn't read good, or get good marks, if I didn't get scared. Like, even if everybody else m-m-m … I can't say it … minded, there, I wouldn't. I mean it wouldn't be so important to me."

I sat without moving, hoping Ben couldn't hear my heart thudding away, praying that we wouldn't be interrupted. Ben understood himself better than anyone else. If I could just listen long enough, hard enough, he would explain it to me.

"I didn't p-plan it all out," he said. "It just sort of happened. See, first I just started walking around the railing on the back porch, just putting one foot in front of the other and b-balancing with my arms. The porch is kind of high up, and I was a little scared at first – but I got pretty good at it, and I was getting so I didn't feel hardly scared at all. But then ole Jessie found out and she always wants to do whatever I'm doing, and I got worried she'd f-f-f …" Ben shook his head in frustration.

"Fall," I said, knowing I shouldn't fill in words, but unable to stop myself.

Ben nodded. "So I had to stop. But I missed being up high, being able to do it and not feel scared – and somehow it got mixed in with thinking about the birds.

"It wasn't that I really planned to fly. At least I don't think I did, or anyway not much. But I liked thinking about it and the feeling – being up so high, all alone, nobody b-bothering me – and so I started climbing out the dormers in the attic onto the slate roof and then walking and balancing around the edge of it. Nobody ever saw me. Our house is way back from the road and there's lots of trees around it, and Mom's never outside. I didn't d-do it on weekends. I guess I was sc-scared Dad might come home then and I knew he'd be really mad. Then the more I walked around out there, the more I began thinking about the birds and wondering how they did it.

"The only d-d-d-dumb thing I did was sneaking out that ole pajama top of Dad's. But it had these great big s-s-s-sleeves, and I liked to f-f-flap, and I could balance real g-g-good in my bare feet. But I shouldn't have gotten his d-d-dumb pajamas. I wasn't really going to j-j-j-jump off the roof, though – honest. I just liked thinking about it."

"Have you told Dr. Golden?" I asked.

"No. Mom's always sitting there. I haven't told anybody b-but Jessie. And you."

I could hear the Mercedes pull into the driveway. There was no beep, but its hum was familiar now. "I don't know what to pay for that, Ben. It's like it's too much for chips."

Ben nodded. "Yeah. Anyway, it doesn't matter. I have enough chips already."

Ben knew as well as I did that our time was up, but still he finished counting his piles of chips. "Two thousand and thirty-five. Can I add it up?"

I pushed the file folder toward Ben, open to the inside back cover. Ben wrote the figure carefully underneath the previous total and added them together, counting softly under his breath.

"Eight thousand one hundred and five."

"Good work." I handed him the Matchbox catalog.

"I already know which one I want," he said, leafing quickly till he came to the little airplane. "This one, right here."

I circled the plane with a red pen and wrote "B.B.A." underneath it. I always write the child's initials so I will remember who ordered what.

The motor still hummed in the driveway, and I looked up to say good-bye to Ben. "As soon as I get it, I'll call you and you can come back, pick it up, and we'll go over your test scores then, too."

But Ben wasn't listening. He was still looking at the picture of the plane – or that's what I thought he was looking at. But instead he pointed to the initials I had just written.

"Did you always know?" he asked. "That they called me that? B.B.?"

I nodded.

"How come you didn't say anything?"

"Because I didn't like it."

"You know what it stands for?"

Again I nodded.

"Mom says I should be proud of my name. Benjamin Bradford – a fine heritage, she says. That's all she knows. Some heritage. Banana Brain."

Phil Golden was in his fifties, tall, with salt and pepper hair and beard. He had been working with troubled children and adults for over twenty years in private practice; he had also been a school psychologist and was presently head of the learning disabilities graduate department at a nearby college. For all these reasons, I valued his opinions and considered the money and time I spent in his office good investments. We also liked and understood each other and had a friendship built on the firm base of working together for many years.

I stood up as Phil walked into the waiting room. He wrapped his arms around me and said, "How are you, Mary? I'm glad to see you. Come in. Come in."

His office was full of leather couches and suede chairs and animal-skin rugs. There was no place to spread out the papers in Ben's folder, so I simply handed him the file, keeping only a blank piece of blue paper on which to make notes. (I had found that using blue paper for my visits to Phil made it easier to pick out his comments when I wanted to locate them quickly.)

"First, before you go through Ben's file, tell me a little about his family," I said.

"An interesting lot. You've met the mother?"

I nodded.

"So you know she's a blueblood – the Bradford name goes back to Plymouth Rock. Lots and lots of money. Her mother is still very much alive and I gather still has a good bit to say about what goes on in the family. Carol, that's Ben's mother's

144

name, is very sweet, very anxious, and very eager to please her husband and her children. I suspect that in the same way we've seen so often there is a tendency for her to overidentify with Ben and that her protectiveness encourages dependency in him.

"The father, Ralph – have you met him?" Phil asked.

I shook my head.

"Well, he's a bit harder to describe. Very intense, very bright. Built his manufacturing company up from almost nothing till now it's one of the largest in the state and has recently made several foreign acquisitions. He was, in the beginning, punctual and outwardly cooperative, but even then there was something guarded about him. I can't quite put my finger on it.

"I'll tell you one interesting thing, though, that just came out. Aylesworth isn't his real name. It was D'Amalio, and he changed it to Aylesworth before he married Carol Bradford and added 'the second' for good measure. I'm not sure he did that legally. My guess is that he is very shrewd and wasn't going into the Bradford clan with what he considered a strike against him. Lately, he's found reasons why he can't keep the appointments. Just sends his wife and kids."

"What about Jessie?" I asked.

Phil smiled. "A doll. A living doll. Cute as a button and smart besides. One of those kids who seem to be born happy and generous, and roll through life no matter where they are, getting all the breaks and giving back as much as they can."

"Ben likes her," I said.

"And she likes him," Phil added. "Neither of them say too much when they're here. But they sit together, over there on the couch.

"Well, now, let's see what you've come up with on Ben."

A Safe Place for Joey

Phil opened Ben's folder and looked up. "Where's the parent form?" We had gone over so many cases together that Phil knew exactly which ten or twelve tests to expect and was immediately aware of any deviation from the usual procedure.

"Mrs. Aylesworth hasn't returned it yet. She's promised several times, but when I called her a few days ago it still wasn't 'quite done,' and she said she'd mail it. It doesn't really matter. We can complete it at the parent conference, although I'd rather not spend our time together that way when there's so much to go over and discuss." Phil nodded. "She probably finds it threatening."

"Well, pretty good score on the WISC-R," Phil commented, almost to himself. "Certainly signs of some LD stuff – interesting how often that ACID acronym turns up."

(Phil was referring to a study that showed that children with low scores on the WISC-R subtests of Arithmetic, Coding, Information, and Digit Span are often found to have some type of learning disability.)

"Also, the Verbal IQ is lower than the Performance, if that means anything. How did he act while he was taking this?"

I reported on the ups and downs of Ben's behavior during the various subtests, as well as his interest in the chips.

Phil picked up the Peabody with surprise. "You don't usually give this." He let out a low whistle. "Mental age, thirteen years, eleven months; ninety-fifth percentile. This kid's no dummy, that's for certain, and yet when they brought in his report card yesterday – one C and the rest D's and F's."

Phil continued leafing through the folder, going over the academic tests, the Bender, the Detroit. "Terrible Bender, rotations, distortions – except for the recall, six out of nine isn't bad. Visual memory seems to be okay, but then look at those

146

low scores on the Detroit. Mary, he's going to need a lot of help."

And then, as always, Phil spent a long time studying Ben's pictures, particularly those of the family.

"Well, not exactly what you'd call a close family. Everybody doing his own thing. See how the father is turned away from Ben. Mmm … I know you've noted the lack of hands and feet on the self figure … the shaded head … and the insecurity that shows in those sketchy lines …"

Phil talked on, going back and reviewing certain tests, asking questions when he could not quite read my writing.

Finally he said, "Well, from these I think we can definitely say that Ben's poor school performance is not due to a lack of intelligence."

I nodded agreement as I made notes.

Phil continued, "There are definite signs of learning disabilities and emotional overlay. Show the parents the tests, the drawings, etcetera. You know how to do that better than I do.

"And tell them," he went on, "that we recommend supportive educational therapy as well as continued therapy with me. Are you going to have time to work with him?"

I nodded. There was no way I could say no now. I told Phil briefly that Ben had started to talk about some of his fears and feelings, about the river and birds and flying, and that I thought Ben needed time alone with Phil. Ben didn't want to talk in front of either his mother or his father right now, and even though I would be seeing him twice a week, most of our time would be spent working on ways for Ben to catch up and then learn how to compensate for his academic problem areas. Also, Phil was the trained psychologist, and some of this was pretty heavy stuff.

"He's so scared," I said. "He tries to cover it, but it's costing him an enormous amount of energy, and I don't think he'll let down his cover in front of his parents, at least not yet. And if he's going to start academic learning, he'll need that energy for work."

Phil agreed to give Ben some time of his own and see how it went. He straightened out Ben's papers and handed me the folder.

"Thank you, Phil," I said. "I'll call you after I've seen the Aylesworths. Now, unless you tell me otherwise, I'm going to play it very straight with them. I'm going to show them all the tests. I'm going to explain why Ben has difficulty with reading and written expression and also how alone and scared I think he feels. And I'm going to tell his father that Ben needs him more now than he ever has in his life, and that Mr. Aylesworth has got to find some way to spend quality time with his son or he's going to lose him."

A grin spread over Phil's face. "Atta girl! I couldn't agree more. I wish I could be a fly on the wall at that conference. I have a feeling that you and Ralph Aylesworth are going to have quite a time."

Ralph Aylesworth walked directly behind me as we went up the stairs to my office. There was an elusive scent of male cologne, and his finely tailored suit made me acutely and uncomfortably aware of my faded jeans. I wished I had scheduled their conference a few minutes later so that I could have changed out of the jeans I always wore with the kids into something else. But into what? I owned nothing more authentic. These were my working clothes.

Without speaking, Mr. Aylesworth sat down in the chair to the left. I stood for a minute waiting for Ben's mother to be seated and then took my place behind the desk. I knew it was not the conventional grouping, that some would feel the desk was a barrier, but I still liked having a place where I could spread out all the child's tests and papers, as well as charts explaining what they meant and examples of some of the tests themselves. Most learning consultants and psychologists do not share the raw data (the actual drawings and answers to the questions) with the parents. But I believe a child explains himself best in his own writing and drawings, and who has a better right to know him than his parents?

"What a nice room!" Mrs. Aylesworth said. "No wonder Ben didn't object to coming. Ralph, look at that handmade quilt. Charming."

Ralph did not even glance in the direction she motioned.

"Thank you," I replied. "And thank you both for coming. Can you stay an hour? As I said on the phone, I think we'll need at least that much time to go over everything thoroughly."

Both parents nodded in agreement.

"I would like to say two things before we start. First, when you receive your written report all scores and scaled subtest scores and percentiles will be included. This is primarily because it's the way I would like it myself. If I took my child to a pediatrician, I wouldn't want to hear that he's of average height and weight. I would want to know exactly how many pounds and inches as well as the range for his age.

"You'll receive the original typed report; I'll keep a copy. If anyone wishes to have another copy, and I do urge you to share information with others who work with Ben, I will ask that they contact you and that you provide them with a copy from your original. I do this because it cuts down the possibility of professionals exchanging information about a child without including the parents.

"Which brings me to my second point – which is that you, as Ben's parents, have known him intimately for twelve years and four months. I saw him at most for seven or eight hours. I can and will tell you how he did on standardized tests compared to other children his age, and I can give you my opinions and recommendations based on tests and observations.

"But …" – and here I looked directly at Mr. Aylesworth and then at Mrs. Aylesworth – "you have the truest, most intimate knowledge of Ben, and it is your responsibility to stop me or any other professional, if something doesn't ring true to you, and say, 'That may have been the way Ben acted on that particular day in your office, but that's not the usual Ben.'"

Mrs. Aylesworth shifted slightly in her seat; Mr. Aylesworth kept his eyes directly on my face.

"Now, these are the tests that I gave Ben." I slid a copy of the evaluation sheet across the desk to Ralph Aylesworth, but he barely glanced at it, as I read the names of the tests out loud.

"I know that these names probably are not familiar to you, but I plan to go through each test and explain it and also show you how Ben did on it."

Mr. Aylesworth turned slightly toward his wife, but kept his eyes on me. "Now, as I understand this," he said, "the reason we're here, the reason Ben came here, is to find out if he's got some kind of learning disability that made him climb out on the roof in the middle of winter in his bare feet. Is that correct?"

"Partially," I answered. "I've explained to your wife and I'm glad you reminded me to explain again the purpose of a diagnostic educational evaluation.

"What I'm looking for when I do an evaluation is, what is the child's intellectual potential? How much do we have a right to expect from him or her? What are his academic achievement levels, and is there a match or mismatch between these two? Are there any signs of learning disabilities such as perceptual distortions or receptive or expressive language processing problems? What are his strengths and weaknesses? Can he use these strengths to compensate for areas of weakness? Is the problem in the receptive, associative, or expressive mode? And how does this child feel about himself and his world?"

Mr. Aylesworth nodded curtly. "All right. Sounds thorough."

I turned toward Mrs. Aylesworth, making sure that she knew I felt her understanding and opinion were of equal importance.

"Thank you for filling out the form. It came in yesterday's mail," I said, addressing her. "There are a few things on which I need a little more information, but we can come back to those after we go over the tests."

I laid the WISC-R out in front of them and pointed out Ben's various scores. I also showed them a chart explaining the scaled scores, IQ's, and various meanings. I explained that I felt the subtest scores were much more important and gave more information than the full-scale IQ score. I drew a vertical line and said that if they thought of 0 as the bottom and 100 as the top, they could visualize how Ben had done on each test. For example, on Block Design, a nonverbal task that is considered one of the best tests of overall intelligence, Ben scored in the 99th percentile (meaning that he did better than 99 percent of the children his age); however, on Vocabulary, also considered to be an excellent test of intelligence, he scored in only the

37th percentile. I also showed them the Picture Completion subtest, where Ben had called a hinge "the swinging part." In simpler terms, Ben could see "the answer," but he couldn't always put it into the right words. After going over each of the subtests, I pointed out that his full-scale IQ was in the 85th percentile. I explained that I felt Ben was even brighter than this and because of that I had administered the Peabody, and that here Ben had scored in the 95th percentile.

"Are you saying Ben is smarter than ninety-five percent of the kids his age?" Ben's father peered at me intently.

"On this particular test, yes. He has an exceptionally high receptive language, that is, the understanding of the meaning of words; but he has great difficulty with expressive language, that is, expressing his thoughts in verbal or written words."

I turned next to the WRAT and said, "This is a brief test of word recognition, and spelling, and arithmetic. The grade scores on this test are somewhat inflated; that is, they come out four or five months too high, but the percentiles are fairly accurate. As you can see, Ben scored in the thirty-fourth percentile in reading, sixteenth percentile in spelling, and eighty-sixth percentile in arithmetic. Both reading and spelling are far below the potential he showed on the WISC-R."

"Ben's always been good in math," Carol Aylesworth said.

"Shush. Let her finish."

"Well," I continued, "obviously Ben does do better with math – which is primarily a visual, nonverbal task – than he does with reading and spelling. It is unusual to have a child's reading and spelling abilities so much lower than his overall intelligence. We need to look closely at the kind of spelling and reading errors he made, both here and on the other tests of reading."

Thirty minutes later I had finished going through the rest of the tests, pointing out his slow rate of reading, his good creative thinking, his difficulty in remembering the things he heard, his comparative ease in recalling what he saw, although there was still perceptual confusion. By "perception" I meant the way Ben organized and interpreted the raw data he received through his senses. I had shown them the Bender, the drawings, the Raven, and the Detroit and Harris. I explained that Ben was left-eyed and right-handed and that while there was dispute in the field over the importance of this mixed dominance, it was present in many of the children whom I tutored. The Aylesworths were paying for all this information, and they were entitled to it. But more than that, I wanted all of us to understand Ben as thoroughly as we could.

"Overall," I continued, "we see a picture of a bright boy – brighter than he (and probably his teachers) suspect. In school he feels his classmates consider him stupid, and rightly or wrongly he feels that at home he is not pleasing you.

"Both Dr. Golden and I feel that Ben does have specific learning disabilities – some prefer the term 'dyslexia' – that account for a large proportion of his academic problems, and that Ben also feels anxious and insecure."

"Anxious? What are you talking about? The boy is only twelve years old. That's a little young to be anxious." There was an angry edge to Mr. Aylesworth's voice.

"Anxious is just another word for scared," I said. "Nobody's too young to be scared."

"All right. All right. But it seems to me that this just confirms what I've been saying all along. He's lazy. You've just proved to me that he's smart. If he's smart, he can learn. Correct? If, and I underline if, he works – and doesn't diddle around up on the roof." Ralph Aylesworth took out a pack of cigarettes, then, seeing no ashtray, laid them on the desk.

"Would you like an ashtray?"

"Do you object to my smoking?"

"No. Excuse me a minute. I'll bring an ashtray up from downstairs."

As I went down the stairs, I could hear Ralph Aylesworth saying, "I told you to stop babying him. I knew he was smart."

I set the ashtray in front of Mr. Aylesworth, watched while he shook a cigarette from the pack into his mouth. He held a silver lighter in his left hand and touched it to the end of the cigarette. He inhaled deeply and then let the smoke out in slow short puffs. The acrid smell immediately filled the room, but it was worth it. Ralph Aylesworth was left-handed. Nothing conclusive about that, but another piece to add to the puzzle.

I turned to the parent form that Mrs. Aylesworth had finally returned, still only partially completed. "You've filled in Ben's birth weight and the fact that he was a full-term baby. But you've left out the age when he first walked."

"Yes … well. I know." Carol Aylesworth smiled appealingly. "It's just that I couldn't remember. You know you think you'll never forget, but somehow I just don't know exactly …" Her voice trailed off.

"How exact does it have to be?" Ralph Aylesworth cut in. "I know it was well before he was a year old. He was standing up, walking around in that rabbit costume you made him for Halloween, and his birthday's not till November. I remember your mother telling everyone about it at Christmas."

"So eleven months?" I said. "Okay. Fine. Now about talking. When did he say his first words?"

"That was later," Mrs. Aylesworth said, seemingly encouraged by the fact that she wasn't expected to remember an exact date. "He made lots of noises, but we couldn't understand any of them. Remember, Ralph, how we used to say he'd made up a language of his own?"

Ralph Aylesworth ground out his cigarette with his left hand and glanced at his watch.

"It's after seven. We've been here over an hour, and I'm still not sure what's the matter with Ben or what we're supposed to do about it."

"I did tell you that I believe Ben has specific problems that make it difficult for him to learn by ordinary classroom methods," I said. "But I also need to know what he was like before I knew him. I need you to tell me that. Did he have any high fevers, broken bones?"

"No, he was a very healthy baby," Mr. Aylesworth said. "In fact, one thing I've got to be thankful for is that the whole family is healthy. Never had to call a doctor in our lives – only see them for checkups."

Mrs. Aylesworth nodded. "That's right. The only time was when we were first married – and I got so sick you had to call Dr. Johnstone, and he put me in the hospital because my fever was so high and I was vomiting so much that he worried about dehydration. But then," she stopped and smiled, "it turned out to be nothing. Well, nothing more than being pregnant with Ben."

I sighed. "Look. I know it's late. And learning disabilities is a vague term – I realize that. And it's vague because a child's brain is not an easy place to explore. Until recently, the only means for internal examinations of the brain have been painful and dangerous. Certainly you can have Ben examined by a neurologist, and I can give you the names of two excellent pediatric neurologists and, in fact, would suggest you see one. I would also recommend an examination by a pediatric audiologist, just to cover all bases. I would also recommend that Ben see someone twice a week who understands children with learning disabilities and knows how to teach him techniques to improve his reading and spelling. Ben badly needs to catch up and start having some success in school."

Ralph Aylesworth stood up. I thought perhaps he was leaving, but instead he lit another cigarette and walked across the room.

"Learning disabilities? What the hell does that mean?" He picked up a pad of white paper from a corner of the desk and tossed it in front of me. "Here – draw me a picture in black and white of what's wrong with Ben's brain."

I pulled the pad toward me and stared at Ralph Aylesworth. Who did this man think he was to order me around in my own office? I started to say this, but then Ben's pale, handsome face imposed itself on the pad, and I forced myself to be quiet. Ben needed his father. I had to help Ralph Aylesworth understand that it wasn't just a question of making Ben try harder. Well, I couldn't draw a picture of Ben's brain, but maybe I could make some lists. I wrote:

Overall Possible Causes
1. Genetic.
2. Organic.
3. Environmental.

Specific Signs of Ben's Learning Disabilities

4. Mismatch between intelligence and academic performance.
5. Difficulty or delay in acquiring language – slight stutter.
6. Mixes up or can't remember words.
7. Reversals – writes d for b – reads "was" as "saw."
8. Poor auditory memory.
9. Poor sound-symbol relationship.
10. Mixed dominance.
11. Poor perceptual and organizational skills.
12. Poor graphomotor skills.
13. Large gap between excellent spatial knowledge and poor verbal and written expression.

Additional information

14. More males than females have these kinds of learning problems.
15. 45 per cent have close relatives who have learning disabilities.

What to Do

16. Examination by a pediatric neurologist.
17. Examination by a pediatric audiologist.
18. Supply educational therapy.
19. Supply emotional support.

This took about five minutes. Mrs. Aylesworth sat folding and unfolding her hands; Mr. Aylesworth paced back and forth across the room, stopping by the desk only to snuff out his cigarette and light another.

When I'd finished I put the pad back on the desk and pushed it to the other side.

"Maybe this will help."

Mr. Aylesworth glanced at the pad briefly, but never missed a stride. Mrs. Aylesworth leaned forward and looked at the list.

"Well, read it," he barked, pacing to the far side of the room.

Mrs. Aylesworth cleared her throat and read: "Causes: one – genetic; two – organic; three – environmental …"

Mr. Aylesworth put out his cigarette and sat down, shading his eyes, looking at the pad.

When Carol Aylesworth had finished reading the page, he coughed and said, "Causes? Genetic? What do you mean by that?"

"Well," I said. "There have been a number of studies done that show there is a tendency for dyslexia – or learning disabilities – to run in families." I hesitated and then added, "And that it occurs more often in the males of those families."

The room was absolutely silent until Mr. Aylesworth spoke. His voice was steady, but very low. "Are you trying to tell me that I gave this damn thing to my son? Is that what you're trying to say?"

"No," I answered. "I said it was one of the possible –"

I stopped. Tears were running down Mr. Aylesworth's face. He sat without moving, without sound, without expression, while tears flooded his eyes and poured down his cheeks. I couldn't believe it. This assured, successful, dominant, demanding man was crying in my office.

Mrs. Aylesworth fumbled in her purse and proffered a tissue. He pushed it away and stood up and took a pristine, folded handkerchief from his back pocket and wiped his cheeks and eyes. He unfolded it, turned away, and blew his nose. He sat back down and bent toward me, the handkerchief still between his hands, his voice unsteady now.

"Did you know I couldn't read? Is that why you made that list instead of drawing? To prove it?"

"No," I said, shaking my head. "I just didn't know how to draw a picture of what you were asking. I was trying to be as clear as I could be."

"Well, now you know. I can't read more than five or ten words on that whole page. I've never been able to. But I can talk. Unlike Ben, I guess. Although almost everything else you said about him you could say about me."

I shook my head. "I don't understand. How can you be president of –"

Mr. Aylesworth interrupted. "I just told you. Because I can talk. I talked myself a high school degree, although I never finished. I talked myself a college degree and an MBA besides. Nobody ever checked. And it has been a living hell, wondering if, when, somebody will find out and call me on it.

"But, besides being able to talk, I can sell and I can make money. I made more sales my first year out than anybody had ever made in that company, and after that it was easy. I just climbed the ladder, moving from one company to another, and finally to president of Zyloc. I had my résumé, my sales record, recommendations, and increasing money and power, and I had Helen.

"Helen is my secretary. She was an English major at college. I hired her the day she graduated, and she's been with me ever since. When I moved, Helen moved with me. She never married. Zyloc, Inc., is her life. Everywhere I go, Helen goes.

In fact, until a couple of months ago, she was the only one who knew I could hardly read and couldn't write even a simple letter. Helen reads to me and I dictate to her.

"But when all this damn business about Ben came to a head, Carol began to fuss about my being home more, spending more time with Ben. Of course, there was no point to that, because I didn't know what to do with Ben. He was acting crazy. Did you know he actually had my pajama top on up there on the roof? He wouldn't talk to me, and it seemed to me that Carol was contributing to the problem by babying him, doing his work for him. He was enough of a sissy as it was."

Carol Aylesworth and I watched silently as Ralph began his steady pacing once again.

"So then," he continued, "Carol got it into her head that I was having an affair with Helen." He shook his head. "Helen has about as much sex appeal as Grandma Moses."

"Well, you did take her every single place you went. Chicago. Los Angeles. London. Brussels. What was I supposed to think?" Carol Aylesworth said defensively, her voice whiny, the way Ben's had been in the beginning.

"I took her, for Christ's sake, because she had to cover for me. Anyway, I hadn't told Carol before," Ralph Aylesworth continued. "I knew a hundred tricks with Carol. I told her I had poor eyesight, so she had to read the street signs if we were going someplace new. Money – she took care of all the bills. The finest restaurants – the captain attended to our order personally, I never used a menu. And every day I sat behind a newspaper and turned the pages for at least a half hour.

"Well, she knows now. In fact, there are three of you who know now. You, Helen, and Carol.

"In some ways it's a relief. And I suppose I knew all along that Ben was having some of the same troubles I did, but I didn't want to admit it.

"You talk about scared," Ralph Aylesworth said. "I can remember screaming at Ben when he first mispronounced 'spaghetti.' How was he ever going to learn to read if he couldn't even get his words straight?"

I nodded. I could see how terrifying it would be to this man who had acquired so much surface success at such cost to think that the same kind of tortured life awaited his son.

"Well, there's no way of being positive that Ben's problems are only genetic." I turned toward Mrs. Aylesworth. "Your high fever and nausea during your pregnancy may have had something to do with it, too. That's one of the frustrating things – no one is sure about causes."

"Is it like a disease?" Mrs. Aylesworth asked. "Can it be cured?"

I shook my head. "No. A learning disability is not a disease. It's a kind of neurological dysfunction. Some very brilliant, famous people have had similar problems – Winston Churchill, Charles Darwin, General George Patton, and John Kennedy among them. You don't cure it, but you can learn how to compensate. And Ben can learn to read and write. I can guarantee that. I also think Ben has a lot of sorting out of his emotions to do, and he should see Dr. Golden by himself for a while. I think you both should continue seeing Dr. Golden, too. It's not easy to bring up a child who has learning disabilities, particularly when there's so much emotion involved.

"It's true that it's not good to baby him. It's also true that it's not a good idea to put too much pressure on him."

A Safe Place for Joey

I turned toward Mr. Aylesworth. "Dr. Golden will be a help on all this – how much is too much, things like that.

"The last thing I want to say is that Ben is at a very vulnerable time right now, and he badly needs a good male model. He needs to start moving away from his mother, becoming less dependent, more independent. And you can be such help." I nodded to Mr. Aylesworth. "You, more than anyone, can understand how he feels. Your problems sound as though they were more severe than Ben's, and yet you've been enormously successful."

"Do you know what that success has cost me?" Ralph Aylesworth replied. "I live in a cold sweat all day, all night, counting the days till I can retire. Move away. Do something else.

"Well, at least Carol knows now. I don't have to pretend in front of her anymore." He reached for his wife's hand, and they stood up together. "I suppose in a way I have Ben to thank for that."

I smiled at him, liking this man who suffered so many of the difficulties that my children did. "Just try to spend time with Ben," I said. "Don't feel you have to teach him anything – just listen to him. Let him know that you value him for being who he is and what he thinks. Do whatever is fun for you to do together."

It was after eight o'clock, and we were all tired and cramped from tension and sitting too long.

"You will be working with Ben, won't you? You do think you can help him?" Mr. Aylesworth asked.

"I think we can help him," I said, emphasizing the "we." "Yes. I'd like to try. I'd also like to speak to his teacher. If she's agreeable, I'd like to talk to her on a weekly basis so we can coordinate what we do."

"Wait now. Don't go too fast," Ralph Aylesworth said. "I'm not sure just how much I want the school to know."

We had reached the front door. I put out my hand. "Well, we can talk about it and then decide, and please call me whenever you have questions, particularly if there's anything you don't understand when you get the report. And I'll call you tomorrow, Mrs. Aylesworth, about setting up Ben's appointments. I want to go over the test results with him, too, before we start working together."

I saw Ben twice a week for two years, and Phil Golden worked with both Ben and his family. Ben's reading improved quickly. His visual memory was so strong that he acquired new sight words relatively easily and learned to use techniques to speed up his reading without losing concentration. His testing scores rose because of this and because he no longer was frozen with fear, sure of his stupidity. We worked on phonetic skills, using specific techniques developed for children with Ben's kinds of learning problems. And when he was taught in short-sequenced segments, he slowly learned to decode unknown words and also to improve his spelling.

Most importantly, he was no longer alone. We all worked with him, making it clear that while we wouldn't do the work for him, he didn't have to do it alone.

It made a difference. Enough of a difference so that "Banana Brain" faded from the school picture as Ben emerged.

At the beginning of eighth grade, Ben went off to a New England prep school experienced in providing individualized education for bright adolescents with learning disabilities, and I'm certain he will go on to college.

And now, Ralph Aylesworth comes to my office every week, determined that he, too, will learn to read and write as well as his son. He arrives early in the morning, before he goes to work and when there's no chance of being seen. He wears his hand-tailored pinstripe suits; I wear my jeans.

He cancels often – when he's out of town (with Helen, of course) or at a board meeting. His problems are far more severe than Ben's, and more deeply entrenched, but he is learning to read. His last test showed his silent reading comprehension at a fifth-grade level. He works hard, sweat pouring down his face, swearing as he sweats. He's defensive and manipulative, but he's also intelligent and courageous, and I'm as proud of Ralph Aylesworth as I am of his son.

Alice

"I hate her," Alice sobbed. "Hate her! Hate her! Hate her!"

She was sitting sideways on the couch in my office over our garage, knees pulled up under her chin. Now she put her head on her knees, and her long, straight, light-brown hair fell forward around her face so that tears dripped from an invisible source, making dark blotches on her long, grey flannel skirt.

"Oh, Alice," I said, sitting down beside her, handing her the box of tissues. "What's wrong? Who do you hate?"

Alice sobbed on. "Both of them, that's who. My stupid mother *and* my stupid teacher. I don't even know which one I hate the most."

I was surprised at the depth of Alice's emotion. On her first visit she had sat as still and silent as a rock for most of the time. But, I loved having Alice in my office. While I enjoyed my boys, there was something special about having a girl there.

I lifted Alice's feet into my lap (she had shed her shoes on the way in the door) and waited. There was no need to ask questions. Since the first visit, words had tumbled out of Alice – there was no language problem here. For a fifth grader she was more than verbal; she was a veritable fountain.

"Nobody ever asks me what I want," she said, mopping her face. "They just run my life as if I wasn't even here. Just because that doctor said I should take Ritalin, Mom assumes she has the right to stick it in my sandwich in my lunchbox. Well, I hate it – never knowing which bite it will be in, having the other kids stare, waiting for me to choke on the pill. She says I'd forget to take it if it wasn't in the sandwich. Maybe I would. But it's my life, not hers. Anyway, I just throw my sandwich out – I'm not that hungry, anyway, and that was fine till stupid Mrs. Robinson decides it's her 'duty to tell your mother.' She called Mom into school, and now there's a whole big hassle and I'm supposed to show stupid Robinson my empty sandwich baggie and swear I've eaten the sandwich and the pill.

"Well, I won't. I'm not some kindergarten baby. I don't care what they do. I don't even want to go to the dumb school anyway."

"I know," I said. And I did. Dr. Volpe had sent me a copy of Alice's copious file before he sent me Alice, and there was a detailed family history along with reports from various doctors and teachers.

The Martins had arrived from Kansas during the previous summer. Mr. Martin had been promoted and transferred to the New York home office of a large insurance company.

The Martins were reportedly thrilled by the "move up the ladder" and delighted with their picture-book pretty home in a nearby affluent community.

However, it was immediately evident to everyone that Alice's previous schooling had in no way prepared her for the highly academic program of this achievement-oriented town, which prided itself on its standards of education and high national ranking.

The small private school in the little midwestern city that Alice had attended had a curriculum based on "developmental milestones" rather than standardized levels of achievement. It was considered to be innovative and less pressured than the public schools, and since Alice had been "high-strung" from the beginning, the Martins thought it was the better option for Alice. And it may have been, but it had left her poorly prepared to enter any other type of school.

Even in her special school Alice had difficulties, and while she was still in kindergarten the school psychologist had tested her.

Her highest scores were in reasoning and abstract thinking. Her lowest scores were in arithmetic and visual moto tasks. Her full-scale IQ score on the Wechsler Preschool and Primary Scale of Intelligence (WPPSI) was 113; the Verbal IQ was 126, the Performance IQ 103 – a 23-point spread. The Bender Gestalt was reported to be "difficult" for Alice, and her drawings showed "signs of stress." Her teachers reported that Alice's feelings were "easily hurt" and that she was often on "the verge of tears – and needed more than the usual amount of encouragement to perform." On the basis of the teachers' reports and the tests, the school psychologist concluded that Alice's difficulties were due to "emotional rather than physical problems" and advised "a more relaxed attitude and less pressure from the parents."

The psychologist never did explain the 23-point difference between Alice's Verbal and Performance scores.

Alice continued to have trouble during first grade, and her teacher noted that she had "awkward left-handed writing, trouble cutting with scissors, and that she reversed letters." However, the teacher said she was not concerned, because she felt these difficulties were simply because Alice was not yet "ready." Since the philosophy of the school was based on "readiness determined by developmental milestones," this was also the advice of the school director, who pointed out that Alice's molars were slow in coming in and that her other problems were undoubtedly related to this fact. Consequently, her parents waited patiently through another year. But when there was no improvement, Alice was taken for a neurological examination.

The pediatric neurologist's report stated that while Alice was slightly older than most first graders – seven years, four months during the spring of first grade – she looked more like a kindergarten child, with "awkward posturing of the hands and fingers accompanying all of her gait performances and twitches of the hands and fingers when she is trying to hold still in the eyes-closed, posture-holding position." The neurologist also noted a "marked mixed dominance with a 50–50 percent left and right in terms of destination of tasks performed with one hand or the other, although the traditional writing task is done with the left hand. There is mixed eye and foot dominance."

The neurological summary concluded that Alice showed signs of a "patchy minimal brain dysfunction marked by unevenness in development" and that while she was "not hyperactive she exhibited elements of the dyscontrol syndrome in terms of lack of organization, lack of self control and low frustration." The neurologist's report further stated that the "emotional problems are secondary reactions to the MBD syndrome" and recommended "intensive remedial help over the summer."

The Martins were understandably confused. The neurologist's findings seemed to be the opposite of the psychologist's. They were relieved that Alice's problems had a physical cause and were not due only to pressures they had applied. Their difficulty lay in the fact that they were not quite sure what kind of "intensive remedial help" was required, and instead of contacting the neurologist for clarification, they followed a neighbor's suggestion and enrolled Alice in a perceptual training program run by an optometrist assisted by graduate students from a nearby university. The optometrist assured the Martins that Alice's basic problem was "divergence excess," and this could be "cured by practice in eye-hand coordination, eye movements, visual memory, and balance."

Alice disliked these weekly sessions and the assorted roster of graduate students, and resisted additional practice at home. She developed gastrointestinal trouble, which increased on the days when the perceptual training was scheduled. Finally, after more than a year, still with no visible improvement, the training sessions were dropped and Alice (and the Martins) struggled along alone through third and fourth grade. Although Alice was absent often and for increasingly longer periods, her academic grades – based, of course, on "developmental milestones" – remained surprisingly high, except for arithmetic.

Now in fifth grade at Bryant Elementary School in Brentwood, New Jersey, not only did Alice have gastrointestinal problems, but her new school psychologist felt there was a "phobic resistance to attending school" and referred her to a Dr. Volpe, psychiatrist. Dr. Volpe confirmed the "school phobia," noting that Alice's symptoms were "always worse on Monday mornings or following a school vacation and were accompanied by hysterical crying and protestations of dire consequences if she were forced to attend school." Alice also had increasing difficulty in concentrating, paying attention, and not forgetting what she had known the day before.

Interestingly, the parents revealed to Dr. Volpe a fact that they had not shared before. Alice had been adopted at five weeks of age through a Catholic charity. A year after Alice's adoption, Billy, a natural child, was born as "quite a surprise" to both parents.

Alice's overall intelligence scores done by the school psychologist had dropped slightly between kindergarten and fifth grade, but the same patterns were evident – full-scale intelligence in the bright average range with highs in abstract thinking and vocabulary, and lows in spatial and perceptual tasks as well as those calling for rote memory. Dr. Volpe commented on Alice's "rigidity, caution, and self absorption," as well as the fact that she appeared "younger than her chronological age." The Rorschach, a projective inkblot test used by psychiatrists, showed "good attention to detail, considerable compulsiveness, constriction, and guardedness." His recommendations were for "family therapy sessions for all members of the family," for mild stimulant medication (Ritalin or Cylert), for Alice to be monitored by her pediatrician to help her maintain focus, and for "specific expert remedial help in the main area of schoolwork where she is weak, namely math." Dr. Volpe gave the Martins my name.

I was far from an expert; I had had my own mathematical struggles, but I was enchanted by Alice. She reminded me of a watercolour illustration in an old black leather, gold-rimmed book of my grandmother's. Her brown hair was almost waist length, held back with a tortoiseshell headband. She was slim, small-boned, and fine-featured. On her first visit to my office she was dressed in a white blouse and an ankle-length blue pinafore that again seemed from another age. There was an overall misty quality about her, almost a physical aura, as if indeed she might have stepped out of another time and place. It was hard to imagine the hysterical storms described in Alice's file.

But appealing as Alice might be to me, I knew she'd be a joke at Bryant Elementary School. Jeans were not allowed during the school hours, but any and every other style of pants were – and this particular year, the tighter they were, the better. This was not only the world of achievement; high fashion began in second grade. Hair was styled, not cut, at sixty dollars a throw. Designer labels bloomed like daisies, nails were long and polished, and hair was streaked. By fifth grade, childhood was a thing of the past.

Alice was a walking anachronism, a terrified one at that. I wasn't sure of how best to go about helping her, but I was sure I was not going to begin by doing an evaluation. Valuable as diagnostic sessions are, it was clear that Alice had been tested enough. The neurologist's report made sense to me. And while we no longer used the term MBD – minimal brain dysfunction – I believed Alice did have some type of neurological dysfunction resulting in what would now be called dyscalculia, or an inability to calculate by ordinary classroom methods, as well as an accompanying dyscontrol. In my practice, language-based problems were far more common than perceptual ones, and, for whatever reason, more girls have difficulties in spatial and numerical tasks. It seemed to me that the major mistake the Martins had made was entering Alice in a perceptual training program, rather than providing her with specific help from a trained learning disabilities specialist.

On Alice's second visit, she wore a dark red pinafore that was an exact copy of the blue one she had worn the time before. I asked the usual questions – address, phone number, parents' and siblings' names, pets.

A Safe Place for Joey

"Yes," Alice said. "I do have one pet."

"Good. What kind?"

"He is a rabbit, a brown and white, intelligent rabbit. His name is Sigmund."

"Sigmund," I repeated. "That's an unusual name."

"Not really. I thought it would be amusing to have a resident rabbit psychiatrist in the house."

I'd listened to hundreds of eleven-year-old kids, but Alice sounded more like she was entering graduate school than fifth grade. And yet she was "school phobic" and failing math – and a social innocent.

"Is he as insightful as his distinguished predecessor?" I certainly wasn't going to talk down to Alice.

She looked up quickly, surprised, and said quietly, "Sigmund doesn't often share his insights with me, Mrs. MacCracken."

"Discreet," I said.

Alice nodded, and then she smiled at me. "And besides, he's only a rabbit."

And blip – we'd made our connection. There was no need to be careful any longer.

"Dr. Volpe told me you were having some trouble with math, Alice. That's why he suggested that you come here. But I don't know what kind of trouble it is, and I really don't want to give you any tests right now. Could you explain it to me more clearly?"

Alice shrugged and studied her hands again. "I don't know," she said, "everything just comes out wrong. Besides, I don't care if it does. I hate school, anyway."

My sophisticated conversationalist of the moment before had reverted to total childishness. Now it was easy to see why the psychologists and neurologist had seen Alice as a much younger child.

"Yes. I heard that you did," I said. "Do you hate all of it? Or are there some parts you like?"

"The whole thing. Well … maybe not every single thing." Alice peeked up at me. "The library really is very nice. It's much larger than the one in my old school, and they let you take out three books at one time."

"You know my idea of heaven?" I said. "An enormous bed with lots of squishy pillows, a mug of hot coffee, and every conceivable kind of book stacked all over the floor and table and bed right within my reach."

"And Sigmund could sleep on one of the pillows," Alice said as I laid out paper, pencil, rods, and blocks and began to explain basic arithmetic concepts.

But now things seemed to have gone from bad to worse, and Alice was dissolved in tears, engaged in battle with both her mother and her teacher. Certainly a solution had to be found for the pill-taking; I agreed with Alice that she shouldn't have to struggle with medication in public. She was enough of an oddity as a new student dressed in out-of-date clothing.

I lifted Alice's feet out of my lap and got up and walked around the office in pure frustration. Dr. Volpe had made it very clear to me that he was referring Alice to me for "tutoring in arithmetic, not therapy" and that he would take care of whatever counseling was needed.

"I don't mean to be rude," Dr. Volpe had said when we had first spoken, his slight accent rolling across the *r*, "but I must remind you that learning disability specialists are just that – specialists in learning, not in therapy. Sometimes there is a tendency to forget."

I had not forgotten. How could I? But what did it matter how well Alice understood math if she was totally miserable both in and out of school?

I sat back down again. "Alice, it doesn't make any sense for you to be so unhappy and constantly fighting with both your mom and your teacher. What does Dr. Volpe say about all this?"

Alice shrugged. "I haven't really seen him for a while. Mom goes there during the day when Billy and I are in school."

Wonderful. Family therapy seemed to have shrunk. Shrunk by a shrink. I debated sharing this with Alice – she could have passed it on to Sigmund. I stopped just in time, reminding myself of my own belief in the importance of working as a team.

Instead I called Dr. Volpe after Alice had left, and he confirmed what she had said. Family therapy had evolved into individual therapy for Mrs. Martin.

"The father is virtually unavailable to either therapy or his family," Dr. Volpe said. "He is away both physically and emotionally most of the time. Alice is getting a great deal of support from you. Billy is doing well by himself. Mrs. Martin is the one who feels deserted and bereft. Alone in a new town with limited support from her husband, constantly facing criticism about the way she rears her children, particularly Alice. She lets Billy dress pretty much as he wants. And, of course, he's not on any medication and doesn't have Alice's learning problems.

"But Mrs. Martin is much more emotionally involved with Alice, which, as you know, is not rare between the mother and the so-called wounded child. In fact, there's a touch of symbiosis on her part, and the fact that Alice is adopted and that

Mrs. Martin was the one who pushed for the adoption seems to heighten her guilt and her involvement. She is also a very tense, anxious person herself, and of course her anxiety feeds Alice's and vice versa. In any event, I continue to see Mrs. Martin because she's the one who's available, and I believe I can help the whole family best by helping her learn to handle her own needs."

"But what about Alice?" I couldn't help asking. "Somebody's got to do something about Alice. It's my turn to apologize to you if I sound rude, Dr. Volpe, but the school psychologist did refer Alice to you for help."

There was a moment's silence on the other end of the line. Then Dr. Volpe replied in a voice even more distant than usual, "Indeed. Indeed. An excellent point. I think you should be more in touch with the school. Certainly that's where learning takes place. Or is supposed to. And as I pointed out earlier, you are the learning specialist, Mrs. MacCracken. I, of course, will be reviewing Alice's emotional state periodically and am in constant communication with her through her mother. Thank you for calling."

I replaced the phone somewhat more loudly than necessary.

I had worked with dozens of clinical psychologists and psychiatrists and was constantly impressed by their knowledge and sensitivity, but I certainly wasn't impressed with Dr. Volpe at the moment. "In constant communication through her mother." Some wonderful communication that was.

By the next morning my blood was a little cooler and my mind a little clearer. The next step was obviously a conference with Mrs. Martin and then with Alice's teacher and the school psychologist.

Mrs. Martin sat in the same place on the couch as Alice had, but her feet were close together on the floor, her slightly heavy body upright and her brown hair pinned into a tight bun across the back of her head. But leaning forward, her face flushed, she was almost pretty in her eagerness. "Dr. Volpe is helping us – well, me – see how to meet Alice's needs. But she is so difficult; she resists everything I try to do for her, even to taking important medication."

I nodded. "I heard about the sandwich."

"Alice means so much to me," Mrs. Martin went on. "She's our oldest, you know, and a girl, and, well, it isn't generally known but Alice is adopted. Mr. Martin was against it, but I wanted a baby so much and I couldn't seem to get pregnant, so he finally agreed. In fact, he fell in love with her, too. He couldn't help it – she was such a beautiful baby. But then before Alice was a year old I discovered I was pregnant with Billy, and with Alice awake and crying two or three times a night, neither of us got much sleep. But I can't complain. Both our families lived nearby. You see, both Mr. Martin and I went to the same grammar school out in Kenoba, Kansas, and our families had been friends for ages, so I had lots of company and hands to help with all that needed doing."

Words continued to pour out of Mrs. Martin. "Besides, Billy was easy. It was only Alice that needed extra care. And I suppose I felt responsible for her because, as I said before, I'd been the one to insist on adopting her. And then, you probably can't see it now, but I always thought we looked a lot alike."

Mrs. Martin leaned further forward, inviting me to inspect her face.

"Yes," I said. "There is a resemblance – the same high cheekbones, the same colour hair. Although your eyes are blue and Alice's are brown."

"Yes," Mrs. Martin said, "and I suppose the likeness is harder to see now because I've put on weight since I've been here.

"Now that the house is decorated and the children in school all day, there's not that much that needs doing. And, I have to admit, I miss home. Although this is supposed to be home. Still, it doesn't feel that way. We were all so close, both families … and it's different here in the East. I mean back home there were neighborhoods. Nobody would think of letting someone move in without taking them some homemade bread or something or other."

I looked at Mrs. Martin's polished navy blue shoes and thought of Alice. I certainly couldn't hold Mrs. Martin's feet in my lap; in fact, it was hard even to imagine her barefoot. But how was I ever going to get through to her? She had been in my office for twenty minutes, and we had yet to get to Alice. Somehow her loneliness had a kind of desperate quality, and I understood Dr. Volpe's view a little better. It must be very hard for Mrs. Martin in a strange town, away from her family and friends. It certainly wouldn't help for me to rush into criticisms of her handling of Alice's clothes and medication.

"How does Mr. Martin like his new job?" I asked, trying to move the conversation along.

Mrs. Martin's face closed, and she leaned back away from me. "He likes it fine," she said. "Too much, if anything, if you ask me.

"Now what about Alice?" Mrs. Martin asked on her own. "I know you've only seen her a few times, but do you think she'll ever understand math? She seems to have it all backward."

"I'm sure she will. Once she's shown in a way she understands. But right now, she's so caught up in trying to fit in at a new school that she isn't focusing on arithmetic that much. Now, the most important thing in the world to Alice is not to seem different. She just wants to be like everybody else."

Mrs. Martin leaned forward again. "But that's just it – she is different. She's not like everybody else. I mean I know she's overly sensitive and she does need medicine to calm her down, but so do I. But what I mean about Alice's being different is that she's special. I mean you should see the books she reads, and the poetry she writes, and the way she talks. She even named our rabbit after Sigmund Freud, so she'd have someone in the house who would understand her. Now, have you ever heard of an eleven-year-old doing that?"

"No, I haven't. And I agree with you that Alice is intelligent and sensitive. But it's because of those very attributes that she needs to fit in at least on the outside, so the others won't make fun of her."

"Make fun of her?"

"Her clothes seem strange to the other fifth graders, and also they think she must be sick if she has to take medicine," I said as gently as I could.

Not gently enough. Mrs. Martin stood up. "It is not my fault or Alice's if those children don't understand quality. Alice is quality, and so are her clothes – the finest materials made by the best dressmakers. As for her medicine, that's none of the other children's business, now, is it?" Her voice was abrupt, and she moved toward the door.

I put out my hand, and only as I said good-bye could I see the tears standing in Mrs. Martin's blue eyes. I covered her hand with my free hand. "Moves are always hard for everyone," I said. "But Alice is smart and you are, too, and we'll get it worked out. Do you think we could have lunch sometime?"

Mrs. Martin patted the tears on her cheeks. "I'd like that very much," she said. "Thank you."

Alice slid out of her shoes and tucked her feet underneath her on the couch. "Thanks for talking to Mommy; it really helped."

"It did?" I asked in genuine surprise. "I thought maybe I'd made things worse."

"Nope. Mom actually told me she'd been here and that you were going to have lunch together sometime. Usually she never tells me anything except what to do and how to live my life. Anyway, it was kind of nice just talking to her. You know what I mean, just talking about something, not arguing. So I discussed it with Sigmund. You remember Sigmund?"

"How could I forget?"

"Well, anyway, I discussed things with Sigmund. He communicates now, and he suggested that I make my own sandwich, put the pill in a corner, and punch that corner with a fork. That way, I can bite off the corner, be prepared for the pill, and get it over with and then be able to relax and enjoy the sandwich, and the other kids wouldn't even notice. And it works. Mom even likes me making the sandwich."

"That's terrific, Alice," I said, meaning it. "In fact, it's so terrific we're actually going to spend the rest of our time talking about math."

Alice groaned.

"It's not so bad. Actually, it's a lot easier than it seems. Most of elementary school math – kindergarten through fifth grade – is made up of four things. They call them operations because they're something you do to numbers, just like doctors do to people. And I imagine you already know these four operations, or their names, anyway – addition, subtraction, multiplication, and division. Adding just means putting things together, subtracting is separating them, multiplying is putting them together in equal groups, and dividing is sharing.

"Later on, in fifth, there's maybe a little fractions or decimals, but I can show you those."

Alice said, "It doesn't sound hard the way you describe it, but when they put those papers in front of me I can't remember anything. It all just looks like some sort of stuff from outer space."

"All right. Let's start with the first operation – addition. Here, take this paper and give me something to add."

Alice hesitated but then wrote:

$$
\begin{array}{r}
23 \\
42 \\
+\ 54 \\
\hline
\end{array}
$$

"Okay," I said, "That plus sign tells me that I've got to put those three numbers together. I start at the top and I run my pencil through the numbers, so if the columns are long I can write it out on the side. Like I'd go three and two are five and write five somewhere out on the side – and five and four are nine. I put that in one place. Do you know about places or place value?"

Alice shook her head.

"All right. We'll talk about that in a minute. Then I go back up to the top of the next column, and one of the things that always used to get me mixed up is that you work right to left in addition – just the opposite of reading. But anyway, add straight down – two and four are six plus five is eleven."

"But suppose I don't know that," Alice said, "that six plus five is eleven, or what thirteen minus eight is, or seven times six. Suppose I don't know any of that?"

"Well, that's my job," I said. "To show you how you can learn them. And you can. But for now write down six (two plus four is six), so you don't forget that, and ask yourself: what's six plus five?"

"I don't know," Alice answered.

"Ask yourself what's five plus five?"

"Ten. Oh, I get it. Six is one more than five, so six plus five is eleven."

"Exactly. Now eventually you'll know it automatically, just like you know your telephone number. But until you do, I'll show you ways to figure it out.

"Now, I'm going to write down a harder one, because I want to explain about places."

$$
\begin{array}{r}
76 \\
24 \\
+\ 23 \\
\hline
\end{array}
$$

"Some of this you probably already know, but remember you have a chart like this: hundreds, tens, ones. Now, the trick to remember is trading. When you add and you get ten ones, you trade them for one ten.

"Sorry, that sounds confusing. Let me try again. We're adding up the problem:

A Safe Place for Joey

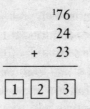

"Okay, I put the boxes down below – a box for the ones, a box for the tens, and another for the hundreds. Only one number allowed to a box. So six and four are ten plus three more, that's thirteen. Okay, I'll put the three in the ones box, but the one can't go there (only one number to a box), so it goes up at the top of the tens. One and seven are eight and two are ten and two more are twelve. Put the two in the tens box (only one number to a box), and put the one up in the hundreds column. It's the only thing in that column, so one and nothing is one and that goes in the hundreds box, and the answer is one hundred twenty-three."

I looked at Alice. She was still looking at the problem. "And if that last number was one hundred twenty-three instead of just twenty-three, then you'd add the two ones and the answer would be two hundred twenty-three?" she asked.

"You got it."

"Well, that's rather interesting. Of course, we're doing things in the thousands in school."

"Same thing. Same for millions, too. I just have to show you about commas. Let's try a little of your homework now."

Alice's homework was a page of "mixed practice" – a little of everything from fourth grade. The four operations we'd talked about plus a couple of word problems.

As I watched Alice copying the problems I could see how difficult the physical writing and aligning of the numbers was for her. She could remember only one number at a time, so she had to look back and forth continually from book to paper; her numbers were uneven and sketchily formed, and her hooked, left-handed grip covered half the numbers she wrote. She would also read a number as 36 and write it as 32, misforming the 6. I'd have to see if we couldn't get a workbook for her so she wouldn't have to waste so much time and energy copying.

Beside the first problem Alice wrote 1 and the problem itself. Unfortunately, her columns drifted to the left so that she added the 1 into the last column and therefore was 1,000 off. Still, she was pleased that she could do the addition, and we skipped most of that, leaving it for her to do at home.

She could do subtraction as long as there was no regrouping (borrowing) involved and she had enough fingers to count.

Multiplication made little sense to Alice. In fact, she hadn't really known that multiplication and "times" were related.

She had never seen a division symbol before.

"Just skip those," I said. "I'll tell Mrs. Robinson you haven't had division yet. Now, listen, Alice – I've got an idea. There's a man in school by the name of Mr. Renner, and he gives kids extra help, just like I do, only he does it in school in a place called the resource room. It might be a good idea for you two to do some work together. I think maybe I should talk to your teacher, Mrs. Robinson, and see how things are going and also see if we can't arrange for you to get some extra help in the resource room."

Alice shook her head. "I'm not sure you should do that. I don't believe you'll hear anything good from Robinson. Besides, I've already met that man – Mr. Renner – he gave me some sort of test. I guess it was arithmetic, but it wasn't any kind of arithmetic I've even seen before."

I knew Mrs. Robinson, Alice's fifth-grade teacher, from having worked with other children in her class in other years. She was in her mid-forties and had two children of her own, and her husband taught in the high school. She used good materials, she understood the subjects she taught, and she was organized and thorough. But any deviation from her way of doing things was regarded as rebellion, so I could understand why she wasn't thrilled to have Alice in her class, as well as her reaction to Alice's medication.

Still, Alice desperately needed a friend and interpreter in her school. I decided to give Mrs. Robinson a call.

"It is incomprehensible to me how they could have let that child enter fifth grade," Mrs. Robinson almost shouted into the phone, as soon as I'd mentioned Alice's name. "I don't care if she is eleven – she doesn't begin to know the first thing about arithmetic. I have the lowest group, you know, so I've seen everything, but nothing close to Alice. The school psychologist tested her and says she's smart enough but has school phobia – whatever that may be – so he referred her to a psychiatrist. Anyway, I can't get any help from the psychologist. His case-load is five times what it should be, and once he's referred a child to what he considers the best source of help, he's onto his next case, and I can't blame him. So I sent her in to Jack Renner – he runs the resource room, you know. I didn't need any more fancy testing, I just wanted to find out what levels she was on.

"He gave her the WRAT – you know that one, the Wide Range Achievement Test. Would you believe she did the wrong section, Level Two? The one for twelve-year-olds and over. Jack didn't notice. He'd already showed her the page she should do. He told her she had ten minutes and to do as many as she could, and then went back to his regular schedule.

"Well, at the end of ten minutes, Jack collected the paper and Alice had done every single problem on Level Two – fifty or so. Averaging, decimals, percents, fractions, algebra equations, square roots, as well as the ordinary addition, subtraction, multiplication, and division. Of course, all but two were wrong – I mean way off. She didn't have any idea in the world what she was doing, but that didn't bother Alice. She just kept her head in the clouds and wrote down whatever she pleased.

"For one-sixth of thirty, she wrote twenty-two. That kind of thing. Well, in my mind, she should be repeating. I mean it's not just that she doesn't know her facts – she lies; she pretends she knows what she's doing.

"And it's not just math. She hasn't ever had cursive, or so she says. She scrawls out these tiny little marks, not even connected half the time, when she's asked to write. Jack says being left-handed may have something to do with it, but in my view, it's a lot more than that.

"And you know, she's lied to her mother about taking her medicine, though that seems to have been worked out, but I simply don't know what we're going to do."

I kept quiet. I knew if I listened long enough, Mrs. Robinson would end up offering to send me Alice's papers, and extra copies of the books and workbooks they were using in class. She really was organized and generous, but she and Alice were not what you would call made for each other.

"I suggested sending Alice to the resource room the very first day," Mrs. Robinson shouted over the telephone, trying to be heard above the noise in the teachers' room, "but you know what that's like – she has to have such and such to qualify for any additional help, forms filled out, evaluations filed. Besides, she is doing better. She eats her sandwich nicely every day now. I don't even ask to see her baggie anymore."

"That's great. Now what do you say if I just call Jack Renner and see if he can fit Alice in for a half hour somewhere in the day? You are absolutely right about how much help she needs – let's see if we can't get that help. The forms will catch up to her, and there's no question she qualifies," I said.

"Go right ahead," Mrs. Robinson said, "if you want to stick your neck out. Your job's not at stake."

"Right. Just promise you won't wave a flag pointing it out."

I'd played tennis with Jack Renner a couple of times at the club. Just pick-up games when one or the other of us had filled in, but I'd known him for a long time, and I'd seen him on the courts and in the pool as he was growing up. He'd gone away to college, then returned, and had been teaching in the resource room at Bryant Elementary for the past two or three years.

I explained the situation to Jack over the phone.

"Sure, why the hell not? She seems like a nice kid, although somebody ought to get her out of those weird clothes before the kids laugh her off the block. Tell you what, tell her to come into my room at twelve thirty. I don't think either Alice or I are the hit of the lunchroom. The ladies can hardly wait to get me out of the teachers' room so they can talk about whatever it is they talk about – and I bet the kids feel the same way about Alice. Besides, if someone tells me I'm 'bastardizing my position' – like happened once before when I took an unclassified kid – I can at least say that I'm doing it on my own time."

I was pleased that Jack had agreed to work with Alice. Not only did she need to catch up and fill in arithmetic facts and concepts, she also needed somebody in the school who was on her side, and I had the feeling that Alice and Jack could become friends.

Also, Jack's feedback would be invaluable to me. There's nothing like on-the-spot reporting, particularly from someone on the same team. He was absolutely right about Alice's clothes. The other kids would laugh at her; in fact, they almost certainly already were.

The snow began about four o'clock in the afternoon – huge, fat flakes that clung to each other and covered the front lawn and driveway within an hour. By morning, the snow was thinner, lighter, but the weather report announced blizzard conditions with the present accumulation twenty-two inches, and up to four more inches predicted. Schools were closed across the state.

An unexpected holiday. We reveled in it, adults and children alike. The children in the neighborhood built snowmen and fortresses and filled the hills with sleds and toboggans. I read and wrote letters, cleaned out a drawer or two, and helped shovel the driveway and paths. Then Cal and I tramped back and forth between friends' houses for good food and drink and talk.

But the holiday ended as abruptly as it had begun. After two days, the sun came out, streets were cleared, schools reopened, reality returned – and the phone rang unrelentingly, requesting make-up appointments. Finally, I decided we'd just have to double up. I tried to make the "double-ups" as compatible as possible and hoped that Tara Hirsch and Alice would work out. They shared the fact that they both were girls, a minority in my office population, and both were in fifth grade at Bryant Elementary School, although in different classes.

A Safe Place for Joey

Tara had short, black, curly hair and the taut body of an athlete. Her math was quite good, but she had the more usual reading and language problems of learning disabled children. I had seen Tara the year before in my other office. In fact, I had been seeing her twice a week for over a year when I moved, and her mother decided to keep Tara with me since the drive was about the same to either office. Tara had been two years below grade level in both reading and spelling when I first saw her – and a snarly little thing besides. Her parents would not let her go out for sports as long as her grades were poor, so her frustration escalated. She was not allowed to do the things she was good at, and she just kept getting worse at the others. But once her parents understood how much she needed to excel at something, they allowed her to enter the after-school sports program, and now she was the star of the acrobatic team and one of two girls on the Little League team – and she was also part of an active social group.

The two girls arrived at the same time, walking up the driveway without speaking to each other. Tara had obviously changed after school and had on jeans, her Little League sweatshirt, and a blue down vest, and she skipped along in her sneakers despite some slippery patches. Alice walked carefully, dressed in fitted brown leather boots and a velvet-collared, dark green wool coat that reached to her ankles.

I introduced the girls, and we proceeded on to my office. Alice hung up her coat; Tara tossed her vest over a doorknob. They both stood staring silently at me.

"Now we have a choice," I said. "You two can work separately – one at the desk, the other at the table by the couch. Alice can work on math, Tara on reading, and I'll split my time between you. Or we can all sit around the desk and have everybody work on the same thing – some of the time on this, some on that, but we'll do it together. Which do you prefer? Alone or together?"

"Together," answered gregarious Tara.

"Is that all right with you, Alice?" I asked.

"Yes," she answered quietly.

"Okay," I said. "Let's go."

We scrunched around the big desk. I sat in the swivel chair they usually used when they worked at the desk, and they pulled up others.

"Let's start with the reading," I said. "Tara, we're on the first column of the last page of fifth-grade words. You go ahead and try the first ten. We'll make our usual cards for the words you don't know."

Tara read slowly, stumbling over "continue" and "astounded," but figuring them out by herself. However, she could not get "opportunity."

"Can you help out, Alice?" I asked.

"Opportunity," Alice said, without hesitation.

"Okay, Alice, your turn. You read the next ten."

Alice whizzed through the words with elegant elocution.

Tara regarded Alice with new interest. "How'd you learn to do that?"

Alice shrugged. "I don't know. It's just always been easy for me."

"How come you come here if you can read so good?" Tara quizzed Alice.

"I have trouble with math. At least I used to. I'm getting better."

"Me too. Isn't it a relief?"

A Safe Place for Joey

Now Alice was the one who was interested. I kept quiet. Nothing is more fun than watching children learn from each other.

I'd been paying out chips all along, and I paid again as we corrected math sheets.

"Time's almost up, but let's do just a little writing. Grab a pad of paper, any size you want," I said, pointing to various-sized pads of white and yellow paper on one corner of the big desk, "and hand me a yellow nine-by-twelve, so I can write, too. Good. Thanks. Now just write whatever you want about your favourite place. It can be indoors or out, maybe some place you go on vacation or maybe your own room. It can be anywhere, but just write what it is you like about it. Try to tell what it looks like – try to make me be able to see it. Okay? Now let's go. We'll take about five minutes."

I wrote about our country house. Tara wrote three sentences with many misspellings about the baseball field and how good she felt out there. Alice wrote three-quarters of a page of printed scratchy words about a place she'd made for herself in the attic where she could go to read and think. Each of us read out loud what we had written, and we were all smiling when we finished.

As the girls were counting up their chips, Tara said to Alice, "Can I ask you something?"

Alice froze and looked at Tara suspiciously. "Like what?" My own complacency vanished.

"Well," Tara said, "like how come you wear such weird clothes? I really thought that you were weird. But you're not. You're really nice. It's just the clothes."

"My mother makes me," Alice replied, head down, stacking and restacking her chips.

I was holding my breath.

"Well, that's cuckoo," Tara said. "Why don't you tell her you need some new clothes like other kids wear?"

Alice shook her head. "She doesn't care. She doesn't even listen."

"Well, I'll tell her," Tara said, her head up, her black eyes blazing. I could imagine her slamming a home run. Nothing on the baseball field or in the social world scared Tara.

Alice and I were both staring at her.

"Well, I will. She's got no right making you look like an idiot."

But when Alice came for her next session she still wore the long green coat with a grey wool pinafore underneath.

"What happened?" I asked, trying to hide my disappointment. "Did Tara talk to your mother?"

Alice nodded.

"Well, come on. What happened? What did your mother say?"

"She told Tara to shut her fresh mouth."

I sighed. "I don't know what we're going to do. I've tried, you've tried, Tara's tried." I sighed again.

"Well, it's not all bad," Alice said, smiling. "First of all, Tara's my friend now, sort of. Mom won't let her come over to the house, but Tara sticks up for me in school when the kids make fun of me. And we eat lunch together sometimes. I told her about the pill, and she understood how gross it was."

Gross? Alice was acquiring a new vocabulary.

"And we do some of our homework together once in a while. Like, I tell her words she can't figure out and she helps me with division."

"That's nice, Alice. Really nice."

"Wait," Alice said. "I'm not done. I discussed the clothes problem with Sigmund." She looked at me closely to make sure I was with her. I nodded without speaking. "And Sigmund suggested that perhaps a compromise could be reached."

"There is no question of Sigmund's brilliance," I said.

"So I proposed to Mom that maybe we could have my dresses and coats shortened. Maybe some of them even made into regular skirts. Sigmund said in that way Mom would still feel in control."

I wanted to hug Alice. Instead I nodded. "Insightful."

"And it worked," Alice continued. "Everything but what I've got on is over at the dressmaker's getting fixed."

"That's terrific, Alice –"

"And you know what else," Alice interrupted, "arithmetic isn't really all that hard."

I kept quiet, loving it, watching it happen.

One of the pleasures of working with children with learning disabilities is that they can learn so much more easily than they think they can.

"Do you realize," Alice said proudly, "that there are one hundred addition facts and one hundred subtraction facts, and that I now know more than three-fourths of both?"

I smiled at Alice. "How did you manage to do that?" Alice made me feel like smiling a lot these days.

"Well, Mr. Renner said the way to do it was to learn the easy ones first," Alice continued, "like the zeros, the doubles, the ten sums, the count ons, the nine pattern. That nine pattern is so neat; anytime you're adding nine to something, the number in the ones place is one less and you put that one in front of it. I don't even have to think about it. Ask me one."

"Nine plus seven," I said.

"Sixteen," Alice said immediately. "See. It's automatic. Oh-h," she sighed, "it's so nice when you can count on something."

Alice continued nonstop. "The rest of the facts are harder, but Mr. Renner said we'll just learn a few at a time. What we're going to do is print them on these Language Master cards; then I run the card through the machine and record it. I will say six plus eight is … whatever it is … one side will have the answer. Mr. Renner says I will remember it better that way because my auditory memory is better than my visual memory. Isn't that interesting?"

"Very." Alice was obviously thriving under Jack Renner's tutelage, and he was evidently a terrific teacher. Or maybe I just meant that he agreed with me; start at the point where the child actually is, teach to the strengths, respect the child's intelligence, break learning into manageable components, and build from there.

"And he says times is going to be just as easy. Do you think that's true?"

"I know it is. Maybe easier. There are one hundred basic multiplication facts, too, and I bet you already know some of those without even studying."

"No, I would doubt that," Alice said.

"Do you know the zeros?" I asked. "They're different than in addition. In addition you're putting together. Three plus zero means three plus nothing more, so the answer remains three."

"Yes, I understand that," Alice said.

"In multiplication you're working with groups. The first number just tells you how many groups. Three times zero means three groups of nothing." I went over to the prize basket and took out a plastic bag of sugarless lollipops.

A Safe Place for Joey

"Okay, reach in and take nothing. Good. How much have you got?"

Alice giggled. "Nothing, of course."

"All right. Reach again and take nothing. That's two. One more time. That's three. How much do you have now?"

Alice simply made a face at me.

"Suppose you reached in eight times?"

"Nothing."

"That's right. So remember in multiplication that the answer to anything that has a zero in it is zero." I wrote 9 x 0 = on the pad of paper and put it in front of Alice, and she quickly wrote 0.

"The ones are just as easy. What do you think three times one is?"

Alice reached for the lollipop bag. "I'll reach in three times and take one each time. Last time I took nothing; this time I'll take one."

Zap! I held onto my chair. I know it sounds a little crazy to get excited about three times one, but that's what happens to me.

"Three," Alice announced. "Three times one has to be three. And four times one has to be four. Oh, I get it. Whenever there's a one, the answer is the other number. Like one hundred and twelve times one would be one hundred and twelve."

"That's right. And you already know the twos."

Alice reached for the lollipop bag again.

"You can use that if you want," I said, "but remember your doubles in addition. The twos in multiplication are exactly the same. Two times three means there are two threes. How much are two threes? Three and three?"

"Six. I know all those doubles. Remember four plus four is the spider fact – four legs on each side. Eight altogether. Yuk."

"Yeah. Yuk. But if two fours are eight, how much is two times four?"

"Two times four is also eight," Alice said without hesitation.

"Okay. This is the two-hundred-dollar question. Last one for today." I wrote 2 x 8 = on the pad, and Alice, without a second's hesitation, filled in the answer – 16.

"Pay yourself two hundred, Alice. And a bonus of one hundred for concentration. That was terrific. Mr. Renner will show you how it's the same with the fives; there's a trick or two for the nines; and then, believe it or not, there are only fifteen other multiplication facts to learn, and you can do those on the Language Master. Or put them on index cards and tape them to your refrigerator door. Don't let yourself open the door until you know the answer."

My weekly phone calls to Mrs. Robinson, Jack Renner, and Alice's mother were all positive. In the past month Alice had been getting C's on math classroom tests, and Jack reported with pleasure her increasing knowledge of math concepts and computation. Mrs. Martin said the best thing that had happened at home was that she had decided to plant a garden in the back-yard, and on her own Alice had asked if she could help. Next thing she knew, Tara was out there working with them – and she had to admit that Tara really was a spunky little thing and a hard worker.

Now Alice stopped just inside the door, and before she took off her moccasins she handed me a folded piece of paper. She wore a yellow turtleneck, her grey skirt ended in the vicinity of her knees, and there was an inch or two of bare skin showing between her skirt and knee socks. Not high style at Bryant Elementary, but not weird, either.

"Here's a poem," she said, holding out a piece of paper. "It's not very good, but … I guess I wanted to give you something, and you know how unbelievably bad my drawings are. Anyway, don't read it now, okay?"

"Okay," I agreed, "but thank you."

I tucked the folded piece of paper in the back pocket of my jeans and patted it. "I'll save it till tonight when I'm through," I said, struggling to keep the catch out of my voice. Presents from children always move me. But when it's something they've made themselves, it's as if they're giving me a little piece of themselves – saying, "Here, I trust you to take care of this piece of me" and "I have enough of me now so that I can share some of it."

But Alice's mind was on practical matters. She was already at the desk with her book open.

"Okay if I turn on the light?" she asked.

I nodded, thinking how pretty she looked as the light picked up the highlights in her hair.

"See," Alice said. "We're working on division now, and I remember what you said about the four operations and division being the one that meant sharing, and I understand that – four cookies, two people, each person gets two cookies when they share them, right?"

"Absolutely."

"I even get harder ones, because I know the multiplication facts now. Twenty-eight pennies, four people, they get seven pennies each, four times seven is twenty-eight, twenty-eight divided by four is seven, and also twenty-eight divided by seven is four."

"Good, Alice –"

"Yes," Alice interrupted, "but what I don't get at all is long division. I mean there are so many steps or whatever you call them, I can never remember what to do when."

"That's not hard," I said, pulling an index card out of the drawer. "Just keep this card taped in the back of your math book till you've memorized it. Think of a family first:

There's the big old Daddy – D for (÷) division.
Next to him is the Mother – M for (×) multiplication.
Then comes the Sister – S for (–) subtraction.
And then the Brother – B for bring down.

"And then when you've done all that, just start over again. Here. Try it."

I wrote on a piece of paper:

$$5 \overline{)\ 2164}$$

Alice said, concentrating hard, "First is D, so I divide. Five can't go into two because it's bigger, right? So twenty-one divided by five is four, and I put that over the one … like this":

$$5 \overline{)\ 2164}^{4}$$

"Right?"

"Right."

Alice checked the card. "Mother. Multiply. Let's see. I guess I multiply the four by five and put it here:

$$5 \overline{\smash{\big)}\,2164} \atop \,20 \qquad \overset{4}{}$$

"Now, subtract, then bring down. Uh-oh. Now what?"

"Same old thing. Just go back up to the top of the card and start again. Daddy, Mom, Sister, Brother. Actually, it's just like your own family."

Alice turned and looked at me. "Yes," she said, "except we hardly ever see Daddy anymore. Do you think he's mad at me maybe? I mean because of school and everything."

"I doubt it. Especially since you're doing better and better and better. Do you realize how much you've accomplished in just a little more than half a year? You've worked out your pill problem, your clothes problem, you're getting good marks in school ..."

"Well, not exactly 'good' in math and not new clothes."

"But much better. You've made a friend, you look terrific ..."

"And I don't have those temper tantrums before school anymore, so that can't be why Daddy doesn't come home at night sometimes."

"That's right," I said. "Whatever the reason that he's away, it sure isn't you. Probably it's his new job and traveling. Maybe you should ask him."

"Maybe. Or maybe," Alice tilted her head so that her sweet, serious face was close to mine, "maybe you could."

I didn't forget about Alice's poem. I was conscious of it all afternoon as I worked with other children, but I waited until I was alone before I took it out of my pocket.

She had centered the lines in the middle of the paper, and the printing was the neatest and clearest I'd ever seen Alice do.

Surrounding the printed words was a border of little hearts and flowers.

Spring
All winter – the ground has been frozen,
And the brook covered with ice,
Hard and white and still,
As if the world was dead.

But yesterday spring came,
The dirt in the garden is warm,
Seeds are sprouting,
Buds are bursting.

Winter is gone – spring is here,
And everything is growing.

I love you, Alice

I sat reading and rereading Alice's poem, smoothing it with my fingers, thinking about her and her own growth, and also about her father and her mother. Alice – sensitive, high-strung, intelligent, brave, lovely, still out of fashion, and always vulnerable. And her mother. I wondered if Mrs. Martin had made any friends yet and made a mental note to follow up on my lunch invitation.

If Alice hadn't talked about her father in the preceding months, she made up for it now.

"You know what he says? He says he'll always take care of us." Alice took off her shoes and slammed them on the floor. "Well, I don't want him to take care of me. I can take care of myself."

A Safe Place for Joey

I waited. Knowing Alice, this was just the beginning.

"See," she continued, "they don't know it, but I can hear every single thing they say at night now. Saturday night they had this big fight downstairs, and I couldn't hear that too well, but when they came upstairs Mom told Daddy not to touch her and she didn't want to be anywhere near him. And he told her not to go so fast, that they had to think of the children, and she says it was a fine time for him to talk about thinking about the children. Anyway, for the last three nights, he's been sleeping – or anyway lying – on this chaise lounge thing where Mom reads in the afternoon. It's way across the room from the bed, so they have to talk loud to hear each other. They think we're asleep, but I can hear everything."

I shook my head. "Are you sure you want to? People say things they don't mean when they're angry."

"Yes, I want to. I want to hear every little thing. I'm mad, too. You know why he hasn't been coming home? He has a girlfriend. He says he's in love with her and wants to marry her – that's when he said it was nobody's fault and that he'd always take care of us."

Alice's rage slipped away as quickly as it had arrived, and now tears welled in her eyes. "What are we ever going to do now? You know what Mommy's like. She doesn't know how to do anything, I mean like anything besides take care of the house."

I sat beside Alice, smoothing her hair, thinking how crisis after crisis arrived in some children's lives. Just when things seemed to be straightening out – crash, something worse happened.

"I'm sure he meant it," I said. "I'm sure he will take care of you and see that the bills are paid, but that doesn't make it any less scary for you and Billy. How is Billy doing?"

"He's okay. Billy's always okay. That's why they like him so much – he gets the best grades in his class. That's all they really care about, anyway, is how many A's you get. That's probably why they're getting a divorce, because I didn't get enough A's."

"Come on, Alice," I said. "You know that's not true. You just told me your father said he was in love with somebody."

"Yes, but if I'd been good enough, maybe he wouldn't have had to fall in love with somebody else. Maybe we'd have been enough."

I stood up and then squatted down in front of the couch so that our eyes were exactly level.

"Don't ever believe that, Alice. Promise me. If your parents get divorced, it's not because of something you did or didn't do. It's between them, and it's not your fault. Okay?"

Alice's eyes never left mine. "But see, it's not just that I have this problem in my brain, it's that I don't really belong to them. I don't belong to anybody. Last night Mommy said to Daddy that maybe they should never have adopted me or had Billy – that way she'd be the only one to suffer."

"Oh, Alice, Alice." I gathered her up in my arms. It was bad enough to hear your parents arguing about a divorce, but to discover you are adopted at the same time is just too much. "Hadn't they told you before?"

Alice waggled her head back and forth against my shoulder.

"Well, they should have. They've told other people, and it's in your reports. They wanted you so much – especially your mom – and they were so happy when they found you."

Alice peeked up at me. "How do you know?" she asked.

"Your mother told me herself. She also told me you were a very beautiful baby."

A Safe Place for Joey

Alice sat up. "Beautiful baby," she repeated. "With holes in her head."

"Alice. That doesn't help."

Alice shrugged. "Well, what are we going to do?"

I shrugged myself. "I don't know. We're just going to have to work at it."

Alice, Billy, and Tara all arrived together at Alice's next session. I stared at the trio in surprise. "What are you guys doing here?"

"Can we come in?" Billy asked, obviously in charge.

"Sure, but tell me what's going on."

All three sat down in a row on the couch, Billy in the middle.

"Well, we have this idea," he said, "and we decided to come and check it out with you."

I had to admit one thing. Alice did seem to be right about Billy. He did appear to be very much okay, especially for nine years old.

I nodded. "Go ahead."

"Well, see, like, we've got this real mess at our house. Alice said she told you about it."

I nodded again, unable to take my eyes off this bright-eyed, verbal kid. Even Tara seemed to be letting him lead the way.

"Well, the first thing we thought of was to track down this girlfriend of Dad's and try to get rid of her – like, poison her or scare her off. But that could end up in a lot of trouble. So then we decided that she sounds like she's pretty young, so we figured we could tell her how old Dad is, and Tara thought maybe if she saw us and thought she'd have to take care of us maybe she wouldn't be so crazy about being with Dad."

Alice said, "Sigmund did not think this was a wise idea. Particularly since I never even want to lay eyes on that person.

But then we thought, I thought anyway, maybe we could talk to Dad's boss or somebody and get him transferred back to Kansas. He never acted like this back there."

"But I told them that wouldn't work," Tara said. "It would just make him mad to get both demoted and lose his girlfriend."

"You're probably right," I said.

"So then we decided to work on Mom instead," said Billy, taking over again. "She's the worst off. I mean Alice was bad in the beginning, but at least she's got us," he said, and Tara nodded. "And being adopted's not such a big deal if you're not alone."

"But Mom hasn't got anybody," Billy continued. "Like, anybody her own age. Except that dumb Dr. Volpe, and she feels even worse when she comes back from seeing him. It's, like, all she does with him is talk about her problems and so that's all she thinks about and it makes her feel even more terrible."

"Get to the plan, Billy," Alice whispered. "Somebody else will be here in a few minutes."

"Okay. Okay. What we decided was that Mom ought to get a job – but the trouble is she hasn't ever worked. So we had to think about what she'd be good at, and Alice got the idea because of the flowers and her garden."

"We have this garden in the back," Alice said.

I nodded. "Your mother told me about that and about how you were helping her with it."

"Yes. It's really nice. I like doing it and Mom's flowers are beautiful, and then she puts them in bowls all over the house and they look wonderful."

"You're the one who'd better hurry up, Alice," Billy said.

"I know. So we decided she'd be good at being a florist – working at a florist's, I mean. So Tara volunteered to go into that flower shop just off Spring Street; she kind of knows the owner. I gave her one of Mom's bowls of flowers, and she showed it to him and he said he'd be interested in talking to Mom."

Alice looked at me hard. "Sigmund thinks it's a good idea, but now we don't know what to say to Mom. So we decided to come ask you."

"Mmm" was all I could get out. I was overwhelmed at how enterprising these three kids were. At least I could tell them that.

"You have been doing some pretty impressive brainstorming – trying out all kinds of ideas, not criticizing each other, being supportive, and I think you've come up with a really good idea."

"Yeah, thanks," Billy said. "But what about Mom? I mean what do we actually say? It isn't like she's ever tried to get a job before."

"Why don't you just tell her the truth, like you did me? It certainly shows how much you love her and how much you've been thinking about her, and she'll be glad to hear that. And then since Tara knows the man who owns the flower shop, maybe she could go along with your mother and take another flower arrangement."

"Yeah, sure. I can do that. You just get me the flowers, Alice."

"All right. That's easy, especially since Mom will know. But what about Daddy?" Alice wanted to know. "I think somebody ought to talk to him and find out how serious he is and everything."

Three pairs of eyes stared at me without blinking. There was no mistaking their meaning.

"How about Dr. Volpe?" I asked.

"Daddy hates Dr. Volpe," Alice and Billy said in chorus.

"Listen," I said. "I'm no marriage counselor. Be fair. I'm a learning consultant."

"Well, that's okay," Billy replied without a moment's hesitation. "Looks to me like Dad's into learning things."

"Billy," Alice reprimanded. "Don't be fresh. But remember, Mary, I asked you once before if you would talk to him. I mean you do have lots of parent conferences, and you could start out talking about me, couldn't you?"

"Yes. I guess I could do that. I could try, anyway."

Alice called as soon as she got home, whispering into the phone. "He's gone. Gone for real now. He left Billy and me a note saying he's staying at a friend's apartment. He didn't say what friend. Anyway, here's the number." She rattled it off and hung up.

At least Alice didn't seem heartbroken about being adopted. I blessed Billy and Tara for matter-of-factly accepting her adoption and for involving her in a plan of action. Problem-solving is the best therapy in the world.

I tried to reach Mr. Martin early in the morning and late at night, but there was never an answer. It seemed unlikely to me that the apartment where he was staying belonged to his girlfriend, since no one seemed to be there. More likely he'd chosen some middle ground – perhaps moved in with someone else who was separated or divorced, or at least had given that number.

I wasn't able to reach Mr. Martin, but I did have lunch with Mrs. Martin. She told me about how the children had come to talk to her about getting a job and how touched she'd been – and that she'd decided to get up her nerve and go with Tara and talk to the florist, and how Alice and Billy waited across the street, and when she got the job they took her to have ice cream to celebrate.

She'd been working at the florist's for only about two weeks, but she loved it. She couldn't imagine being paid for something that was so much fun. She said the only thing that had worried her was not being there when Alice and Billy got home from school. But then Alice had suggested that she talk to Mr. D'Ippolito, the florist, and he'd been so nice. He'd arranged her hours so she worked from eight o'clock until three and could eat a sandwich right there at the shop instead of taking a lunch hour, and that also meant she'd lost a few pounds. So she, Alice, and Billy all left together in the morning, and they either walked home or waited for her to pick them up after school. Of course, the school year was almost over, and summer would be a problem.

I told her I didn't think she needed to worry with Alice, Billy, and Tara around.

"Sorry you had trouble reaching me," Mr. Martin said apologetically, ducking a little as he came through my office door, surprising me. Somehow I hadn't expected him to be so large. "I've been out of town a good bit the last month," he said.

I stretched out my hand. "Well, I'm glad you're here now. Alice was eager for us to meet."

Mr. Martin shook my hand, almost pulling me toward him in his eagerness. "Yes. Tell me how she is, how she's doing."

"She's just fine," I said, smiling. "In spite of everything – your separation, even the discovery that she was adopted – she's kept on growing, doing better in school and better at home."

Mr. Martin sat down on the couch, his big, lean frame collapsing. He sank back against the cushions. "You know," he said, skipping over the separation and adoption, "I never have understood what's wrong with Alice. Everybody we took her to, and we took her to a lot of people, seemed to come up with a different opinion."

I nodded. "That often happens with children who have very mild learning disabilities. The problems are so subtle that they go undetected until the child herself or himself begins to feel that something's wrong, and then the emotional problems set in and grow and grow until they disguise the original learning problem.

"In Alice's case the neurologist was right in her evaluation. Alice does have a mild learning disability; some would call it dyscalculia, which only means the inability to learn math by ordinary classroom methods. The neurologist called it minimal brain dysfunction – MBD – a term rarely used now. If Alice were seen by a neurologist today, he would probably diagnose ADD – Attention Deficit Disorder. But by whatever name it's called, it's not something in Alice's imagination or yours, but rather some small, very real disruption in the neural connections in her brain, probably in the parietal lobe. It doesn't affect her overall intelligence, but it does make processing of spatial and mathematical information more difficult.

"And then, as you know, Alice's early education was … well … unorthodox at the least, and there were lots of emotional traumas going on as well. But you can really be proud of the progress she's made … I'm sorry," I interrupted myself. "I'm talking too much."

"No. No, not at all." Mr. Martin leaned forward, large hands clasped between his knees. "I want to know. I want to know everything. I don't get much news nowadays."

A Safe Place for Joey

I sat quietly, finding myself liking this big, open-faced man. "Since you called me at Bob's apartment – he's a friend from work – you obviously know I'm not living at home. And knowing Alice as I do, I suspect you know a good bit more."

I nodded.

"I call home often," he went on, and I was interested that he still thought of his former living quarters as "home." "But nobody is very eager to talk to me. I don't blame them, but I want them to know I never meant for this to happen."

Mr. Martin cleared his throat, hesitated, then started again. "Sometimes I wish … I mean I just can't seem to … I don't want to get you involved with personal things, but I just want to make sure they're all right. Alice and Billy and Edna, too."

Edna. I realized I had never heard Mrs. Martin's first name before. I found myself feeling unexpectedly sympathetic toward both Mr. and Mrs. Martin. His concern for his family certainly appeared to be sincere (I had to remind myself he'd gotten himself into this situation), and I loved Mrs. Martin's courage in finding a job.

"They're all fine," I said.

"Thank you. I wish you could talk Alice and Billy into coming out to dinner with me some night, but I know that's not fair to ask." Mr. Martin stood up. "But please tell Alice I love them both very much."

"I will," I promised as I followed Mr. Martin to the door.

Alice plunked her books on the desk, took off her shoes, and sat cross-legged, Indian style, on the couch, feet tucked beneath her.

"Wait till I tell you. First of all, Mom and I went shopping. Mom's lost so much weight she needed a new bathing suit, and I got one, too, and some other summer stuff. It's really cool.

Even Tara says so. And Mom promised I can have everything new for school next fall. There's only two days of school left now, so she said it wasn't worth getting too much now.

"Anyway, while we were at the mall, Mom decided all of a sudden to get her hair cut. They cut it really short and it looks so good I'm thinking maybe I'll get mine cut, too, but maybe not. Tara doesn't want me to. Incidentally, we're all going to both tennis and day camp so we don't even have to get a sitter.

"Anyway, more good news. We haven't got our report cards yet, but Mr. Renner says I've passed everything and gotten really good grades in some subjects."

"Congratulations, Alice –"

"Wait, now listen to this. On Saturday afternoon, Tara and I were up in my bedroom playing some new records I got when Mom and I were shopping, and the doorbell rang. Billy was over at his friend's house swimming, and Mom was out shopping with these two friends of hers from work. So I went down to answer it, and it was Daddy.

"I didn't know what to do, but he looked so sort of sad that I forgot about being mad at him, and so I asked him if he wanted to come in. But then once he was in I didn't know what to talk to him about, so I got Tara to come downstairs 'cause she's really good with people, and she found our Monopoly board and the three of us started playing.

"I guess we must have been having a good time, 'cause all of a sudden Mom was back and Billy was back and it was almost six o'clock.

"I was really scared, 'cause I was sure Mom was going to have a fit. But you know Mom. You never know what she's going to do, especially these days, and she didn't even act mad one little bit. In fact, she even asked him to stay for supper.

"Daddy said he was sorry, he couldn't – but then, listen to this, he asked if he could come back the next day and she said yes.

"Well, he came back and he stayed for dinner and he was still there in the morning, and Billy and I are pretty sure he didn't sleep on the chaise lounge, either. I checked when they were all downstairs having breakfast. The bed was all made, but Mom's book was still in exactly the same place on the chaise lounge that it had been the afternoon before."

Even Alice had to stop talking for a minute to catch her breath.

I smiled at her. "That's a lot of good news, Alice. I hope things work out for your mom and dad. He stopped by here, you know, and I certainly got the impression that he missed you all. He especially wanted me to tell you how much he loved you. But no matter what happens with your parents, however that goes, I'm really proud of you. You've sure come a long way, babe."

Alice smiled back at me, hair glistening, skin glowing. She smoothed the pleat in her new short, split skirt. "You know what I've been thinking lately?"

"What?"

"Well, what I think is that maybe the reason I was so easy to fix is that there just wasn't that much wrong with me in the first place."

Hallelujah! Hallelujah! Hallelujah! A hundred choruses went off inside my head simultaneously. Some days I think I'm going to work forever.

Charlie

Charlie arrived at our first tutoring session carrying a large piece of paper, dropping it twice on the way up to the office.

At the top of the stairs he handed it to me, peering up through round, foggy glasses, his black hair plastered down on his forehead with water, sections of hair rising slightly upward as they dried into black pointy spikes. Charlie was tall for an eight-year-old and slightly pigeon-toed, often stumbling over his own feet. Now he stood one foot on top of the other as if to keep them from getting tangled up with each other, looking like an oversized crane. And it wasn't just Charlie's feet that got tangled.

"Mom said I should show you this. She said to tell you it was tiptical."

I had a sudden impulse just to gather Charlie up and somehow smooth him out and untangle him. But it was too soon for that. Instead I asked, "Typical? Why, Charlie? What is it?"

Charlie shrugged. "Just a story I wrote last year at the end of third. It's called 'The Fiery Bird.'"

I looked closely at the paper. There was some sort of yellow, red, and black picture on the top of the wide-lined primary paper with letters printed underneath. I tried to decipher the words, but I couldn't.

A Safe Place for Joey

"Could you read it to me, Charlie?"

"Sure. I've already read it to Mrs. Hawes – you know, my last year's third-grade teacher. She said it was very exciting."

Charlie began reading. "The fiery bird has struck again at the city. The city is wrecked."

"Wait a minute," I said. "Let me write it down." I realized that Charlie's story was totally incomprehensible without his translation. "Okay, I'm ready."

"The fiery bird has struck again at the city. The city is wrecked," Charlie read again. "All the people are evacuating. The president is very mad so all his bodyguards are going there with guns to attack the fiery bird and capture the fiery bird and then put it in a zoo so more people can see it. But the zoo man had to put it in a giant metal box so he doesn't melt through. But the president can't get it so his bodyguards are very mad so they are killing themselves."

Charlie looked at me when he'd finished.

"What do you think?"

I hesitated. It was a classic example of the writing of a dysgraphic, dyslexic child. Vocabulary and story content were good, but the written words themselves seemed to come from a foreign planet. Charlie wrote "apen" for "again," "retk" for "wrecked," "rea" or "r" for 'are," "vakuwede" for "evacuating." Poor Charlie; I could almost feel his pain and humiliation. What must it be like to be able to use a word like "evacuating" and yet be unable to remember how to write a three-letter word like "are"? No wonder his story had guns and anger and killing, and I knew that sometime soon I had to try to explain to Charlie why he was having trouble in school.

"Well," I said. "Your teacher's right. It is an exciting story, and I sure couldn't have figured it out unless you read it to me."

"Yeah. I know. The teacher said spelling didn't count. She just wanted us to write a good story. But …" Charlie stared at the floor. "Why is it like that? I mean, the other kids make mistakes, too, but not like mine. I'm the only one that has to read it out loud. I hate it."

"I know. I don't blame you. That's one of the things I'm going to try to do – teach you how to write down some of the good ideas you have. Not just write them, but spell the words so that other people can read them, too, and then you can hand in your papers like the other kids."

Charlie looked up from the floor and then moved his chair over toward mine, pushing his face close, too close for comfort, to my own.

"Listen," Charlie said. "I'm not like the other kids. I know it. I've always known it. But I want to know why. What's the matter with me?"

It hadn't been easy for Charlie from the beginning. He was born six weeks prematurely; he was slow to walk, slow to talk, and subject to high fevers.

He was referred to me by the headmaster of Chapel School when he was eight years old and just finishing third grade. The hope was that a diagnostic educational evaluation would shed more light on whether Charlie should be promoted to fourth grade or repeat third.

It was a difficult decision. Charlie had transferred out of public school to Chapel in the middle of second grade. His parents hadn't wanted to put him in private school. They believed in public education, but, as his mother had explained to me, "We had no choice. It was like Charlie was drowning. Every day he'd sink a little further. He was the one everybody else picked on. I don't know why – maybe it was his glasses, maybe because he was clumsy, couldn't seem to get the hang of how to catch or throw a ball. He couldn't really read, he seemed to get things mixed up or backward. He was tall for his age, so maybe people, the teacher as well as the other children, expected more from him. Anyway, we knew we had to do something. We didn't want to move. We'd been lucky enough to buy our dream house the year before. Charlie's dad is an engineer, but I used to do some real estate and the agency I worked for let me know about their old estate that was coming up for sale. We made an offer on the stone studio cottage and a piece of land, and it was accepted. We absolutely love it, and we'd never be able to afford anything like it anywhere else.

"So, the only alternative was to put Charlie in private school, even though it was the middle of the year. He had trouble at Chapel, too, but his teacher loved him and thought that his difficulties were due to 'lack of exposure' and that he just had a lot of 'catching up to do.'

"Now they're not so sure."

My formal evaluation showed the same uneven profile that had been noticed by his teachers. His full-scale IQ score was in the high average range. But while the subtests that measured reasoning, abstract thinking, and spatial relationships were superior, the tests requiring rote memory were very poor. Testing showed that Charlie's intelligence was in the 90th percentile; his academic achievements were in the 30th and 40th percentiles. His reading was a good year and a half behind, and although his stories were imaginative, his handwriting and spelling were almost indecipherable. His speaking vocabulary was good, although he often talked in a circumlocutory fashion, calling a knob on a bureau a "drawer puller thing"; a hinge, "one of those thingamajigs that hold the door on." He had difficulty pronouncing words such as "preliminary" or "circumstantial." He was unable to skip, confused about left and right, awkward, and distractible, and he had a great deal of difficulty switching from one activity to another.

If there is such a thing as a classic learning disabled child, Charlie was it. He could talk on an adult level, although he mispronounced the words or couldn't quite find the one he wanted. When he read out loud, he omitted or substituted words and phrases, skipped lines and lost his place, reversed both letters and words – and yet, somehow, he could answer eight out of eight comprehension questions correctly. He could do analogies and solve complicated mathematical problems. Yet he scored poorly on math tests because his math facts were not automatic, and when he counted on his fingers he would be just slightly off, or else he would reverse numbers and write down 21 when he meant 12. He could talk at length about the solar system, but he couldn't say the months of the year in correct order. He was gentle, appealing, and affectionate, but he was also disorganized and distractible and had no friends his own age.

Charlie could easily have benefited from repeating a grade when he had switched schools. With a November birthday, he was one of the youngest in his class even though he was tall. But now he had been at Chapel for a year and a half. He was shy and thought of himself as "stupid" and "weird." "Please," he begged me, "don't let them make me do third again. Please! The kids will really think I'm retarded if I repeat."

In the end my recommendation that Charlie be promoted to fourth grade was based primarily on the feeling that "more of the same" wasn't going to do it for Charlie. He could repeat third grade three times and still not know his multiplication tables or be able to hand in a legible book report. Charlie needed to learn new ways of learning. Most of all, he needed to learn to believe in himself.

I strongly urged Charlie's parents to rethink the idea of moving. Several of the surrounding towns had good public school systems with excellent resource rooms, and I felt Charlie was going to need ongoing support, at least through elementary school. But the Hammonds couldn't bring themselves to part with their house, and Charlie was terrified at the thought of moving.

"What I think is, I'd be even dumber in a new school. I'd be scareder and I wouldn't even know anybody. At least here me and Sam can go exploring the woods after school."

It was true that Charlie got great pleasure and comfort from his quiet, familiar neighborhood and from Sam, a six-year-old who lived on the next street.

Finally, we worked out a compromise. I'd see Charlie over the summer and twice a week during fourth grade. Charlie's mother felt that she could handle the cost by once again doing a little real estate work.

Charlie had three major problems interfering with his learning. His auditory processing was exceptionally weak, although examination by a pediatric audiologist found his hearing acuity to be within normal limits. Try as he would, he could not match letters and sounds. He would make the sound of *p* when trying to spell "put" and then write a *b*, or even reverse the *b* and write "dut." The differences between the short vowel sounds were too subtle for him to discriminate between them.

Second, Charlie became overwhelmed when too much material was given at once. If there were thirty math problems on a page, he might do the first one or two and then just push the paper aside. If four directions were given at once – such as "Take out your reading workbook; turn to page seventeen; read the top half of the page; and then use your green and red crayons to do the puzzle at the bottom" – Charlie either turned to the wrong page, or used the wrong colour, or had to go to the teacher and ask her to say it all over again.

Because Charlie was so unsure of himself, he had gotten in the habit of trying to forget his problems instead of trying to solve them. His teacher told me that he rarely completed assignments. When I talked to Charlie, it became clear that what happened was that he would "forget" that he had to read the book by the end of the month until two days before his report was due. Then panic struck, and he turned his household upside down while his mother tried to help him get it done.

Third, Charlie was lost in time and space. He could not remember the months or even which day of the week it was. He could not remember which was the right or left side of the football field. He could not judge the distance between himself and other objects, so he tripped over obvious obstacles and missed even the easiest of the balls that were thrown to him.

But how was I going to explain all that to Charlie? He still had his face close to mine, and he was breathing hard. He peered at me from behind the foggy lenses of his glasses. The only thing I was sure of was that I had to be honest.

"There aren't any windows in your head, Charlie. I can't look in and say, 'Ah hah! There! That's the spot that makes it difficult for Charlie to spell things right. And sure enough, that big area over there is why he can reason and think things out so well.' Someday soon there will be instruments that can see inside our brains and report back just how we learn –"

"Well, tell me what you know now," Charlie interrupted. "You must have found out something after all those tests you gave me. And you've talked to Mom and Dad. I got a right to know, too."

"Okay. First of all, I know that the troubles, the failures you have in school, are not because you're dumb. You're plenty smart enough.

"Also, I know you'll remember things better if they make sense to you rather than just strings of unrelated words and numbers – and that you remember what you see better than what you hear, and you'll remember best of all if you see it and hear it and then say it out loud or write it. We call that multi-sensory learning.

"Next, I know you learn better when things are presented to you a few at a time, so you can digest them. Your brain sort of goes on overload if you put too much in all at once. Like, say you have a TV, a toaster, and a microwave oven on the counter in the kitchen all plugged into the same circuit. If you turn them all on at once, you blow the fuse and none of them work. If you turn them on one at a time, they're all okay.

"And I know you get mixed up about right and left and which way is which, and that you will have to teach yourself to be constantly alert for clues to give you the right signals."

Charlie took a deep breath. "But why? Why me? What happened to me? Is it like when kids used to get polio?"

"No. It's not a disease. Educators like me call it a learning disability, or dyslexia, if we're forced to put a label on it. A friend of mine who's a pediatric neurologist – that's a doctor whose specialty is studying children's nervous systems and brains – doesn't think there are any good labels. She says it's due to a lag in neural development, and then she describes it like this: 'Everything's fine in New Jersey and things are all okay in New York City, but there's some kind of tie-up on the George Washington Bridge.' I like that, because I know you can always use the Lincoln Tunnel as an alternate route."

Charlie smiled, and his body relaxed a little.

"It won't get any worse," I said. "In fact, if anything it will get better as you learn new ways to learn. I don't think anybody knows for sure exactly why it happens to some people and not to others. I could pretend I did, but I don't want to pretend with you."

Charlie nodded. "Yeah. I know. I don't want you to, either." He shook his head. "It sure is confusing, though."

"Well, Charlie, remember we do know this. You're smart enough to learn whatever you want to learn. There are reasons for the failures you've had, and something can be done about it, but you'll have to work longer and harder than some kids because you have to make the imprint on your brain very clear and very strong so you can remember whatever it is you need to remember."

"Well," Charlie said, pushing his chair back, "I guess maybe it's worth a try."

It was decided that I would see Charlie twice a week beginning the first of July. Summer vacation would have to wait this year.

"Thank you all for coming in," I said, nodding at Charlie and each of his parents. Charlie sat behind the desk; I sat beside him. June and Jim Hammond sat on the chairs in front of the desk.

"I'd just like to go over what we're going to try to do this summer, and I think it's easier if we all talk about it together.

A Safe Place for Joey

"We've been through Charlie's evaluation, and Charlie and I have already had a teaching session together. We know his strengths and weaknesses. We also know that he's going into fourth grade in the fall and that there's a lot to do to be ready for it.

"I'm going to talk for a few minutes and tell you what I think we need to work on, and then I'd like to get your ideas.

"First of all, Charlie has to get organized. In order to do good academic work, you have to have a good workplace. A fine woodworker has his workbench and tools in prime condition and order.

"It's the same for you, Charlie. You need a desk in your own room, a good light, a supply of various kinds of paper, index cards, paper clips" – I stopped as June Hammond reached for a pad, took a pen out of her jacket, and began making notes – "pencils, pencil sharpener, pens, a digital clock or stopwatch, bookshelves, coloured tape, a book bag, a notebook, and an assignment pad."

"You know," June Hammond said, "I'm as anxious to help Charlie as anyone. Maybe more. But I have to tell you that he has never studied in his room in his life. Whatever work he's done has been on the floor of the den with the TV on full blast. Isn't that right, Charlie?"

Charlie nodded, eyes down.

"Look," I said. "Let's not waste time talking about the way it used to be. We need to plan for the fall."

I turned toward Charlie. "I'm going to give you between fifteen and thirty minutes of homework each day this summer. I won't give you any once school starts. Do you think you can handle that in your room?"

"Yeah. I think so. Can I play my radio?"

"I'd rather you didn't. What you're trying to do is train yourself to concentrate. I think you'll do better without any kind of noise while you're studying. Later on, if you want to try some music without words, you can."

I explained that Charlie needed a large, well-made book bag. He also needed a special place to keep it. I asked Mrs. Hammond to help Charlie mark out a large square on one of his shelves with brightly coloured tape. Any time Charlie wasn't studying, his book bag and his books were to be inside the square. This was to avoid the last-minute scramble that I was sure happened in Charlie's house: "It's gotta be here. I saw it just a minute ago …"

I talked for a few more minutes, answered a few questions. It wasn't until after they'd left that I realized Mr. Hammond hadn't said a word other than good-bye.

Mrs. Hammond called the next morning. "I'm so sorry to bother you so soon again, but there are two other things I wanted to talk to you about and I didn't want to mention them in front of Charlie.

"First of all, he lies constantly, and it's getting worse all the time. It's not just about his schoolwork, but outright lies about things he's seen and done."

"I know what you're saying," I said. "Every once in a while I get a child, usually a boy, who has to make everything bigger, brighter, louder than it is. Try to ignore it for now. Let's see what happens. You said there was something else bothering you."

"Yes, but I'm not sure you can do anything about it. I love Charlie so much, but he is so aggravating. I took him shopping yesterday to get the things for his room – you know, the things you said. Well, I was a wreck by the time we got home. First he fell over a perfectly obvious chair, then he knocked a lamp off a table. Fortunately, it didn't break, but it certainly was embarrassing. And then while I was getting my charge plate, he asked the sales-clerk for something to drink. I mean, he acted as if he was a four-year-old, and a dumb one at that. I'm sorry to sound like such a witch."

I smiled into the phone. "You sound just fine. But what you've described to me is as typical of many dyslexic children as the Fiery Bird story Charlie brought in. Just try to remember he doesn't do it on purpose. He honestly doesn't judge distances correctly – that's why he has a hard time catching and throwing – and he hasn't assimilated social amenities. We have to try to teach those, too. Now, can I ask you something? How does Mr. Hammond feel about all this? He was very quiet at our conference yesterday."

There was a pause. "All I can really say is that he wasn't entirely in favour of your tutoring Charlie, but he says he's willing to give it a chance. Anyway, Charlie loves all his new stuff. I don't know if it'll do any good, but at least it's the happiest I've seen him in a long while."

Charlie was still smiling when he arrived at my office the next day, a navy backpack across his shoulders. "What do you think? Is it okay to use this for a book bag? I got the assignment pad inside." Charlie's straight black hair was every which way across his forehead, but his black eyes were shining through his glasses.

We did a quick run-through of the best thing and the worst thing that had happened to him since I'd seen him last – a perfect opportunity for Charlie to indulge in a few exaggerations. His best was all his new stuff, but his worst was that he'd been attacked by three high school kids when he was walking home from Sam's last night. This seemed highly unlikely to me, considering Charlie's neighborhood, but I let it pass without comment and paid fifty for the best and the worst.

"Now, Charlie, we need to get started. Do you know how many letters there are in the alphabet?"

"Mmm … maybe about thirty-eight."

"How about vowels?"

Charlie said he wasn't exactly positive what I meant by a vowel.

"Okay, Charlie," I said. "In English eighty-five percent of the words are words that you can figure out and spell if you know the rules. The other fifteen percent you have to memorize. That will be easy for you because you have a good visual memory. In fact, that's the way you do all your reading now – from having memorized the words or making a guess according to the meaning of the sentence. And that's fine. Even unknown words that I teach you to figure out will become sight words after you've read them a few times.

"We'll do the easy part first." I took out a red folder that contained graded lists of sight words, about four to six hundred words for each grade. I handed Charlie the first-grade list. "I think you know all these," I said.

He skimmed the pages quickly. "Yeah, I think I do," he said slowly.

"And most of these, too." I handed him the second-grade words.

Again Charlie looked over the words. "You're right. I didn't know I knew so much."

I put the third-grade list in front of him. The lists are labeled VT21 for first grade, VT22 for second grade. This one was VT23. I didn't cover up the numbers, but I also didn't stress the grades. "These are a little harder. Just read the first column out loud, and put a dot beside any word you don't know."

Charlie had ten dots before he'd read twenty words. Together we copied the words he didn't know onto separate index cards and went over them again. With just one review he knew seven of the ten words. I put an elastic band around the cards and put them in an envelope. "Review them at home with your mom and dad. If you forget, have them tell you the word. You're not supposed to figure it out." Charlie got out his assignment pad and carefully wrote, "1. Rid wrds." He pushed it over to me. "See. Read words."

"Okay. Fine. Now, I'll tell you what I'm going to do. I'm going to pretend that you're Chinese and that you don't know how to read English. I'm going to begin at the beginning. Okay?" I picked up a pack of white cards, each about the size of a regular playing card. "There are twenty-six letters in the alphabet – I have a card for each one. Twenty-one of the letters are consonants; they always look the same, except when they're written as capitals. And they almost always have the same sound. The other five are vowels – sometimes six, if you count *y* – and I'm going to take those out of the pack for now," I said, lifting out the *a*, *e*, *i*, *o*, *u* cards.

"What we're going to do now may seem too easy, but remember, you're Chinese. When I put a card in front of you, just tell me the sound of the letter and a word that begins with it. I'll do it first."

Charlie knew the sounds of all the consonants except *q*, *w*, *y*, and *x*, and he reversed the *d* and gave the *b* sound. We separated those five from the pack and I wrote each one on a separate index card and Charlie traced it with a Magic Marker. We practiced those five again.

"This time, Charlie, leave those five cards in front of you and I'll make the sound, and you give me the letter that goes with the sound."

Charlie had it by the second try and put the index cards in another envelope in his backpack, dated his assignment pad, and made a note to study them: "2. Stude letrs."

Next I handed him lined paper and a pencil and asked him to write his name and the date. Charlie was right-handed (although he threw and batted like a lefty). He made his *o* from right to left and his *d* from the bottom up.

"This time I'm going to dictate about fifty letter sounds to you. Just write the letter that goes with the sound you hear me say: *m, h, b, s, b, t, m, b* ..."

Charlie was struggling. He could easily point to the card representing the sound, but when it came to transcoding what he heard into written symbols, he had great difficulty.

"Take your time. There's no rush." When we'd finished I put his paper in a folder in his bin. In a month or two we'd look back, and he'd be amazed that this had once seemed so difficult.

He had his assignment book open. "What do I write?" he wanted to know.

"Nothing. We'll do that part here." I certainly wasn't going to set Charlie up for failure at home.

I took out the five vowel cards. "These are the key cards. The vowels. And they're also tricky. They can have several different sounds, and the position of a vowel in a word is of prime importance. You must notice this carefully in order to understand the code.

"Now. This is important, Charlie. Every word must have at least one vowel, or it isn't a word. So when you go to spell something, remember that it has to have at least one of these five letters.

"Now, here's another important thing. There are short words like 'ran' and long words like 'transatlantic.' The short word has one part, the long word has four parts. We call the parts syllables."

I wrote the vowels across the top of the page and the words "ran" and "transatlantic." "Okay, there's one vowel sound in 'ran.' I'll mark the *a* and colour it yellow to make it stand out. Now here, you mark the vowels in 'transatlantic,' and tell me how many syllables."

Charlie got it right away. "Four," he said. "Four silly bulls."

I hugged him. "You're one terrific kid, you know that, Charlie? Four is exactly right." I could explain about the silly bulls later.

"Now, listen to this. Even when you can't see the word and count the vowels, you can still tell how many syllables there are. I'll show you how. What we're really talking about are vowel sounds. I'll explain more about that later."

I put my hand under my chin. "Cat," I said. "I could feel my mouth open once. Now, catcher. It opened twice. That means it has two syllables. Try it."

"Yeah," Charlie said in surprise, imitating me. "You're right. Give me some more."

"Christmas," I said. "How many syllables?"

"Two."

"Baseball."

"Two. Harder."

"Electric."

"Three."

"Blank."

"One."

"You've got it, Charlie. Okay. Your assignment is to think up two words of one syllable, two with two syllables, and so on. You don't have to write them. Just know them and be able to tell me."

Charlie wrote in his assignment pad, "3. No sily bul – 1, 2, 3, 4."

I kept quiet. Charlie knew what it meant. That's what assignment pads are for.

"All right. Now one more thing. Tune in to me, Charlie. This is important." I took the *a* card. "This letter, this vowel, can have several sounds. The sound I want you to learn now is called the short *a* sound." I wrote *a* on an index card and drew an apple on the other side. "Like the sound that begins apple. Say it. Okay. Good. Now you can write Martian words."

"What do you mean, Martian?"

"Come on, Charlie. You're through being Chinese. You got to move a little. I'm just fooling around. This stuff can get enormously boring, you know."

Charlie bulged his eyes at me behind his glasses. "You're telling me?" he asked incredulously.

"So, okay," I agreed. "As I was saying. Now that you know all the consonant sounds, the truth about syllables, and the short *a*, you can write Martian words."

Charlie shrugged. "Anything you say."

"Good. Write 'zad.'"

"Zad? What are you talking about? There's no such word."

"That's all you know. Martians say it when they're surprised – like, if they step in a puddle they didn't see. That's what they say. 'Zad!'"

Charlie laughed in spite of himself. "That's nuts."

A Safe Place for Joey

"Don't insult the teacher," I replied. "Just write it. Think of the sound that you hear in the beginning, the sound in the middle, and the sound at the end." I pushed the pad toward Charlie.

"Zad," he said to himself, "Z-z-z … okay." And within a minute he'd written it exactly right.

I gave him three more nonsense words to make sure he was writing out of his new understanding of sound-symbol relationships.

"All right, now, this is the last one. 'Zatbam.' Now, think about it, say it to yourself. How many times did you open your mouth? How many syllables? Remember, a syllable is just a short word and it has to have a vowel. Okay, go ahead and write it."

Charlie worked industriously, saying it, hearing the sounds, writing them down.

"One hundred percent right, Charlie. Pay yourself ten chips for each word and a bonus of fifty for 'zatbam.'"

I also gave Charlie two easy workbooks for homework – one math, one reading – with an assignment in each. He wrote the assignments in his own sweet style in his assignment book, counted his chips, bought a pack of sugarless gum, stuffed half the pack in his mouth, and at the door turned back. He shoved the gum to one bulging cheek and said, "Zatbam."

"Zatbam?" I asked.

"Yeah. Zatbam. That's how they say good-bye in Martian. Remember?"

"How could I have forgotten? Zatbam to you, too, Charlie."

I loved working with Charlie. He was intelligent, gentle, and thoughtful, and he understood that continuing on to fourth grade at Chapel was going to require a lot of hard work on his part. I promised I wouldn't ask him to do anything he didn't understand, but he would have to practice what he did understand in order to improve. He wouldn't have to do it alone; I'd be there and so would his family, but the major part of the work would be his.

Charlie wasn't turned off and he wasn't hyperactive, but it was true that he did lie. The lies grew smaller, though. As his reading improved and he felt better about himself, the need to exaggerate diminished, and what was left I used in language experience stories. For a few minutes of each session I had him dictate a story to me – anything and everything was okay. No limits. I wrote down all Charlie's thoughts; whatever he wanted to say was what I wrote. The resulting stories were an odd mixture of immaturity and sophistication, war and peace, but he loved it and so did I.

By the fourth week in July, Charlie was able to decode and encode (read and write) all phonetically regular words of one or two syllables (including silent *e* words). He had learned and internalized another seventy third-grade sight vocabulary words. He had learned the days of the week, the months of the year, and the zero, one, two, and five times tables.

During the last session before he left for a two-week vacation, Charlie asked, "Are you going to give me homework to take down to the shore?"

"Do you want some?"

"No-o! But Mom said you'd make me. Because there's so much I have to learn."

"Your mom's right, Charlie. You will remember the things you've learned better if you keep practicing every day. Like baseball players. The more they practice, the better they get.

The more you work, the more you practice, the more you'll remember. That is really true.

"But, on the other hand, there are a lot more things to learn than arithmetic and reading. Things that are much more important."

Charlie looked straight at me, his eyes widening behind his glasses. "Like what?"

"Like friends. Nothing's more important than learning how to be a good friend. People sometimes give it fancy names, like they call it learning 'socialization skills.' But what it really means is learning how to have fun with other people, caring about them, helping them when they hurt, sharing things, telling the truth, brushing your teeth and changing your socks so you smell good, keeping your promise, showing up when you said you would. Things like that."

"Could you say that over again?"

"I'm sorry, Charlie. I think I kind of got carried away."

"No. I liked it, but I just can't remember it. Could you make a list?"

I studied Charlie. He was obviously entirely serious. "I can certainly try."

After I'd written down as much as I could remember, with Charlie reminding me about the socks, he went over each item carefully.

"I'm pretty good at most of those. Like with Sam – you know, he lives across the street – I share and keep my promises and stuff. But I don't know if he's my friend. Dad says he's only six. That's why he puts up with me." How many times can a child be hurt and stay intact, whether the hurt is intentional or not? How many walking wounded kids are out there aching, hurting, feeling inadequate, with nobody to talk to? Where's the immunization for interior pain? Where's the pill for loss of confidence? "Well, I don't know, Charlie. I don't think it matters how old somebody is if you enjoy doing things together. It's the liking each other that counts.

"Anyway, down at the shore, you'll be fishing or out on the beach, and even though it's early, there'll be other kids around. It would probably be a pretty good place to work on making a friend."

Charlie sat without speaking and then finally said, without looking up, "I can't work on that. See, working on something is like practicing it, right? Practice is when you know what to do, but need to get better at it. But I don't even know how to start. Making a friend, I mean."

Charlie was right. He needed someone to show him what to do, not just tell him. I searched for some practical advice.

"All right, let's see. The first thing is just to look around. You don't have to say anything. You just look at the other kids on the beach, and you look for somebody who is doing the kind of thing you like to do.

"Say you like to fish or collect shells. Look and see if there's anybody else doing that. Just keep on walking and looking around, and if after a while the person seems nice, then go over and do your fishing or collecting somewhere near him. See, first you sort of do it near each other. Each of you doing your own thing. And then after a while you get so you do it together.

"Anyway, Charlie, have fun, and I'll see you in two weeks."

On the second Thursday in August, Charlie arrived at the office sunburned, nose peeling, but grinning from ear to ear. He put a shoebox in front of me.

"It's a present," he said.

A Safe Place for Joey

Inside the box was a slightly fishy-smelling double length of green yarn about two feet long with shells glued or tied to it at even intervals.

"One for each day I was there," Charlie said. "See, this is a horseshoe crab. This one is called a double sunrise. They're some of my best ones."

I stood on a stool to hang the shell-studded yarn in a swag across the wall and then stepped down and back to admire it. "I love it, Charlie. It's just exactly what this office needed. Thank you."

"Yeah," Charlie said, admiring it too. "And I made a friend. I mean a real friend, and I made him on purpose.

"He's nine and he's going in fourth – just like me. He lives down there at the shore all year long, and he knows everything there is to know about that ole beach.

"I saw him out there the first day, walking along picking up shells. Most of them he put back, but he'd keep one or two. I mean, he wasn't just grabbing any ole thing. He knew what he was doing.

"So the next day I did like you said. I sort of started picking up shells further down the beach, and then after a while he got down to where I was and we were both doing it. Then he showed me a sand dollar he'd found, and before he went home he gave me a snail shell, a good one, 'cause he already had a lot of them.

"Then the next day we did it again, and then he said whyn't we go over to his house so he could show me the rest of his shells. He came back to Gram's house with me so I could ask if I could go, and it turned out she knew his mom from church and right where his street was.

"His name's Eddie, and I'll see him again when we go down Labor Day weekend. He said he'd write, but I don't know about that part of it. Most people can't read my letters so good."

"Charlie, that's terrific. Of course you can write to him. Anybody who can make a friend that fast can write a letter. Just make a one-line note every night in your notebook of something that happened that day – like it rained, or your teacher got sick and you had a substitute, or you watched your favourite TV show, or your fish died. Then after a couple of weeks you can put the lines together, add a couple of words here and there – I'll help with the spelling – and you'll have a great letter."

"Yeah. Well, maybe," Charlie said. "There's only one trouble."

"I don't have a fish," we said in unison.

Charlie had a very concrete approach to life.

We admired the swag of shells one last time, and then I said, "Okay, Charlie. Time to get back to work."

After five or ten minutes of review, it became obvious that Charlie had forgotten at least 25 percent of the sight words he had learned. Multiplication was shaky, too. He mixed up 2 x 7 and 2 x 8 and got lost somewhere in the middle of the five times table. I wasn't particularly concerned. Kids with learning disabilities are notorious for knowing it one day and not the next, so it wasn't surprising that Charlie had forgotten some things during the two weeks he'd been away. What he'd learned was far more important.

But not to Charlie.

Gone was the sunny, confident boy who had walked in less than a half hour ago. Now his arms were on the desk, his head on his arms.

"See, I am stupid. I'll never be able to do it. I can't remember anything. My brain's like a sieve. Everything falls right out of it."

A Safe Place for Joey

"I know," I said. "It feels that way sometimes, but it will come back. I promise you. And learning how to make a friend is one hundred percent more important than two times seven. But I know it's frightening when you try to remember something you knew just a few days ago and you can't think of it at all."

Tears stood in Charlie's eyes. "You know what one kid told me when I was in second grade in that public school? He said somebody fed me ground-up glass when I was a baby and that was what made me retarded."

I pushed the tissues toward Charlie and said, "And you know that's not true. Right? You remember I showed you your test scores that showed you are smarter than ninety percent of the kids your age."

"I remember," Charlie said, blowing his nose. "And I believed you. Things seemed like they were going to be all right for a while. Like, I was doing pretty good before I went away. But now, I'm still the same."

"Yes. You are still the same and that's good. You're you and you're going to stay you always. You don't want to be somebody different every day, that would be too confusing. You'll grow, you'll learn how to do new things, you'll get bigger and older, but you'll always be Charlie Hammond. Nobody else can be you.

"It's true that it's harder for you to remember some facts than it is for other kids. That doesn't mean you can't learn. You just have to use different techniques, and not get mad at yourself if it takes you a little longer or you forget sometimes. Gradually, it's going to get easier, believe me, and then the parts that you're good at will take off – whammo – and you'll be right on grade level or above."

A car honked in the driveway, and Charlie walked to the lookout window. "It's Mom. Does she know all this stuff about me?"

234

"Yes. I've told both your mom and dad everything I've told you. I've told you before, too, Charlie – it's just hard to remember it all."

"You're telling me," Charlie said.

I walked out to the car with Charlie. June Hammond looked rested and tan and pretty.

"A good vacation?" I asked.

"The best we've ever had." She smiled.

"Good. I came out because I wanted to tell you that we didn't get Charlie's homework written down in his assignment pad this time. We got talking about why Charlie has trouble remembering things sometimes, and time ran out before we got to the homework. So would you just review the cards in his word bank with him? Divide the words he doesn't know into piles of five and go over them, a pile at a time. If he forgets, just tell him the word and have him say it, trace it, and use it in a sentence. And if you could get a dollar's worth of pennies and nickels and let Charlie practice counting by twos and fives, that would be a real help. Thank you. We'll be back in the groove next time." I touched Charlie's shoulder. "See you then."

Charlie's mother called early the next morning. Her voice certainly didn't match her sunny face of the day before.

"I know how busy you are," she said, "but I wondered if I could make an appointment to come in and talk to you sometime this week?"

"I have time up until eleven thirty today. There isn't anything open tomorrow, but I have lunch time on Friday."

"Would ten this morning be all right?"

"Yes. Fine. I'll see you in a little while, then."

* * *

Mrs. Hammond's eyes roamed across my desk and then around the room. "Uh … what I wanted to talk to you about … uh. I'm sorry, would you mind terribly if I smoke? I'm trying to give it up, but …" her voice trailed off.

"I'll get you an ashtray," I said. "Just let me bring one up from downstairs."

Cigarette smoke was already curling to the ceiling when I got back, and she dropped the used match into the ashtray.

"I'm sorry," she said again. "It's just that I didn't sleep much last night. We … uh … had a big scene at the house. Charlie's father is very upset. He says Charlie is worse now than before he came here. I know that's not true, but I don't know what to do about it. He wants Charlie to stop coming."

"When you say scene, do you mean argument?"

Mrs. Hammond nodded. "Yes. Worse. We were all yelling. Charlie was crying. So was I after a while."

"How did it begin? What happened?"

"Well, you know how you said to get the pennies and the nickels. It was too late to go to the bank, I mean the bank was closed and I wanted to get started right away. I do that sometimes. I want to help Charlie so much that I try too hard or go too fast or do too much and just end up making things worse.

"Anyway, when I got home I began going through my purse, and then we opened Charlie's piggy bank and we found some nickels and a bunch of pennies, but you had said a dollar's worth and we still didn't have enough. When Charlie's father came home I asked him for his pennies and nickels, and he wanted to know why, and when I told him Charlie was supposed to count them, that's when it started."

I nodded.

"Jim said that Charlie knew how many pennies made a nickel years ago and that he had been able to count before he ever heard your name, and you were making Charlie worse by having him think he didn't know things that he already did know."

I sighed.

"I can see why it was confusing, and I really am sorry," I said. "I should have explained more clearly. The idea was to have a concrete way of helping Charlie with multiplication. He was feeling a little panicked because he couldn't remember two times seven or five times eight, and he had known them before he went to the shore. Multiplication is really just a quick way of counting, and I thought it would help Charlie if, for example, he could see the eight nickels and count by fives to forty."

"I know," June Hammond said. "'Well, I mean I didn't know, but Charlie did. He really did, and he tried to tell his dad about how you had laid out bottle caps to explain multiplication, but Jim never let him finish. He said the next thing he'd be hearing was that you and Charlie sat around drinking beer and trading bottle caps.

"Jim doesn't really mean it when he talks like that. It's just that he's upset about Charlie. We both are. He's all we've got now."

Tears welled in Mrs. Hammond's eyes.

"Charlie's brother died before Charlie was born. We lived in the city then. I'm sorry."

Mrs. Hammond stopped and wiped her eyes.

"It's hard for me to talk about it. Jason was four years old, and I was pregnant with Charlie. Jim had called me from the office one afternoon and said he had some good news. He wanted me to call Mrs. Edgars, our baby-sitter, and meet him for dinner at Mario's. We didn't have much money, but we'd gotten engaged at Mario's and we always went back there when we had something to celebrate.

"I really didn't want to go. I'm always sick to my stomach when I'm pregnant, and besides, I was almost seven months and it was hard to sit in one place too long."

June Hammond stopped and lit another cigarette.

"I'm sorry I'm taking so long. I don't know how else to tell you."

"We have plenty of time," I said.

"Well, anyway, I called Mrs. Edgars. She lived in the next building over. I'd met her when Jason was a baby and I'd be out walking him in his carriage. Jason loved Mrs. Edgars – she was sort of like a grandmother to him, and we'd stop in to see her on our walks. And when Jim and I went out to the movies or someplace, though we didn't go out often, she'd baby-sit for Jason.

"Anyway, she said she couldn't come because she had to go to her church circle meeting, but that her sister was visiting from Rochester and she'd ask her. She, the sister, I mean, had heard Mrs. Edgars talk so much about Jason.

"So the sister came, and I left Jason with her." Tears slid down Mrs. Hammond's face. "He was dead when we got home," she sobbed.

"Dead?"

"Well, not really dead, but as good as. It was boiling hot – Indian summer, I guess; I still get sick every year when it comes. So Mrs. Edgars's sister opened a window in our apartment. The super had just taken the screens off that day to paint the trim and she didn't notice, and the phone rang and she went out to the hall to answer it, and Jason must have climbed on a chair.

Nobody really knows. Anyway, he fell out the window and dropped two stories into the side courtyard."

"Oh, no."

"She couldn't find him," Mrs. Hammond continued. "By the time she came back she thought he was hiding, playing a game, and she kept calling him. 'Jason. Where are you, Jason?' And then she heard people yelling, and she looked out into the courtyard and there was this little boy …"

Mrs. Hammond's sobs filled my office.

I couldn't talk.

"I'm sorry," she said again. "I can't stop now. I have to finish now that I've started. I'm sorry. We never talk about it at home.

"The sister, Mrs. Hale her name was, was so upset she couldn't find the pad with the phone number I'd left her, so no one knew where to reach us till Mrs. Edgars came home. She knew we usually went to Mario's.

"Jason had been in the hospital for two hours before we got there … all the time we'd just been eating, talking about Jim's raise.

"Anyway, Jason lived for almost another month. He was home for the last week. Jim wanted him to die at home. He took care of Jason. Jason could only take nourishment through a bottle and most of that he threw up. But Jim never once lost patience. He moved Jason's old crib into the living room, and he slept there on the couch with Jason next to him in the crib.

"Charlie was born six weeks early, three days after we buried Jason."

Tears were forming in my own eyes. "I'm so sorry," I said. "So terribly sorry."

Mrs. Hammond sighed. "I thought I would die, too. I thought I would die in childbirth. I wanted to. Charlie's delivery was very difficult. But somehow I didn't. I was still there, and Charlie was, too. This little, tiny, black-haired baby. In an isolette – like a little glass coffin.

"You know, I didn't even want to go see him. I never told Jim, but I didn't want to go down to the nursery to see Charlie at all. I thought I'd hate him. Since I'd lived I thought maybe it would feel like he'd killed Jason. But Jim made me go the next day, and I don't know, the minute I saw him, I loved him." She smiled – a sad, tired smile.

"Have you and Jim – do you mind?" I asked. "It's difficult to call him Mr. Hammond now."

"Oh, please, and call me June."

"Have you and Jim seen someone – a counselor or therapist?"

June Hammond nodded. "Our minister was wonderful. We still go back into the city to see him. And we also went to a therapist for a while, but Jim didn't think it was doing any good so we stopped."

"What did you think?"

"Oh, I don't know. It's true what they say about time being a great healer. It's been over eight years now. I know I'll never forget it, but I try to be grateful for everything else."

I stood up. The emotion in the room was so high that it was almost tangible, and we still hadn't really talked about Charlie. June Hammond lit a cigarette, and I cleared my throat. "Would you like a cup of coffee?"

Five minutes later I handed her the steaming mug and asked, "How much does Charlie know?"

"I'm not really sure. As I said, Jim and I never talk about Jason now. But there are some photographs in the album, and Charlie's asked questions. So he knows he had a brother and that he died. I think that's probably all he knows. Why? Do you think that's part of what's wrong with Charlie?

"You see, I couldn't ask you before because Jim was always with me, and he doesn't like other people to know about Jason. But please tell me, do you think Jason's death – I mean, me getting so upset – did something to Charlie before he was born?"

Slowly, carefully, I repeated once again what I knew about the causal factors of dyslexia and learning disabilities.

"Nobody knows for sure what causes a child to have a learning disability," I said as gently as I could. "Most of us who work with dyslexic kids feel that it has something to do with the neural development and how the brain is wired. It's true that stress or use of drugs during pregnancy can cause changes, but so can lots of other things, such as heredity. In fact, some think now that the human chromosome fifteen may carry genes associated with learning disabilities. And I have always had a suspicion that eventually the neurologists will discover that the corpus callosum, that bundle of tissues that connects the right and left sides of the brain, will turn out to be even more important in the transfer of information and learning than we've expected.

"But look, let's talk about what we can do to help Charlie now." I pulled a yellow pad toward me and said, "Maybe it would be clearer if I made a couple of lists. Column A will be Charlie's strengths, and column B will be his areas of weakness." I wrote:

A Safe Place for Joey

A. Strengths	**B. Areas of Weakness**
1. Above average intelligence.	1. Below average in reading, writing, arithmetic.
2. Above average visual memory.	2. Large gap between academic achievement and intelligence.
3. Good abstract thinking.	3. Below average in auditory memory.
4. Good reasoning skills.	4. Below average in graphomotor skills.
5. Good understanding of spatial relationships.	5. Below average gross motor skills.
6. Attractive personality.	6. Disorganized.
7. Motivated – wants to learn.	7. Lacks confidence in his abilities.
8. Not hyperactive.	

"Now, roughly, the plan is to use Charlie's strengths to help him compensate for his weaknesses – and he can do it, I know he can; he's doing it right now.

"I can understand your worry, maybe even some feelings of guilt and also Jim's impatience. But you've done so wonderfully well. Charlie is one of the nicest boys I've known, and he's learning so much so fast. Really.

"Try to convince Jim to let me keep working with Charlie. I'd be happy to talk to Jim myself if you think it would help, although I don't seem to have done very well so far.

"But now that Charlie's been promoted, we can't just let him flounder in fourth grade. And besides, Charlie and I like each other, or at least I like him."

"Oh, Charlie loves to come here. I thought he'd hate being tutored, but it's just the opposite."

"All right," I said. "Then I don't think it makes sense to switch to another tutor. Ask Jim if he'll give us half a year and then we can reassess the situation."

Charlie plunked his book bag beside the desk and said, "Mom says just to tell you that it's okay. She says you'll know what that means."

I nodded.

"Well, what does that mean?"

"That it's all right for us to keep on working together."

"Well, that's good. The house has been a mess the last couple of days. Everybody's yelling. Now Mom's got all these books out of the library, trying to figure out what's the matter with me. She said you explained it to her and she understood it while she was here, but when she tried to tell it to Dad she got all mixed up, and he got madder than heck and said if Mom wasn't paying your bills I certainly wouldn't be coming here. And then he yelled at Mom, 'I don't want to discuss this any further,' and slammed the door on the way out to work."

"I'm sorry, Charlie," I said, and I really was. And not just for Charlie, but for Mr. Hammond and myself as well. Lack of paternal support made my job much harder.

"It's okay," Charlie said. "I've been thinking about it, and I don't think anybody can really explain. I think I'm just somebody nobody knows."

"That sounds pretty lonely," I said.

Charlie nodded, his sweet face serious. "It is," he agreed. Then he smiled, just a little, black eyes lighting up. "But I think maybe it's going to get better."

"I called Mr. Dalwig yesterday," I told Charlie at his last session before school began, "and he let me talk to your fourth-grade teacher. She sounded nice, but I had to promise not to tell you her name. They don't want any of the kids to know who they're getting until the first day of school."

"I'm glad it's a she, anyway," Charlie said. "At least that rules out old frog-face Hogan."

"Just forget I said 'she,' okay? Anyway, your teacher said that September will be mostly review in English and math, and that if I go over to the school they'll lend me copies of the social studies and grammar books. So that sounds good."

And it was good. Charlie's teacher, Mrs. Yager, was intelligent, confident, and creative. There were four fourth grades at Chapel, two with only ten children. Charlie was in one of these, but the work load was still heavy.

Charlie took all his books home from school every night, whether he had homework in the subject or not. This was Charlie's own idea, because to him the extra weight was worth the lack of worry. One of his problems the year before had been that even if he did remember to write down the assignment, he invariably forgot to bring the right book. We had worked out an alphabetical system of organization for schoolbooks, and I checked his book bag each time.

"English grammar, math, reading, science, spelling, social studies, vocabulary. Good, Charlie."

"Yup," Charlie said. "E, M, R, three S's, and a V. Pencils and pens here in the zipper pocket and my assignment pad in the front. Here's today's."

Charlie had listed his assignments one under the other:

1. Scnse – Rd C.2. No Q 1–6
2. Sp Bok – Xse 10 11
3. Math – qj 20 NM 1–15
4. R – C3 nex F
5. Enq – pj 10 und nons

It might look like a foreign language to me, but it made sense to Charlie.

"I had to write fast, so the spelling isn't so good. I'll read it to you. One. Science. Read chapter two. Answer questions one through six. Two. Spelling book. Do exercises ten and eleven. Three. Math. Page twenty. Do numbers one through fifteen. Four. Reading. That's this." He held up a paperback, *The Riders of the Pony Express*. "We have to read up to chapter three by Friday. Five is English. Page ten. Underline the nouns."

I was overwhelmed. How was Charlie going to handle all that work? He'd been doing a half hour of homework during the latter part of the summer, but this looked like a lot more than a half hour.

"Are you going to be able to get all that done?" I asked.

Charlie nodded. "I think I can. See, I already checked off science. We get to do most of that in class. I'm half done with math – it's just addition and subtraction."

Charlie did a half page of nouns with me, and it was clear that he spotted them with no trouble. "Person, place, thing, or idea. Ideas are the only hard ones."

We alternated reading pages of *The Riders of the Pony Express*. Charlie either skipped the words he didn't know or made a passing shot based on the shape of the word and the meaning of the sentence. I didn't correct him. He was able to tell me what was happening in his own words, so I knew he'd understood what he'd read. I also knew he'd never get through the two chapters if he had to stop and figure out every word he didn't know. I told him to try to write down the words he didn't get and I'd teach them to him, but I wasn't going to insist. He had enough to do as it was. We divided the remaining pages of chapters one and two in *Pony Express* by three (Tuesday, Wednesday, and Thursday nights) and separated them with paper clips so Charlie would know how much he had to read each night.

Spelling was Charlie's Waterloo. The two pages in the spelling book were intended to review the long *a* sound. The problem was that in the book there were no rules to follow and no consistency. For example, four of the words were "rain, payment, tale, and neighbor." There were twenty new words a week and a test every Thursday. I copied the next six pages of Charlie's spelling book on my copy machine, resolving to figure out some way to help him.

"For this week, just write them out. Learn the easy ones first, and memorize as many of the others as you can."

Mrs. Yager and I conferred on a weekly basis. She was wonderful about adapting assignments for Charlie. She accepted shorter written reports, corrected his spelling, allowed him to copy reports over after she'd corrected them, and, whenever possible, let him shine in class by talking about all the information he'd acquired. Charlie's mom was good, too. She encouraged him and tried to practice "planned ignoring," deliberately not noticing the dozens of annoying little things Charlie did – just concentrating on one or two changes at a time. I tried to clarify and reinforce as creatively as I could the things Charlie was learning in school, and Charlie himself was trying to improve his concentration, to focus, and to sort out the important from the unimportant.

Because it was so important to Charlie not to look "dumb" in front of his classmates, we spent an inordinate amount of time on spelling. Charlie got so that he earned "High Pass" on most tests, although that didn't mean he would remember how to spell the same words if he had to use them in a book report a few days later.

Mrs. Yager had actually offered to let Charlie skip the spelling test or else cut down his number of words, at least during the first trimester. But Charlie wouldn't hear of it.

"Whadda you mean, not take the test?" Charlie was fuming. "What am I gonna do while everybody has the spelling test? Play tic-tac-toe with myself? There are only twenty words, you know. Now that I know how to study them, I'm not ever going to miss thirteen again, like that first time. I'm not that dumb, you know."

"Okay," I said. "I guess I didn't remember you telling me that before."

Charlie smiled. "All right. I get it. I did used to think I couldn't do it. I don't know why. It just seems like it used to be harder, but that couldn't be it 'cause that was third and third has got to be easier than fourth."

"Well," I said. "You're older and that makes a difference."

"And I'm not so mad," Charlie said softly, "so I can think better."

It was true. Charlie's dictated stories had less violence, and he had also learned to concentrate for longer periods of time. Charlie was doing his homework, passing his tests, increasing his academic skills, and even smiling a little more. I suppose it was because things were going relatively smoothly that I forgot about Jim Hammond. However, Jim Hammond did not forget about me.

The first day of November was grey and cold – a reminder of the long winter yet to come. On impulse I decided to light a fire in the living room fireplace and bring my office work down there.

But the phone rang as I struck a match, and I blew it out and walked to the kitchen to pick up the phone.

"Mrs. MacCracken? This is Jim Hammond, Charlie's father. It's been almost a half year since you first saw Charlie for his evaluation, and I wondered if you had retested him yet and what the results were?"

Tested Charlie? When would I have had time to test Charlie? Every minute of every session was crammed with extra explanations of things Charlie was encountering in school, plus my own steady building of his reading, writing, and math skills. But I couldn't say that. If there was one key missing member of Charlie's team, it was his father. Motivation mellowed my voice.

"Mr. Hammond. Hello. I'm glad to hear from you. You're right. Your wife and I did talk about seeing what kind of progress Charlie was making. I haven't had a chance to formally test him again, but I am in touch with his teacher every week and she tells me that he's holding his own. Would you like to come in and see what he's been doing here?"

"Holding his own? What does that mean, Mrs. MacCracken? I have Charlie's typed educational evaluation done by you here in front of me. The report gives me specific information as to Charlie's IQ and reading and math scores. I appreciate the specifics of that report, Mrs. MacCracken …"

There was a long pause in which neither of us spoke. Then Mr. Hammond resumed. (It was remarkably easy to start thinking of him as Mr. Hammond again, rather than Jim.)

"It has been five months," he said. "I think it's time to re-evaluate the situation as we discussed previously and see exactly how much, if any, progress has been made."

There was another long pause. I was holding my breath. I wanted to scream, "Damn it, Mr. Hammond. Do you have any idea how much energy, how much courage, how much effort it takes for Charlie to do his homework every night? To go to school and keep his mind focused on what's being taught in class? To strike out in softball every day and still play again the next day? Can't you see with your own eyes the progress he's making?"

I let out my breath and instead said, "I understand your concern about Charlie's progress. It's just that testing takes time. We only have two forty-five-minute sessions a week. To repeat the academic tests I gave Charlie in June would take two hours, or a week and a half. I don't think this is the right point to spend that amount of time on testing, particularly since things seem to be going along pretty well."

"I don't mean to sound rude, Mrs. MacCracken, but are you trying to tell me that Charlie, our son, cannot be successful in school without your help for even a week and a half?"

"I am trying to tell you, Mr. Hammond, that at this stage of the game Charlie needs all the help he can get, and to use the time we have for testing rather than teaching would be ill-advised."

"Then I suggest you see him two extra hours and get the academic testing done."

"I'm sorry, Mr. Hammond, I don't have any extra hours after school, and I don't think we should take Charlie out of his classes now."

"May I ask, then, what you do suggest?"

I wanted to say, "I suggest you get off Charlie's back and on his side," but underneath my annoyance I knew from what his wife had told me that Jim Hammond was a kind, loving man who cared for his family. And Charlie needed that caring.

I studied my appointment calendar and Charlie's school calendar. "How about the Friday after Thanksgiving? I've canceled most of my appointments for that day."

"That's almost a month away. But if it's the best you can do, all right. How soon can we have the results?"

Push. Push. Push. You're driving me nuts, Mr. Hammond. Out loud I said, "Saturday. Not a written report. But I can certainly score the tests and give you the results the next day."

"Thank you. I appreciate that. My wife will call you to set up the times."

When June Hammond called to arrange the appointments for the testing and follow-up conference she said, "I'm really very sorry to cut into your holiday like this. I apologize. And I hope you'll understand, but I'm not going to come to the conference on Saturday. I know how I feel about Charlie and I know how I feel about you, and whether he goes up or down a few points on some tests doesn't have anything to do with it. Besides, I think you'll be able to talk to Jim better if I'm not there. I can't explain why I think so, but I just do. So I'll make the appointment on Saturday for whatever time you say, but just know ahead of time that I'm not going to be there.

"My sister's coming down from Boston with her family, so it'll be easy enough to have something come up."

* * *

"I'm sorry to make you come in on a holiday, Charlie. How was your Thanksgiving?"

Charlie yawned. "Okay. My cousins came down from Boston. We're going into the city when I finish here."

Charlie yawned again, and I wondered how much sleep he'd gotten the previous night.

"What we have to do today is check and see how much more you know now than you did last June. There's an oral reading test, a silent reading test, and a short spelling and math test."

"What's oral?"

"Out loud."

"Criminy! What do I have to do tests for? I have enough tests in school."

"I know. I usually don't give any till the end of the year, but it's important to your dad, Charlie."

"Oh, I get it. He wants to see if I'm still a dummy."

"I don't think he thinks you're a dummy. He may think I am, but not you."

Charlie smiled. "All right. Let's get it over with. How long is this going to take?"

"A couple of hours." He screwed his face into a pained expression. "I know," I said. "I'll pay double for unfair pain and cruelty. Start with the math. Do as many as you can. Skip the ones you don't know how to do, but remember they get harder as you go down the page."

"Oh, I remember doing this. What did I get last time?"

"Well," I said as I checked Charlie's file, "it came out at third grade, first month."

"How many do I need to get right to get fourth?"

I considered. Would answering be illegal? I decided that it was a fair question, studied the teacher's manual, and told

Charlie how many he needed to get right to be scored at a fourth-grade level.

"But I'm not going to correct your tests till this afternoon, so I can't tell you till Monday how you did. Agreed?" We followed the same procedure on each of the following tests, and at least Charlie's yawns disappeared.

Mr. Hammond was at my office door at exactly two o'clock on Saturday afternoon. A mixture of rain and sleet had begun in the late morning and by early afternoon had turned into a cold, heavy, drenching rain.

Mr. Hammond shrugged off his raincoat and brushed imaginary rain from the narrow lapels of his dark pinstripe suit. I took his raincoat from him and motioned to the stairs that led to my office.

"Why don't you go on up? I'll be right with you. Just let me hang this down by the furnace so it can dry out."

He started to protest, but a small puddle was already forming by my feet. "Can I do it for you?" he asked.

"No, no. I'll be right up."

Mr. Hammond was still standing when I entered the room. He pointed to some charcoal drawings on the wall behind the desk. "Any of those Charlie's?" he asked.

I silently thanked God that "The Fiery Bird" was not still on the wall but in Charlie's file. It would have antagonized Mr. Hammond even more to see his son's inadequacies displayed. I thought about pointing out the swag of shells and then decided against it.

"Actually, most of Charlie's work is here in his bin," I said, lifting out a pile of papers and the black and white notebook where we kept track of the work we did each day.

Mr. Hammond pushed the papers aside without looking at them and sat down in front of the desk. "Mrs. Hammond regrets she is unable to be here today. Her sister is visiting from Boston and an unanticipated doctor's appointment came up, and so June had to drive her in. If they finish early enough, she'll come by. So we might as well get started. How did the testing go?"

I opened Charlie's file folder.

"Fine. Here are the tests I gave him last June. These are the ones he took yesterday. I thought you'd like to compare them. I've also drawn up a chart on this page to point out the differences in grade scores and percentiles."

This time Jim Hammond pulled the papers toward him and pored over them intently. While he studied the papers, I studied him.

Who was this small, black-haired man? How did he really feel about his son? How much did he understand? We had spent two hours together after Charlie's evaluation and another hour before the tutoring sessions began, but his wife had done most of the talking both times.

Charlie was built on a bigger scale than his father – taller, broader shoulders – but he had the same black hair and eyes, although Mr. Hammond's eyebrows were heavier, almost meeting above his nose. I searched in vain for a glimpse of the man who had cared so tenderly for his other son when he was dying …

The papers rustled as Mr. Hammond flipped them back and forth. "How is this possible? To have made over a year's improvement in reading comprehension in less than half a year?" His tone implied that perhaps I'd altered the scores in some way.

A Safe Place for Joey

I chose my words carefully. "I think that there are several factors involved. First, Charlie has learned a great deal about decoding unknown words. He has also increased his sight vocabulary, and he reads much more easily and quickly than before.

"Second, Charlie is much more confident. He really believes he can read better now, and that helps. He actually reads the longer paragraphs instead of just skimming and guessing. The test you're looking at is a silent reading comprehension test. Twenty-five minutes are allowed. See, when Charlie took the test last June – Level C, Form One (Level C is for third grade) – I wrote here in the corner that he had finished in eleven minutes, which meant he had to be either an awfully fast reader, or a guesser. The score – second grade, eight months – says he was the latter. Yesterday he used the full twenty-five minutes to do the comprehension section on Level D (D is for fourth grade), Form One; I'll use Form Two when I do the regular testing at the end of the year."

I hesitated, suddenly realizing I'd implied that Charlie would still be with me. I knew I had made a mistake. Only five minutes into the conference and already a mistake. But I couldn't think how to correct it, so I continued. "He concentrated and was willing to invest a lot of energy into trying to figure out as many words as he could. And as you know, once Charlie can read a word he has no trouble understanding it."

"And it is a different test? It's not just that he's had it before?"

"Yes, Mr. Hammond. It is a different test."

He nodded. "How else do you account for the difference? Not just reading comprehension, but the others, too. On the math test he scored on a fourth-grade level."

"When Charlie took the tests last June he was frightened. He was getting further and further behind. He didn't know why, and he didn't know what to do about it. Now that he sees he can learn, he's willing to try.

"It helps him to know that I know what to do about his learning problems. If he broke his leg and was having trouble walking, you'd take him to a doctor – find out what was wrong and get him help. It's the same thing for a child in our society who is having trouble reading –"

"Are you saying Charlie has a broken head?" Mr. Hammond interrupted, "comparing it to a broken leg? Is that what you think is wrong with Charlie?" Mr. Hammond shoved the papers back across the desk and stared at me.

Another mistake.

"No, of course not. I was just using that as an example."

"An example. I see. Well, then if it's not his head, what is it? And perhaps it would be best if you kept examples and emotions out of it and we just discussed facts.

"In fact, let me start this discussion by saying that none of this makes sense to me at all. Oh, I know. I know. You explained after the evaluation. You've talked to my wife. You've talked to Charlie, but I'm not sure they understand any better than I do." He paused. I had a feeling he wanted to add, "though they may like you better," but he left the words unsaid.

"Now, let me tell you what makes sense to me," Mr. Hammond continued. "Intelligence means that you have the ability to acquire knowledge and the ability to use the knowledge you've acquired. Now that's the truth. I've looked it up in the dictionary, and it also makes sense to me personally, so let's accept that statement as fact.

"Now, reading, spelling, math are all knowledge that you can acquire and use. At least some people can. Charlie doesn't happen to be one of those people, so therefore it follows, or at least it seems very clear to me, that Charlie is not intelligent."

He stopped to clear his throat. "Unfortunate as that may be."

"You're very wrong," I said. I had difficulty controlling my voice. How could he say that? "Charlie is intelligent. Look at his answers on the WISC-R intelligence test." I took the test out of Charlie's file and thrust it in front of him. "He can think abstractly, he can reason, he can solve problems, he has acquired a great deal of …" I stopped myself in midsentence. What was I doing? I was actually arguing with this man – this man who was Charlie's father and whom Charlie needed so much. I should be listening, not arguing.

"I'm sorry," I said. "You've known Charlie so much longer – you have so much more information than I do. Why do you think Charlie lacks intelligence? Is it just the school work or is it also because of the way he acts at home?"

After a small pause Mr. Hammond said, "Well, both. Not being able to read is a terrible thing, although you seem to think he's doing better at that now. But there's more to it than that." Mr. Hammond leaned across the desk. "He always needs help. He's in and out of our bedroom or living room twenty times a night, asking June to help him do this or help him do that. She never says no. He's like a little baby instead of nine years old. Nine – remember that. He turned nine last week and he can't do anything for himself.

"Please understand. It's not that I don't love him. I do. You have to ask yourself what kind of a life it is for Charlie, too. Always behind. Always at the bottom of everything. In sports, too. He'll never make a team – you try to throw him a ball, it hits him in the head. I tell you, he'll be better off away."

"Away?" I could hardly get the word out.

"Yes, away at school. I've been looking into it. At one of the football games this fall I ran into an old friend from college, and he told me how he'd gotten his son into this new school, boarding school, that's just opened in Pennsylvania. It's not cheap, but he says it's worth it – it's made all the difference in their lives."

"But –"

"No. Let me finish. Please. I wanted June to be here when I brought this up because I thought she could be less emotional about it here than at home. But since she's not here, I'm going to put it to you bluntly.

"I think she's covering up – doing Charlie's work for him. I think you're covering up – trying to make both of them feel better. I think the school is probably in on it, too, somehow. Anyway, I've had enough. It's time to face facts. Charlie isn't right. He's never been right, and he's never going to be. I don't understand all the ins and outs of it and I'm not saying he's retarded, but he is defective, and he'll be better off with his own kind."

I sat silently. Something terrible was going on, and I had no idea how to stop it.

"We lost one boy, you know. I'm sure June told you. And something happened to Charlie, too. Some people just aren't meant to have children. You have to face up to it."

"You don't think you're meant to have children?" I repeated.

"It seems that way," he said in a measured voice. "I tried as hard as I knew how to hold on to Jason. I've tried with Charlie. I never got through to either of them. The only way I can figure it is, it wasn't meant to be.

"Look now, I'm not talking about putting him in some institution. Just a school. Lots of kids go away to school. Nothing wrong with that."

"He's only eight. Nine, I mean. What's the name of the school?"

He took a card from his wallet. "High Mountains. High Mountains Boys' School."

"It must be very expensive if it's as good as your friend says."

"It is. But June has just closed a fantastic deal. She's lived here all her life, you know, so she has many contacts, and now she's sold a five-hundred-thousand-dollar estate up on the hill, and the commission from that will go a good ways and I'm sure there will be more to come. So the picture's changed as far as money goes. That's not the issue now."

I wanted to say, "But you didn't earn the money and June doesn't even know your plan," but I had made enough mistakes for one hour.

"You obviously have done a great deal of thinking about this." I wasn't going to be able to change his mind in the next few minutes, and yet I knew it was the wrong thing to do. Wrong for Charlie – but also wrong for his father. I needed time to think.

"Well," I said, glancing at my watch, "let me copy these test scores for you so you can share them with June."

The old copy machine whirred noisily for a minute or two as I copied the papers in the small adjoining room. I expected Mr. Hammond to be up and waiting by the door, but he still sat opposite the desk.

I suddenly felt very tired. The rain pelted against the windows, and I leaned against the side of the desk, holding the copies out to him, not trusting myself to speak.

Finally, he reached for the papers but made no motion of rising.

But I was the one now who couldn't stand it any longer. I forced the words up out of my throat. "I'll get your coat and meet you at the door."

Monday morning, the phone rang at seven o'clock.

"This is Jim Hammond, Mrs. MacCracken. I'm sorry to bother you so early. I'm just on my way into the office now, and I wanted to be sure to get you before you saw Charlie this afternoon. I … uh … haven't had a chance to talk to June – or Charlie either, as a matter of fact – about the school as yet, so I'd appreciate it if you didn't mention it to him just yet."

A reprieve.

I heard nothing further from Mr. Hammond for the next three weeks. My talks with Charlie's mother and teacher were the same as always – brief, specific. We all felt that Charlie was continuing to make progress.

Then just before Christmas vacation I had another seven o'clock phone call from Mr. Hammond, asking if I was going away over the Christmas holiday and, if not, if he could "come by." Cal and I were to be away for only a week, and so we arranged a time to meet three days after Christmas.

Mr. Hammond opened the conversation as soon as he had settled himself in the chair across from the desk. "June doesn't know I'm here. Neither does Charlie. And I'd like to keep it that way, at least for now."

I nodded and waited for him to continue, but he was silent, studying his hands for several minutes. Then he said slowly, "I'm not a humble man, Mrs. MacCracken, nor can I put my feelings into words easily. I'm an engineer and have much more faith and knowledge in how things work than how people work. It's very difficult for me to come here. I tell you this not because I want your sympathy, but so you will understand how important this is to me.

"I've been doing a lot of thinking since I was last here, and I've been observing Charlie very closely. And I'm not sure this makes any sense, but I think that I may not have been fair to Charlie. Somehow he's all muddled together in my mind with Jason – it's as though they're this one person, my son. And when I told you I'd tried as hard as I could with Charlie, I meant it. I honestly felt I had.

"But now, I don't know, I've been thinking maybe I've been a little confused, and all the work and effort was for Jason. He was so sick – you couldn't believe how hurt and little and frightened he was. Anyway, I've been asking myself to be specific. It seems as though I'm always asking other people to be specific, so I thought perhaps I should ask the same of myself. What specifically have I done for Charlie?

"I couldn't think of very many things. Do you know what I mean? It felt like I'd worked tremendously hard with him, but now I can't think of what, if anything, I've done.

"So that's why I'm here. I want to know if there are things I can do and if there are, what they are.

"I'm not giving up on that school. I don't want you to think that. It's just ... well, to be truthful about it, I want to send Charlie off with a clear conscience. I want to be sure I've done everything that could possibly be done."

I watched the sun shimmering on the snow in the woods behind the office windows. I wasn't sure I liked what I'd heard; it almost sounded as though Mr. Hammond were doing it for himself rather than for Charlie. A clear conscience. Did I want to get into the business of helping Mr. Hammond clear his conscience?

"Well," he said, "are there things I can do?"

"Yes. Of course." Who was I to judge anybody else's conscience? Charlie needed his father. Sometimes the way things begin doesn't matter. If Charlie and his dad could get to know each other, trust each other, what difference did the reason behind it make?

"To begin with," I said, "you can listen to Charlie, and let him know that what he says and thinks are important to you.

"Get to know his room. What kind of posters does he have on his wall? What kind of music does he listen to? Make it a point to get to know his turf and meet him there a lot of the time. You don't have to stay forever, but have it get so it's comfortable for both of you. Whatever rules you have about making beds and picking up, discuss at some other time in some neutral place. When you stop in to visit, don't harp.

"Take over some of those things June does. Lighten her load, and also show Charlie you want to be involved. You said or implied that she babies Charlie by doing things for him that he ought to be able to do for himself. I think that's probably true, but if you're involved in helping him then you can gradually show him how to do things for himself.

"Gradually is the operative word here. If he has to do a report on Alexander Graham Bell, don't just tell him to get busy and do it. He can't. He doesn't know how, and he's more confused and frightened by having to produce quantities of words than most kids are. Go with him to the library. Show him how to use the card catalog. Talk to the librarian. Ask which of the reference books are the clearest, the easiest. Help Charlie find the book. Help him copy the pages of pertinent information so he can take them home. He writes much too slowly to try to do it in the library. Help him organize. Help him when he gets stuck with the writing. Help him rewrite. Let his teacher know you're helping.

"Don't expect too much. Even with a rewrite, there will be lots of mistakes. But praise him. Praise him for the effort that he's put in, not just for the result. And he will get better at it gradually. And, as he does, you can cut back on the amount of help you give. Don't ever do the work for him, but also don't let him flounder.

"Teach him as much as you can. Get him to watch the news with you. Talk about it later. Get a world map and a US map. Put them up in the kitchen or hall and use pushpins to locate the places you talk about.

"Read to him from the books that interest him and from magazines, books, and newspapers that interest you. If someone develops a new vaccine, tell him about it. If the stock market drops, explain. Keep it short, and don't put him on the spot or criticize or get impatient if he forgets what you've told him. Be polite. Tell him again. The main thing is that you interact and expose Charlie to as much of the world as possible."

Mr. Hammond was taking notes, his black eyebrows knit tightly together.

"Look. You don't need to write this down. It's all stuff you know, anyway. I'm just sort of pointing it out again."

"Mrs. MacCracken, as I told you before, I am an engineer, a chemical engineer, and I work in the research department of a chemical company. I'm good at my job, but I'll never go further because I can't, or don't know how to, get along with people. I accept that. I don't particularly like most people, anyway.

"But please don't presume what it is I know or don't know. Charlie is the first and probably the last nine-year-old boy other than myself that I'll ever know. Where do you think I would have learned? Certainly not from my father. He believed bringing up children was women's work. Now, please keep on."

He waited, pencil poised. My head was blank. Suddenly it seemed too awesome a task, and too presumptuous of me to assume to know.

"I don't know. A lot of it will just come naturally once you start. But you can never go wrong telling him you love him and that you don't care whether he bats zero or a thousand. Tell him about some of the things you couldn't do when you were nine.

"And you could get him an electric typewriter and get someone to teach him to type. The keyboard is practically the same as a word processor's. Word processors and computers are going to be big in education. Charlie could use a head start. And maybe you could make a list" – I was off and running again, embarrassed but too excited to care – "of all the things you like about him. You don't have to show it to Charlie, but you could just remind yourself. And you could make a list of every good or decent or intelligent thing he does.

"Try to find something that he's good at – a place where he can excel easily. This will convince him more than any words that he really is a bright, capable person.

"And have fun with him. Go fishing, or swimming, or watch a ball game or a movie, or eat a hot dog, or tell a few jokes.

"See, other than June, Charlie is the most wonderful thing that will ever happen to you. You belong to each other. He's yours, you're his, and you hold an excitement for each other that can't be duplicated.

A Safe Place for Joey

"I'd probably be saying this even if Charlie were blind, deaf, and dumb, because children, including other people's children, give me enormous pleasure.

"But Charlie is attractive, and he's bright and loving; he's a lot like you in lots of ways – and he's yours. You're going to have a wonderful time."

Finally I stopped.

Mr. Hammond was smiling at me. I had never seen him smile before. "I think you like your work as much as I like mine," he said. "Good-bye, and thank you."

He turned to go and then turned back.

"About that school, the one my classmate's boy attends. I think that in all probability its enrollment is full, considering that it's already the middle of the year. Probably no openings. I doubt that there is any point in even applying."

"No point at all," I agreed, and returned Mr. Hammond's smile in spite of myself.

During the winter months Charlie and I continued our attack on spelling and decoding skills. He had mastered the basics of sound-symbol relationships – the sounds of consonants, blends, vowels. Now I included digraphs and reviewed the meanings of closed, open, and silent *e* syllables. I taught him how to recognize and read and spell the four other types of syllables: the vowel team, such as p*ai*l or d*ay*, t*ea* or s*ee*, p*ie*, t*oe*; the *r* controller syllable; the diphthong syllable, like *oi* or *au* in *oi*l and *Au*gust; and the consonant *le* syllable, like bu*bble*, cra*ckle*.

The seven syllables made sense to Charlie. They gave organization to a previously mysterious mass. He learned to locate the vowels in the word, mark them, decide which type of syllable they formed, and then read it – or sometimes write it. Words that did not follow the rules were still designated *red words* and written on cards and memorized, but Charlie was amazed at how few he had to memorize now that he had the tools to break words into syllables, figure them out, and put them back together.

At school Charlie was holding his own. His grades for the second trimester were up to "Satisfactory" in all subjects except spelling and written expression. Even more important, Mrs. Yager felt that Charlie was really trying hard and that he deserved a lot of praise.

The school's biggest concern about Charlie was that he still hadn't established any close relationships or made a group of friends. His poor physical coordination was a handicap, and his lack of social awareness was embarrassing.

Somehow Charlie clapped too loudly or in the wrong places during plays in the auditorium. He laughed at things that didn't seem funny to the other children. He interrupted during class or forgot where he was supposed to stand when he lined up at gym. He tripped on his way to the stage when it was time for his class to sing at the March concert. Fourth graders are self-conscious anyway, and being around Charlie made them more so. But Mrs. Yager tried to help Charlie learn the social amenities, and so did his mom.

I also tried to help Charlie understand the meaning of gestures, facial expressions, and various tones of voice, and how to get along with people. Once in a while I made up open-ended stories for Charlie to complete or did a little role playing.

"All right, Charlie," I said, "let's say you're giving a birthday party. My name's George. I just moved here, but you invited me anyway 'cause I'm in your class and you're a nice guy. Now say this is your living room, this is the front door, you're inside with a couple of other kids. Here I come." I crashed through the door past Charlie and the other kids, looked around, and yelled, "Where's the cake? I thought you said it was your birthday?"

"Nobody's that dumb," Charlie said in disgust.

"Dumb? Whadda you mean?" I said, still being George.

"Come on, Mary. Nobody just yells for cake."

"Oh. What should George have done?"

"Just have waited. The cake comes at the end."

I smiled at him. "You're right," I replied, thinking but not saying anything about his mother's complaint about Charlie asking the salesman for a drink when they went shopping. "When you're at somebody else's place, you wait for them to offer the cake or whatever.

"Also, I think George could have said hello, at least to you, before he did anything else."

And all the while I was working with Charlie and talking to the school and his mother, I waited silently but impatiently for a sign that there were changes at home. Was Mr. Hammond studying his lists or was he actually doing something?

The first hint came not from Mr. Hammond or Charlie's mother or teacher, but from Charlie himself. All of a sudden, Charlie was doing things. He told me that he had gotten out all his old Lego sets and was making all sorts of things. He had to take money out of his savings account to buy more complicated designs. From Lego he moved to mobiles; he had half a dozen swaying from his ceiling.

As winter gave way to spring, Charlie's building erupted into the outdoors. Charlie and his friend Sam were building a clubhouse on weekends – a two-story clubhouse in Charlie's backyard. Charlie drew me a floor plan, and I was amazed at his understanding of space. I was even more amazed when he brought me a photograph, for now Charlie was involved in photography. He said he had gotten a small camera, and now he was walking the neighbor's dog to earn enough money to keep him in film. Charlie certainly seemed to be expanding his world, but whether this was because of Mr. Hammond or not was hard to tell. I could have asked, but some reticence held me back. Whatever was happening in Charlie's world was good and did not include me. I wanted to be careful not to interrupt the chemistry of whatever it was that was evolving. But still, all that wood for the clubhouse and that camera had to come from somewhere.

April slipped into May, and now all Charlie could talk about was the upcoming class trip. The two small fourth grades were going to the Museum of Natural History. The big excitement was not the museum, however, but the fact that they were going by regular public transportation instead of by chartered bus. Many of these girls and boys had never been on a bus or subway. Their mothers spent hours each day carpooling their children to school, piano lessons, guitar lessons, karate class, dancing class, hockey games, and swim meets. After much discussion, parents agreed that travel by bus and subway would be a "learning experience" and signed letters of permission.

The day before the trip Charlie had it all memorized. "See, we'll walk to the bus stop, everybody's going to have a buddy and we'll walk in pairs, and each class will take a different bus across the bridge. Then we're going to take the express – that's what the subway's called – to One Hundred Twenty-fifth Street, and then change to the local and take that to Eightieth Street, and then walk to the museum. It's only a couple of blocks."

I couldn't help smiling. Charlie was so excited. "You certainly sound like you're ready."

A Safe Place for Joey

"Yeah," Charlie said, "we've been studying it at school. I just hope I don't get carsick or get a girl for a buddy."

"How'd it go, Charlie? Did you have fun?" I asked when he came in after the trip.

"You wouldn't believe. Wait'll I tell you what happened." Charlie's eyes were shining through his glasses, and a cowlick of hair stood straight up at the crest of his head.

"First of all, I drew Rick Tower for a buddy and he's practically the most popular kid in our class, and he even said it was interesting when I was telling him about Mr. Ammann, you know, the guy who designed the bridge. Dad and I had just finished reading an article about him.

"And the subway was cool. There was this man who'd made the bottom of his shoes out of newspaper, and one girl had her hair cut like an Indian and coloured pink."

"Sounds different, anyway," I said, loving it, especially reading about Mr. Ammann with his dad.

"Yeah. Well, and then we got to the museum. I'd already been there with Mom and Dad. But the dinosaurs are really neat, especially that Riceratrops."

"Triceratops?"

"Yeah, that's the one – and the other one with the little front legs and great big head. Tyrasoranus Rex – something like that. You know."

I nodded.

"The Indian room was pretty neat, too. Then we had lunch in a special lunchroom and afterward got to buy stuff in the gift shop. I got some postcards of Africa and some stamps for Dad's collection and a little pink stone for Mom."

"That was thoughtful of you, Charlie. Buying presents."

268

"Yeah. Well, wait till you hear the bad part. I guess Rick got tired of walking with me, and on the way back to the subway he just moved up and started walking along with these two other kids who are really his friends.

"I felt really bad, so I just sort of took Mom's present out to look at while I was walking. I knew she'd really like it and that made me feel better, but then this big kid knocked into me and I dropped the stone and I couldn't find it."

"Oh, Charlie. What happened?"

"Well, I kept on looking for it, and then all of a sudden I realized that I was all alone. Well, not alone exactly. There were lots of people – but my class was gone.

"I started running. It was only supposed to be a couple of blocks to the subway, and I thought I could catch up, but I guess I must've made a wrong turn or something and boy, did I ever begin to sweat."

"I don't blame you, Charlie," I said. "All alone in New York City in the afternoon, night coming up."

Charlie nodded. "But you know. I just decided I had to get a plan. And once I decided that, it kinda calmed me down. My first plan was to get directions to the local at Eightieth, but I ran into this creepy guy when I went into a store to ask for help, so I just decided, man, I better get out of there. I found a phone booth and the operator called Mom, but nobody was home. That was because Mrs. Yager had called her, and she and Dad *and* the police were out looking for me. I didn't know that then.

"Anyway, I didn't know Dad's work number, but I remembered the name – Cartan Chemicals – and the operator got it. And I asked for Dad and his secretary told me how Dad was already out looking for me and to stay where I was. I had to go out and look at the street signs – Amsterdam Avenue and

A Safe Place for Joey

Seventy-fifth Street – so I could tell her where I was. Boy, was I glad I knew how to figure out Amsterdam. Anyway, she said Dad was calling in every twenty minutes for news and for me to just stay there and he'd come get me. And he did. He and Mom drove right up to the phone booth in our station wagon. Mom was all upset and crying, but you know what Dad said? He said I'd handled myself well."

Charlie sat up a little straighter behind the desk. "I got this feeling that he was really kind of proud of me."

"I bet he was, Charlie. Getting lost can happen to anyone. What you do about it is what's important," I said. I had a very clear feeling that Mr. Hammond didn't need lists anymore.

Jim Hammond figured more and more prominently in Charlie's conversations. Their latest project was videotaping. They'd gone together to buy a VCR and a video camera, and they were out taping something every weekend – animals at the zoo, kids skateboarding. It turned out that Rick Tower was really into video, too, and now Charlie and Rick were figuring out how to make a space movie using his Lego people.

Most important of all, Charlie told me that his dad had talked to him about Jason.

"See," Charlie said, "I always thought the reason Dad acted so mad at me was because he wished I'd died instead of Jason. He was only four, but they have all these pictures of him and only a couple of me and he looks so good, and I'm such a … well, I used to be such a mess … anybody'd rather have Jason than me. But Dad said no, it wasn't like that. He wished he could have us both and he'd probably seemed mad, but anyway, he said I'm more important to him and Mom than ever now that they don't have Jason. It's like they still miss him some, but they love me, too."

The fourth-grade science fair was coming up. It was a big deal at Chapel. The fifth grade had a social studies exhibit; the sixth grade had an academic Olympic decathlon; but the fourth grades capped their school year with an all-day science fair.

The fourth grades, sixty boys and girls in all, took over the whole gymnasium. The two janitors and groundsmen carried in sixty desks and arranged them in a U in the middle of the gym, and then covered them with red cloths that grew a little more faded with each year. I had attended a half dozen or more science fairs, and the setup was always the same.

But it was all new to Charlie. Each fourth grader created a project for the fair. It had to be related to something that had been studied during the year. Originality was stressed, and Mrs. Yager stretched the limits of science to accommodate enthusiasm as much as she could.

Charlie knew from the beginning what his project was going to be. No event during the year meant more to him or had a bigger impact on his life than the trip to the museum, so Charlie was going to make a model of a dinosaur. Mrs. Yager approved the project, and Charlie agonized over which species to select, finally settling on the huge Tyrannosaurus Rex.

Charlie worked fervently on his dinosaur, racing through his homework to get to the basement, where he was fashioning "Rex" out of coat hangers and wire and green plastic garbage bags, with touches of leather from an old purse of his mom's to add reality.

"How's he coming, Charlie?" I asked a week before the science fair.

"Good. Real good." Charlie's eyes shone, his cowlick zinged up from his head. "It's almost done. He's almost three feet high and Mom and Dad both helped me last night and we even got his head fixed on so that it will sort of wobble back and forth. And now we're going into the museum and I'm going to take pictures of lots of different kinds of dinosaurs, and then I'm going to make this tape about them that plays over and over for people to listen to if they want to. I really wanted to do a videotape, but Mrs. Yager said that was too complicated. I guess she's right. We got a big enough problem just getting ole Rex set up."

I arrived at the science fair at about ten thirty. Nothing had changed since I'd been to the science fair two years ago. Rosebushes still surrounded the parking lot, matching the pinky red of the low brick buildings. Boys in navy blue blazers, girls in coloured cotton dresses, mothers looking much the same as the girls, fathers in business suits, and teachers in skirts, blouses, and low-heeled shoes filled the slate walkways and the gym itself.

The desks had been covered with the rose-red cloth and set in the usual U, with approximately sixty fourth-graders sitting or standing behind their exhibits as teachers led the other classes past and parents talked in little knots around the room after going through the line.

I leaned against one wall, soaking it all in, liking the school. Despite or maybe even because of the formality and rules and dress code, creativity flourished amid respect for learning.

I couldn't actually see Charlie, but it was easy to tell where he was. At the far end of the exhibits, Rex waggled his huge green plastic head above a constant crowd of gawking children and parents. Obviously, Charlie's exhibit was the hit of the show.

I knew I should just get in line, go shake Charlie's hand, and then get back to work, but I put it off, taking pleasure in looking at all those people admiring Charlie and something he'd done.

A hand touched my arm, and I turned to see June Hammond beaming at me. "Aren't you nice to come," she said. "Isn't it wonderful? Have you talked to Charlie yet?"

"No, but I will. I wouldn't have missed this for anything."

Jim Hammond had been talking to a group of parents; now he turned toward me and I stretched out my hand. "Congratulations."

"Thank you," Mr. Hammond said, smiling. "You know, Charlie did most of it himself. He drew a plan first, and then made a small-scale model. I mainly helped getting the big one assembled." His strong hand closed around mine, and I knew we were both thinking the same thing.

June Hammond turned as more parents stopped to say how proud she must be. Jim Hammond released my hand, but his black eyes were still intent on mine. "I've wanted to tell you … thank you, I mean," he continued, "and to apologize. You were right about Charlie. I don't know how I could have missed it all these years. He's incredible when it comes to building things. You know, I'm beginning to think he could actually be an architect or an engineer someday."

I nodded agreement.

Jim Hammond reached out and pulled June toward us. "And it's not just Charlie. June made another big sale, and now they're hinting at a partnership. She's the best salesperson they have."

"And you?" I asked. "How are you doing?"

"Fine. Just fine," he said. "I'm still not adept at understanding people, but June's good enough at that for both of us and I get a lot of satisfaction from my work." He smiled at me. "Like you. But the main thing is, you were right about my getting to know Charlie – and June. I'm glad I didn't miss either of them."

"Me too," I said, and went off in search of Charlie.

As I worked my way around the exhibits, I thought about how one thing leads unexpectedly to another. June Hammond was blooming like the proverbial rose now that Jim had joined the support team for Charlie.

Finally I got to Charlie and reached across the faded-red-covered desk to shake his hand. "That's one terrific dinosaur," I said.

Charlie thanked me, but it was obvious he really didn't have time to talk.

"Good-bye, Charlie. See you later," and I grinned at him as I left. "There sure seem to be a lot of somebodies who want to know you now."

A Safe Place

I had thought when we first bought our house that I needed a separate entrance and waiting room for my office. But any structural change would require a re-evaluation of the entire house with an accompanying increase in taxes, and Cal advised waiting. Maybe he suspected something more as well. In any case, it turned out to be good advice. I wouldn't even consider a separate waiting room now.

Our side door opens directly into the kitchen, and from there it's only a few steps to the stairs that lead to my office. The kitchen is ours during the morning and evening hours, but in the afternoon it belongs to the kids. From after school on, there's an ever-changing flow of children through the kitchen. They open the door for each other; they drape their coats across the chairs; they pile their book bags, their boots, and sometimes their shoes on the floor or cellar landing; they make the popcorn if I haven't had time; they debate the virtues of various television shows or turn the television off entirely if somebody has a paper that's due or a test coming up. Some children walk straight from school and wait in the kitchen for an hour or more before their appointment. The big ones help the little ones with their homework, and they share their prizes while they wait for their parents or taxis to come and pick them up. I have never heard an argument or seen a mean act in the kitchen. The kids have made it a very safe place for themselves.

Nan, my youngest daughter, works with me now. She's a learning specialist herself and a superior grower of children. She has the little upstairs room right next to mine. So now the kitchen is twice as full, and deliverymen and unexpected visitors do double takes when they view our crop of children.

They let each other in, but Nan or I let each child out, and the children that are waiting call to us as we pass through the kitchen.

"My turn now?" David asks.

"Almost," I say.

"What day is it, anyway?" Bob inquires. "I gotta put it on my homework here."

"Friday," David answers. "Are we going to write today like usual, Mary?"

Upstairs, David settles himself behind the big old desk, and I sit beside him in a smaller chair.

"Anything good or bad happen since I last saw you, David?" I begin our ritual.

"Two goods. One bad."

"Which first?" I ask.

"The bad. John whacked me on the head in school today."

I wrote it down in David's book.

"But I didn't whack him back. That's one good, and the other is that it's the weekend and tomorrow I got karate."

"Pay yourself one hundred and seventy-five for your goods and bad, and add an extra bonus of fifty. It took control not to hit back, and that's not easy."

David bent his handsome seven-year-old head over the chip box and deftly extracted the chips. He was in second grade and had been coming to us twice a week for a year and a half, so he knew the ropes. He had arrived as an angry, acting-out, nonreading first grader. He lied; he hit; he cried as well.

But now I was about to cut his two sessions a week to one. He was a natural athlete, his math had always been good, and now he was on grade level in reading and getting good grades on the weekly spelling tests, if he studied hard. But he still had a lot of trouble with spontaneous writing, so every Friday we worked on this.

David passed me a pad of paper and my favourite pen and did the same for himself.

"I already know what I'm writing about," he said.

"Well, you're ahead of me, then."

"Yup."

David already had the first word down, but I wasn't in any hurry to start. I liked looking at him – I liked the vibes in the room. David exuded confidence and grace, and I thought about child expert Urie Bronfenbrenner's statement that every child should spend part of each day with someone who loves him and whom he loves in return. David was lucky. He had both a father and a mother who loved him a lot. Theirs was a busy, hectic family that included two other boys besides David, one older, one younger. Both parents worked and loved their jobs, but they also loved their kids and took time to show them that they did.

I could hear Bob reading softly to Nan in the next room. A light glowed under their door, and I thought how lucky we were to be able to work in such a good place. Happiness was almost visible.

A Safe Place for Joey

"Aren't you even starting yet?" David asked, emphasizing the last word.

"I've almost got it," I said, referring more to what I was thinking than to what I was about to write. David had the loving and also help from us while he was still young, and we all tried to give him a safe place where he could practice and not get down on himself if he made a mistake. Love, specialized help, and a safe place. That seemed to do it.

David put his pencil down. "I'm waiting for you now," he said.

"Okay. I'm ready. What are you writing about?"

"Karate. That's what I'm working on. I'm going to take my brown-belt test tomorrow. And that's what I'm writing about."

Karate – that's what David was working on. Children and my book – that's what I was working on.

I picked up my pen and wrote. "I'm having a lot of trouble finishing this book I'm trying to write."

David was busy writing again, too. He paused for a minute. "We'll trade and read them when we're done, okay? What's yours about?"

I read my first sentence to him out loud.

David nodded. "That sounds pretty good. 'Member to print so I can read it.

"Okay," David announced a few minutes later. "Let's switch. I'm done and yours is long enough. You go first. Read mine out loud, okay?"

"I like karate," I read. "You have to know weaponry, martial arts, fighting, and karate. I hope I get my brown belt tomorrow. Mary, I will show you how to do karate when we're done writing. This is a picture of me fighting."

David had to help me decipher some of the words, but his paragraph was over forty words long. It hung together and made sense, and the illustration was clear and full of action.

"Good," I said. "Pay four hundred and twenty."

David counted out the chips quickly and then bounced out from behind the desk to demonstrate karate blows, leaps, and vicious kicks.

"There," he said with satisfaction. "Now I'll read yours." He read my two paragraphs out loud and then turned to me. "Is your book about us? I mean about kids like me?"

I nodded.

"Well, I know what you ought to call it, then."

I studied David carefully. "You do?"

His turn to nod. "See, you just draw a big bubble like this." David demonstrated on the pad of paper. "And inside the bubble you write HELP! – like in capital letters with a 'splanation thing. Now you draw a line down to this kid at the bottom of the page so you can tell he's saying it. This will be like on the cover."

I watched in fascination as David returned to the bubble and drew curving lines around it.

"See," he said. "You gotta be sure to make the bubble all wiggly. That way everybody will know the kid is thinking it, not saying it out loud. I mean like he's screaming. That's why you gotta write it big, but he isn't making any noise."

"Is that what he's saying ... screaming, I mean? Help?"

David nodded.

"Why doesn't he just say it out loud?"

"He doesn't know ... I mean he knows something's wrong, and he wants somebody to help him, but he's scared that maybe whatever's wrong can't be fixed. So he figures he better not say it out loud – in case."

A Safe Place for Joey

I nodded, not able to find equally good words for an answer. But I knew then that I would – had to – finish this book. Somebody had to say David's words out loud.

I lingered in my office after Nan and the last of the children had gone, reliving the day, relishing the time with David, trying to recapture the thoughts I'd had while I sat beside him. He was doing so well. Why? I needed to understand in order to help other children.

Love, help from someone specifically trained to remediate learning disabilities, ending every session with success, and a safe place. "A safe place," I repeated softly. I liked the sound of the words. I remembered thinking that this was why the children rushed to our kitchen, lingered there, even bringing brothers, sisters, or friends to wait for them till their lessons were done. The children had made themselves a safe place in our kitchen, and they knew it.

I pulled a pad of paper toward me, feeling the urge to try to write it down. Could I take the unwritten rules of the kitchen, understand them, expand and translate them into the principles, the ingredients, of the kind of safe place that these children needed in their homes and schools?

I worked every night for a week, staying in the office after the children left, going back up after dinner, filling page after page with stories of the children – their successes and failures, trying to crystallize their needs – then cutting, paring down the words, until less than a page was left.

Mary MacCracken

A Safe Place

1. In a safe place people are kind. Sarcasm, fighting, backbiting, and namecalling are exceptions rather than the rule. Kindness and consideration and forgiveness are the usual way of life.
2. In a safe place there is laughter. Not just the canned laughter of radio and television, but real laughter that comes from sharing meaningful work and play.
3. In a safe place there are rules. The rules are few and fair and are made by the people who live and work there, including the children.
4. In a safe place people listen to each other. They care about each other and show that they do, with words and also with body language.
5. In a safe place the adults are the models for the others.

I printed the words on a new piece of paper and then read them out loud. Each sentence set off a remembered montage of children, and I walked over to the shelf that held the children's bins and read the rules of a safe place out loud once more to the absent children. Did I have it right? Were these the ingredients of a safe place?

I put the paper on my desk, walked to the back window, and looked out over the dark woods and up to the stars above them.

Which of us doesn't need a safe place somewhere in our lives? Which of us hasn't gone searching for it if we haven't found it in our homes or schools?

I believe that we must explore and dare and discover.

But we also need to know that there is a safe place where we can find the comfort, courage, and confidence to conquer our feelings of inadequacy, pain, sadness, and failure so that we can go out and risk again.

Children with learning disabilities experience humiliation and hurt earlier and more often than most. Their need for a safe place is great.

I left the stars, and picked up the piece of paper and tacked it to the wall behind my desk. I would keep it there as a kind of creed to live by. A creed given to me by the children.

Appendix

Evaluation Summary Sheet

INTELLIGENCE
WISC-R: Wechsler Intelligence Scale for Children Revised

Verbal Section:

Information	measures acquired knowledge
Similarities	measures logical and abstract thinking abilities
Arithmetic	measures numerical reasoning and concentration
Vocabulary	measures word knowledge and language development
Comprehension	measures practical knowledge and common sense
Digit Span	Measures short-term auditory memory and concentration

Performance Section:

Picture Completion	measures visual alertness to details
Picture Arrangement	measures social judgment, perceptual organization, and sequencing

A Safe Place for Joey

Block Design	measures perceptual organization and knowledge of spatial relationships
Object Assembly	measures perceptual organization, spatial relationships, and ability to assemble puzzles
Coding	measures clerical speed and accuracy, visual motor ability, and short-term visual organization
Mazes	measures ability in following a visual pattern; foresight

ACADEMICS ACHIEVEMENT

WRAT: Wide Range Achievement Test	brief test of reading (word recognition), spelling, and written arithmetic
SPACHE: Spache Oral Diagnostic Reading Test	word recognition; oral reading of sentences and paragraphs; phonetic analysis
GATES MACGINITIE: Gates MacGinitie Silent Reading Test	speed, accuracy, vocabulary and comprehension in silent reading
GRAY ORAL READING KEY MATH	oral reading and fluency math skills in numeration, fractions, geometry, symbols, mental computation, reasoning, addition, subtraction, multiplication, division, money measurement, time, word problems
WRITTEN EXPRESSION	dictation from grade level and spontaneous paragraph

LEARNING MODALITIES

DETROIT: Detroit Test of Learning Aptitude — various subtests of visual processing, auditory processing, eye-hand motor speed, and memory

WEPMAN: Wepman Auditory Discrimination Test — measures ability to differentiate between sameness and difference of forty different word pairs

HARRIS: Harris Test of Lateral Dominance — determines whether right- or left-eyed, -handed and -footed

BENDER: Bender Gestalt Test — measures perceptual motor ability and development

SENSE OF SELF

H-T-P: House-Tree-Person — drawings of a house, tree, person, and family

FREEMAN: Freeman Sentence Completion — completions of partial sentences such as "Books are …"

SOCIAL HISTORY

background information form and parents' perception of child

Additional and alternative tests and procedures

(Used when a child is under age six or when additional information about specific areas is needed)

WPPSI: Weschler Preschool and Primary Scale of Intelligence — measures intelligence of children ages four to six and a half

McCarthy Scales of Children's Abilities — measures overall development of children ages two to eight and a half

Goodenough Harris Draw-a-Man — measures intellectual maturity and ability to form concepts of abstract character of children age three and up

Gates MacGinitie Readiness Skills Test — measures listening comprehension, auditory and visual discrimination, visual-motor coordination of children in kindergarten and beginning first grade

Zeitlin Early Identification (ZEIS) — short, multidimensional screening instrument for children ages four and five to detect strengths and weaknesses in learning abilities

Slingerland Pre-Reading Screening Procedures — to screen for difficulties in auditory, visual, and/or kinesthetic modalities and first-grade academic needs

Slingerland Screening Tests for Identifying Children with Specific Language Disability — to screen for specific language difficulties in grades one through six

Mary MacCracken

Peabody Picture Vocabulary Test (PPVT)	measures receptive vocabulary
Progressive Matrices (Raven)	measures ability to reason by analogy and to organize spatial perceptions
Purdue Perceptual Motor Survey Revised Visual Retention	measures perceptual and motor skills
Test (Benton)	measures visual memory, visual perception, and visuo-constructive abilities
Peabody Individual Achievement Test	measures academic achievement for grades kindergarten through high school

About the Author

Mary MacCracken, a learning disabilities specialist, authored four bestselling books about her work with emotionally disturbed children, two of which have been made into television specials. Mary was Honorary Chairman of the National Mental Health Association in 1979 and lectured for them around the country.

More inspiring memoirs by
Mary MacCracken